PAKISTAN UNDER BHUTTO, 1971–1977

Also by Shahid Javed Burki

A STUDY OF CHINESE COMMUNES

PAKISTAN UNDER BHUTTO, 1971–1977

Shahid Javed Burki

St. Martin's Press   New York

© 1980 Shahid Javed Burki

All rights reserved. For more information, write:
St. Martin's Press, Inc. 175 Fifth Avenue, New York, NY 10010
Printed in Great Britain
First published in the United States of America in 1980
ISBN 0–312–59471–2

Library of Congress Cataloging in Publication Data

Burki, Shahid Javed.
    Pakistan under Bhutto.
    Bibliography: p.
    Includes index.
    1.   Pakistan – Politics and government — 1971 –
    2.   Bhutto, Zulfikar Ali.   I.   Title.
DS384.B88   1979   954.9'1'050924   78–31358

ISBN 0–312–59471–2

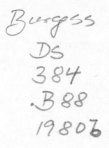

Contents

To Maryam, my mother and Jahanara, my wife

Preface

In 1970 Professor Samuel Huntington of Harvard University invited me to join a group of scholars who were studying the process of change in developing countries. This group of political scientists and economists represented a number of very different points of view about not only the nature and dynamics of the development process but also about the motivation behind it.[1] Within this group, my task was to study Pakistan. The only reason for studying Pakistan was that the Cambridge group was intrigued by an article that I was about to publish in *Public Policy*.[2] In this article, I had analysed West Pakistan's massive public works programme not in terms of its economic results but in terms of the motivation of the decision-makers that had launched it. The main conclusion that I had drawn from this article was a simple one: even in those societies in which interaction between individuals and groups of individuals is not encouraged, the decision-makers have only a limited range for manoeuvre; there are social, political and cultural boundaries that cannot easily be crossed. At least in theory, I could distinguish between three different types of reactions on the part of leadership groups to these societal constraints. Some leaders can be expected to respect these boundaries. Not always familiar with the nature and extent of the constraints imposed on them, it is possible for these leaders to take actions that would be resented by some powerful elements in the society. In that case, these leaders would respect the society's constraints and be quite content to draw back into the area of permitted discretion. But not all leaders and leadership groups behave so passively. Some will use charisma, moral suasion or political intrigue to expand this area of permitted discretion, to create a little more room in which they could move and manoeuvre. Others may refuse to be inhibited at all by societal constraints. This latter group is likely to use force to change the rules of the game, to demolish the boundaries that society erects against radical behaviour.

During my year at Harvard, I applied this analysis to understanding the dynamics of decision-making in Pakistan. As I reflected on the important decisions that had shaped Pakistan's history, I came to realise that group conflict and conflict between individuals is a novel – and in my opinion, better – perspective to understanding change in Pakistan. Politics in Pakistan had been dominated by a succession of powerful personalities. Some of these men had wielded power because of their exceptional ability and charisma. Some had gained power because of their ability to reconcile or manipulate group interests. Many had been exceptionally conservative in the choices they had made for the society. Only two – Mohammad Ali Jinnah and Mohammad Ayub Khan – had made any attempt to expand the area of discretion available to them. Not one of them had been a revolutionary. All of them had had a profound impact on making Pakistan's history.

But, as I searched for the motivation behind the decisions and actions that had made Pakistan's history and as I began to understand their implications, I also came to realise how easy it was to exaggerate the role of strong men in Pakistan's history and how important it was to recognise the part played by social and economic groups. It was all too easy to identify Mohammad Ali Jinnah, the *Quaid-i-Azam* (the Great Leader) of Pakistan, with the movement that led to the creation of a separate homeland for the Muslim community of British India. But could the *Quaid* have succeeded without the help of the Muslim urban middle-classes who saw a better economic and social future in a nation whose destinies they would control rather than in a country in whose management they would have to be content with the role of a junior partner? Was the Industrial Policy of 1948 Prime Minister Liaqat Ali Khan's master stroke to gain economic independence from India or the product of pressure from a group of merchants who had migrated from India to Pakistan in search of new investment opportunities? Governor General Ghulam Mohammad's dismissal of the Constituent Assembly could be interpreted as the action of a strong man determined to preserve power in his hands. Or, it could be seen in terms of an attempt by Pakistan's indigenous leadership groups to recapture some of the power that they had lost to the refugee groups from India. And so on.

There has been a tendency among economic and political historians of Pakistan to view the past as a series of unrelated events. My own approach to understanding events taught me not to treat them as isolated occurrences with little connection to the past or with little relevance for the future. As I searched for meaning in the events that had shaped Pakistan's history, I became convinced that this history was not made up of loosely connected periods, the Jinnah-Liaqat era, the Ayub era, the Yahya interregnum and the Bhutto period. It should be viewed, instead, in terms of the forces, social, economic and political, that made Jinnah, Liaqat, Ayub, Yahya and Bhutto possible.

I was still engaged in this reinterpretation of Pakistan's history when Zulfikar Ali Bhutto fell from power. In the eyes of many in the West, the movement that led to Bhutto's fall was unexpected and undeserved. In the opinion of many in Pakistan, the Prime Minister deserved not only to be thrown out of power but also the treatment that he received once he was deposed. In both cases, Bhutto's fate was interpreted as that of a man with some exceptional qualities, good and bad. However, by now I knew that the political turmoil that resulted in the exit from power of Zulfikar Ali Bhutto in July 1977 was not simply a reaction to some personal quirks or whims of leadership. It was a reaction from a number of social and economic groups who had been hurt by Bhutto's pursuit of Bhuttoism. I decided to attempt an explanation of Bhuttoism, the circumstances that had produced it and the consequences that followed from its application to Pakistan's polity, society and economy. This book is the result of that attempt.

I was helped in this effort by a number of people, friends and colleagues. Shahid Yusuf and Paul Streeten – sometimes to help sustain my argument and sometimes to refute what I was saying – introduced me to a body of literature from various disciplines that I was unlikely to have encountered without their help. Shuja Nawaz, Manfred Blobel and Robert LaPorte read a number of chapters of my draft and helped improve my presentation as well as my analysis. Josephina Valeriano diligently kept track of the sources I used and prepared the bibliography. Fely Favis typed and retyped – patiently deciphering foreign names from hand-written drafts that became increasingly more illegible. Jahanara, my wife, read through all the drafts and discussed with me their content, never failing to point out when I slipped from analyses to assertions. To all these I owe many thanks.

10 July 1979   SHAHID JAVED BURKI

1 Introduction

On 20 December 1971, Pakistan's second military government handed over the country's administration to Zulfikar Ali Bhutto, chairman of the Pakistan People's Party (PPP). On 5 July 1977, the military, after deposing Bhutto, reassumed political and administrative control over the country. During the sixty-seven months that Bhutto was in power – first as President and later as Prime Minister – he introduced some important changes in Pakistan's society, in its economy and in its political system. The main purpose of this study is to present an analysis of these changes – why they were introduced and what were their consequences.

From Bhutto's point of view, the circumstances that brought him to political power could not have been more favourable. The very poor handling of the political situation created by the election of 1970 and the speed with which the Indian army was able to overrun East Pakistan even though the best units of the Pakistani army had been deployed there thoroughly discredited the top military leadership. The prolonged military domination of the political arena had inhibited both the development of political parties and the emergence of any kind of civilian leadership. Bhutto, although himself a creation of the military rule, was the only civilian leader who had succeeded in cultivating a political constituency for himself. Therefore, when the army leaders were persuaded to surrender power to the civilians, Bhutto and his party walked into what was virtually a political vacuum.

Bhutto should have benefited not only from the combination of very fortuitous circumstances that made possible his quick ascent to power: his handling of the very difficult domestic and external situation should also have contributed to political longevity. Within fifteen months of assuming power, he had very shrewdly dealt with a number of problems that he inherited from his military predecessors. A vast majority of the people found his solutions satisfactory. Mujibur Rahman, the leader of the Bengali secessionist movement, had been released from prison and sent to Bangladesh to become the Prime Minister of the new state. Arrangements had been negotiated for the return both of the territory captured by India from West Pakistan and the over 90,000 prisoners of war brought over by India from East Pakistan. The economy, which had faltered very badly during the civil war, had shown signs of recovery. A number of economic reforms had removed the more glaring examples of unequal distribution of national wealth that had been accumulated during the military period. By April 1972, therefore, Bhutto felt confident enough to say that he would 'last longer than anyone else who's governed Pakistan'. Why? Because:

> I know the fundamental rule of this profession. What is the rule? Well, in politics you sometimes have to pretend to be stupid and make others believe they're the only intelligent ones. But to do this you have to have light and flexible fingers, and . . . Have you ever seen a bird sitting on its eggs in the nest? Well, a politician must have fairly light, fairly flexible fingers, to insinuate them under the bird and take away the eggs. One by one. Without the bird realizing it.[1]

Within five years of this statement – by no means an exceptional one, for Bhutto hid neither his contempt for most of the politicians that he dealt with nor the high regard that he had for his own intelligence[2] – a group of essentially second-rank political leaders managed to get Bhutto out of the Prime Minister's house in Rawalpindi and into 'preventive custody' in the resort town of Murree.

What caused the relatively early demise of the Bhutto regime? The main purpose of this study is to find an answer to that question. Bhutto was not alone in predicting that he would last a long time in office. Political observers inside and outside Pakistan were generally impressed with the firm control that he had established over all the important institutions in the country. And yet it took only four months of an admittedly violent but not a very well organised campaign to dislodge him from the prime ministership. The descent from power proved to be as precipitous and quick as his ascent had been six years earlier.

The reasons for Bhutto's fall can be traced to a complex set of circumstances. The most important conclusion to be drawn from this study is that Bhutto and his associates, in seeking to remould Pakistani society, also sowed the seeds of their own political destruction. In this respect Bhutto's conduct and performance in office were not very different from that of Ayub Khan, his one-time mentor. The political situation that Ayub Khan faced, especially during the second half of the 1960s, was much more difficult than the one Bhutto had to deal with. The conflict between East and West Pakistan that had occupied so much of Ayub's time in the 1966–9 period had been resolved before Bhutto came to power. The question of provincial autonomy that remained after the creation of Bangladesh could be handled much more easily in the context of the Pakistan of the post-1971 period. At the time Bhutto took office there was a widespread feeling that he would have learnt from his experiences – first as the closest political adviser of Ayub Khan, and later as his most determined and articulate enemy – and that his administration would not perpetrate the mistakes of his military predecessor. There was great expectation – encouraged by Bhutto during the 1970 election campaign and also during the time that he was putting pressure on the Yahya regime to abdicate in favour of a civilian administration[3] – that once in power he would rebuild the political institutions that had crumbled during the long army rule. Having taken an active part in the anti-Ayub movement, he was conscious of the importance of institutions for maintaining political tranquillity. The expectation that Bhutto would learn – or perhaps had already learnt – from the mistakes made by his military predecessors, when combined with the perception that the task of political and economic reconstruction that he faced was, in many ways, simpler than the task of political and economic development that Ayub Khan had assumed in 1958, led people to believe that Pakistan in 1972 had finally overcome most of its serious problems. Bhutto, too, encouraged this belief.[4]

But it would be wrong to suggest that Bhutto's fall from power was the result of total failure to learn lessons from history. He was too shrewd a politician and his involvement in the history from which he could learn was too deep for him to have remained totally uninfluenced. The fact that he responded to history's teachings is quite clear from the way in which he formulated public policy. As I will argue in Part II of the book, most of the important objectives of decision-making during his administration were those that were explicitly ignored by the Ayub regime.

Perhaps the most important reason for Bhutto's fall was a failure not of substance but of process. It was the failure to comprehend that in implementing a number of the economic and social measures adopted by his administration he needed the full backing of the broad coalition that had helped him into power. This support would have been available if the constituencies that Bhutto had cultivated assiduously during 1969–71 had been consulted not only in determining the objectives the administration was to adopt, but also in deciding on the manner in which they were to be achieved. Since this was not done there occurred a quick attrition in Bhutto's political support and a number of his followers walked out of the PPP camp and went into that of the opposition, the Pakistan National Alliance.

While it is possible readily to identify the policies that alienated Bhutto's supporters – in fact, a major part of this study will be devoted to a description of those policies and an evaluation of their impact – what is not so easy is to provide an assessment of the motivation behind their adoption. But no work on the Bhutto era can be complete without an assessment of those motives, no matter how speculative such an assessment turns out to be. This emphasis on the identification of the factors that influenced policy-making is important for two reasons, one peculiar to Bhutto's Pakistan and the other important for all those countries that share Pakistan's characteristics.

As I will show in Part II of the book, Bhutto's return to political power was made possible by a populist programme put together by a person who prided himself on his ability to read the public mind. The manifesto of the Pakistan People's Party – issued for the elections of 1970[5] – Bhutto's rhetoric in the campaign preceding the election, his public pronouncements during the Bangladesh crisis, the explanation provided by him of his role in the political drama that drew the curtain on the union between East and West Pakistan[6] and his performance at the United Nations Security Council Session during the Second Indo-Pakistan War all contained elements of a political programme with which a vast majority of the people seemed to sympathise. Accordingly, a powerful public sentiment helped him into power. An equally powerful sentiment swept him out of office. What were the reasons for the souring of the public's attitude towards him? I will argue in this study that a major reason for Bhutto's loss of public support is to be found not so much in the political and economic objectives pursued by his administration, but in the policies that were formulated to achieve them. That is why his failure was more one of process rather than one of substance. In both substance and process, the Bhutto administration differed a great deal from the military regimes before it. In adopting the broad objectives of Bhutto's policies, the civilian administration was much more mindful of the interests of the various groups of people involved. It was less mindful in formulating policies and strategies. The military regimes had fully assumed the task of setting the objectives of and priorities between policies; the civilian administration – or, more accurately, the group of people around Prime Minister Bhutto – assumed the task of designing policies. The military did not consult the people in determining objectives; Bhutto, while aware of the peoples' interests, did not consult with them in formulating policies. It is conceivable that a set of policies different from those actually adopted but aimed at more or less the same goals would have gone down better with the people and possibly would have prolonged his stay in power. The question 'Why were their policies adopted?' can be answered only by understanding the motives behind those that were actually implemented by the government.

In a much-quoted passage, Keynes thought 'that the power of vested interests is vastly exaggerated compared with the gradual encroachment of ideas'. Marxians think it is the power of class interests that is reflected in ideas. In those developing countries in which social and political institutions are still in their embryonic stage, powerful men become powerful by making both ideas and vested interests subservient to them. The interests that supported Bhutto and the ideas that motivated him are clearly stamped on the policies that his administration adopted and implemented. But, in their design and implementation, these policies also have the stamp of Bhutto's personality. It is that personal touch, as much as the social and economic interests that supported him or the ideas that inspired him, that makes Bhutto's conduct in public life so different from that of, say, Mohammad Ali Jinnah and Mohammad Ayub Khan. I should, however, emphasise that my preoccupation with the analysis of the 'idiosyncratic element'[7] in decision-making is not aimed only at establishing a psychological profile of Bhutto. I will also argue in this study that we can gain a great deal of understanding of the remarkable twin phenomena of

Bhutto's rise and fall by identifying the peculiar touches that Bhutto lent to policy-making and implementation and their impact on his political support.

The Bhutto period cannot be described or analysed without placing it in a historical setting. The main purpose of Part I is to provide this perspective. In doing so, however, I have found it necessary to reinterpret a number of developments in Pakistan's history; in other words, to challenge conventional wisdom in many ways. Let me provide some examples. I do not accept a purely nationalistic or religious explanation for the momentum that the Pakistan Movement gathered during the mid-1940s. It is correct that the perception that Muslims in India were a separate nation with not a great deal in common with the non-Muslim subjects of the British *raj* had a great deal to do with Jinnah's success in bringing about the creation of Pakistan. In my view it is also correct that social and economic circumstances convinced a number of urban professionals in the Muslim minority provinces that they would face stiff competition in a united India, while they would be able to dominate a largely rural Pakistan. This perception turned them into ardent, almost fanatical supporters of the Pakistan idea. Similarly, it is only partially correct to argue that a number of Pakistan's problems can be traced to the institutional poverty of the country that was created in 1947. This explanation is only partially correct because Pakistan did inherit a number of institutions that had worked very well in keeping the countryside economically and socially tranquil over a period of one century. What Pakistan lacked in 1947 was not institutions, but 'modern' institutions. I believe, and I will show in this study, that a great deal of the economic and political conflict that has characterised Pakistan's short history can be analysed only in the context of a clash between the traditional institutions that the country inherited and the modern institutions that some groups sought to develop. It is also a conventional wisdom that economic stagnation during the pre-military period (1947–58) and economic dynamism during the Ayub period (1958–69) can be adequately explained in terms of the 'correctness' of the policies that were adopted by the regimes during these two periods. I will show that policies are 'correct' not only because they succeed in achieving certain objectives – some of them defined *ex-post* by analysts – but also because they are the product of a certain environment. In that respect a number of policies adopted during the 1950s were

'more correct' than those adopted during the 1960s. These illustrations of some of the conclusions that I reach in this book should
serve to show that the analysis in Part I is not only for the purpose
of setting the stage; in my view, it also sheds some new light on the
way Pakistan developed during the period before Bhutto.

As should be apparent from this brief introduction, I will draw
on a number of disciplines to tell the story of Bhutto's Pakistan. In
so far as the ebb and flow of political support is concerned, this is a
political study. But, to some considerable extent, political support
was built and lost on account of economic decisions taken by this
administration. A detailed account of economic policies – the
factors that motivated them, the manner in which they were
implemented, the goal they pursued, and the results they
achieved – would make this a study of Pakistan's economic
development during the Bhutto period. The emphasis I place on
the peculiar imprint that Bhutto's personality left on both the
process of decision-making and the way decisions were implemented, would lend a flavour of psycho-history to this study,
while the long discussions of the evolution of various kinds of
economic and political organisations that dominated decision-
making at various times in Pakistan's history should make this a
study of institutional development. The reason for straddling a
number of disciplines lies in my belief that satisfactory explanations for what happened in Pakistan during the period under
study cannot be found in one field of academic inquiry. An
economic interpretation of Bhutto's rise and fall is as unsatisfac-
tory as a political one. A description of the social changes is not
complete without understanding the nature of the economic and
political forces that brought them about.

A work such as this cannot be written in strict chronological
order. For instance, it is not possible to describe Bhutto's ascent to
power without analysing, albeit briefly, the conduct of the military administrations that he succeeded, even when some elements
of that conduct had been discussed before in describing the nature
of political and economic change during the Ayub and Yahya
periods. But a total disregard of time in analysing the developments that have shaped Pakistan's history would be equally
confusing. Accordingly, to help the reader along, I have, by and
large, ordered the chapters in a chronological sequence. Thus
Chapter 2 sets the stage for the developments that took place
during the Ayub and Yahya periods (Chapters 3 and 4) by

providing a brief overview of the developments during the pre-military period. In Part II of the book, the more important policies adopted by the Bhutto regime are described as they happened from the time that the military relinquished power in 1971 to the time when they re-entered the political arena in 1977.

In compiling this study, I have drawn on a number of sources. Since this is an exercise in contemporary history, there is considerable reliance on newspaper reports and analyses, especially in dealing with those developments that have not been studied from some perspective or other. I have also tried out my ideas and hypotheses on a number of people, both Pakistanis and foreigners interested in Pakistan. While no formal interviews were conducted, I consulted a number of knowledgeable people about several important events that shaped history during this period. All written, published and unpublished materials are cited in the work. By and large, I have not attributed oral explanations of events or information received in that way.

In writing about contemporary developments, there is always the possibility that a disproportionate weight may attach to some actions and events that future historians will judge to be of considerably less importance. Such an emphasis can, of course, lend a bias to the story being told. My hope is that if my story has biases they will serve to illuminate rather than obscure.

Part I

The Backdrop

Heed not the blind eye, the echoing ear, nor yet the tongue, but bring to this great debate the test of reason.

Parmenides

2 Insiders and Outsiders

Between August 1947, the month Pakistan emerged as an independent state, and April 1951, the month that the open borders
between India and Pakistan were finally closed, some 14 million
people moved between the two countries. Pakistan lost 6 million
non-Muslims to India, receiving 8 million Muslims in return.
These 8 million migrants – mostly from the Indian states of East
Punjab, Uttar Pradesh, Bihar, Gujarat, Maharashtra and
Hyderabad – in 1951 constituted nearly a quarter of the population of what is now Pakistan. The majority of these outsiders
settled in towns and cities; Karachi became not only the capital of
the new state of Pakistan but also its largest centre of refugee
population. Of the city's 1951 population of 1 million, over
600,000 were refugees from India.[1] Lahore, Hyderabad, Lyallpur
and Rawalpindi also received a large number of refugees. In 1951,
Pakistan's 19 largest cities had a population of nearly 4 million, of
which more than 46 per cent were refugees from India (see Table
2.1).

The refugees brought with them a culture and a set of economic
and political institutions that were totally alien to the areas of
British India that were carved out to form the Muslim state of
Pakistan. But they moved into a society that was predominantly
rural not only in an economic sense, but also in a political and
social sense. Pakistan society was, therefore, born polarised. On
the one side were the rural people with their own customs and
traditions, their own history and institutions. On the other side
was an urban population with relatively more modern institutions
and with goals and aspirations that were completely different
from those of the people who had hitherto dominated the areas
that had now become Pakistan. The conflict between these two
groups determined the course Pakistani society was to take on the
road to economic and political development.

TABLE 2.1   Proportion of refugees in the population of
major Pakistan cities, 1951

City	Total population (thousands)	Refugees (thousands)	Refugees as percentage of total
Karachi	1065	608	57·1
Lahore	849	386	45·5
Hyderabad	242	156	64·5
Rawalpindi	237	95	40·1
Multan	190	83	43·7
Lyallpur	179	126	70·4
Sialkot	168	56	33·3
Peshawar	151	18	11·9
Gujranwala	121	62	51·2
Quetta	84	24	28·6
Sargodha	78	53	67·9
Sukkar	77	42	54·5
Jhang	95	36	37·9
Mardan	78	3	3·8
Sahiwal	75	33	44·0
Kasur	74	12	16·2
Gujrat	60	7	11·7
Bahawalpur	84	21	25·0
Wah	37	7	18·9
Total	3944	1828	46·3

Source: Government of Pakistan, Ministry of the Interior, *Population of Pakistan,
1951* (Karachi 1955).

GROUPS IN CONFLICT

For the purposes of this analysis, it is necessary to identify the
main attributes of the rural milieu in which Pakistan was born.
The attributes of this rural society that should be of interest to us
are a strong institutional base; the factionalised character of its
leadership that could, nevertheless, work most of the time in
harmony; and the ability to adjust to changes in the political
environment by switching the spotlight in the concert of factions
from one set of leaders to another. These characteristics made it
possible for the rural society to withstand challenges by accepting
some minor adjustments for itself. These adjustments, accepted
over a period of more than six centuries, had produced a remarkable stability in the rural society.

The production system around which the rural society was organised dates back to the fourteenth century, when a central authority began to exert influence over what were essentially autonomous village communities. Influence was exerted in order to extract three kinds of surpluses from the rural economy: food for feeding an expanding urban population, savings for financing the central authority and manpower for the armed forces. But these surpluses had to be produced before they could be extracted: the output of the agriculture sector as well as the productivity of the workers engaged in it had to increase before food, revenue and labour could be made available for use outside the village economy. To bring about this increase in output and productivity the central authority helped the village society to organise itself to become a better unit of production. This organisation involved linking vertically the various classes in the village. At the apex was the landlord, at the bottom the people who tilled the soil, with the space in the middle occupied by moneylenders, merchants, artisans, teachers and priests. The only meaningful horizontal interaction between these micro-production and social systems developed when a higher power – the tribal chief, the prince, the king or the state – gathered their members into armies. But armies were not maintained on a permanent basis and these horizontal linkages did not develop a life of their own.

The advent of the British into this area, beginning with the annexation of the Punjab in 1848, proved to be very significant for the institutional development of the rural society. There were at least three reasons for this. First, British rule brought about tranquillity to the region, thereby reducing the need for military service. With opportunities for horizontal contact thus lost altogether, the rural micro-system became even more autarchic. Second, the school of administration founded by John Lawrence in the Punjab[2] provided an elaborate legal cover for all the traditional links that ran between different rural classes. Thus the rules of custom that governed the relationship between the landlord and his cultivator acquired legal sanctity, as did those that linked the landlord with moneylenders, artisans with cultivators, merchants with landlords, and so on.[3] The *mahalwari* system of land administration devised by the British for managing the *mahals* (villages) and integrating them into one rural economy eventually turned these micro-systems into autonomous 'little republics'.[4] Third, the British introduced a system of political representation that further transformed the 'little republics' of the countryside into political factions. At the head of each faction was a big landlord who now commanded the political support of all members of his system. This confluence of a traditional economic set-up with new legal and political systems produced a highly stable environment that was able to accommodate itself to changes at the national level.

This stability was not disturbed even by the Indian Mutiny of 1857.[5] In fact, the British recruited a large force from the Punjab and the Northwest Frontier to put down the mutineers in other parts of India.[6] Again, during the 1940s, these provinces of India remained mostly quiet when the agitation against the British *raj* was taking the rest of India through a period of political turmoil. The Muslim League, to which a number of landed aristocrats belonged, had declared in 1906 that its main purpose was 'to promote, among the Mussulmans of India, feelings of loyalty to the British Government and to remove any misconception that may arise as to the intentions of Government with regard to any of its measures'.[7] When the League changed its objective and adopted the Pakistan resolution, a number of influential Punjabi landlords remained steadfast in their original purpose.[8] Even the Pakistan Movement did not cause a great deal of stir among the people of the Punjab, Sind and the Northwestern Frontier. These provinces became Pakistan because a majority of their populations were Muslims and not because the politically powerful landed aristocracy gave Jinnah's movement overwhelming support. At the time of independence, these three provinces were dominated politically and economically by eighty landed families, which together controlled nearly 3 million acres of land or one-tenth of the total cultivated area and, directly or indirectly, were responsible for the livelihood of half a million households.

The emergence of Pakistan as an independent state would not have destabilised the society had it not also resulted in the influx of 8 million people from what was now India.[9] Whereas the indigenous population of Pakistan was mostly rural, the migrants were mostly urban.[10] And since the migrants had spearheaded the Pakistan Movement, they not only moved into the new country but also took over the command of its political, social and economic life. Accordingly, independence for Pakistan was much more than a surrender of power by the colonialists; in its case, by disturbing the equilibrium the society had achieved, it brought about a traumatic change.

It was a trauma because it resulted in a clash between two systems based on totally different traditions, beliefs and values. The much older indigenous system was rigidly hierarchal, that imported by the migrants broadly participatory. The first was a tightly organised and stable system with vertical linkages between different participants; the second was a loosely clustered system of horizontal linkages between members of different social groups who did not owe allegiance to any particular individual. The principal actors in the first were individuals (landlords); the principal actors in the second were not individuals but social and economic groups (merchants, industrialists, lawyers, teachers, etc.). The indigenous system was stable but archaic, its members were linked together by traditional economic, social, political and cultural forces that reinforced one another; the migrants' system was unstable but modern, its participant groups, having been created by modernisation, were often in conflict with one another. The older system espoused political and economic paternalism; the newer system had embraced *laissez-faire* economics and liberal political institutions.

The system that the migrants brought to Pakistan found its home first in the city of Karachi and later in some other large urban centres of the country. It prevailed over the traditional system because the more powerful amongst the landed aristocrats took time to recover from the shock of India's partition into two nation states. Having opposed Jinnah's two-nation theory, these natural and indigenous leaders of what became West Pakistan were held suspect, their loyalty towards the new state too uncertain for them to be accommodated fully into the new political society. With the indigenous leaders thus excluded from the political arena, the migrants had little problem in structuring the institutions and organisations for the new state that conformed to the system of beliefs and values they brought with them. In economics, the dominant role of the state as established under John Lawrence's school of paternalistic administration and developed by such disciples of his as Montgomery, Darling, Bayne, Jacob and Abbot was now assumed by private entrepreneurs. During the days of the British, the state had created the highly complex and sophisticated irrigation network in the Indus plain. The government constructed the barrages, weirs and canals that constituted the network and also oversaw the settlement of the new lands that were brought under cultivation in 'state colonies'.[11] After the emergence of Pakistan, the regimes of Jinnah and Liaqat

Ali Khan adopted a series of policies that promised almost complete freedom of action to the private entrepreneurs.

AN URBAN BIAS IN POLITICS AND ECONOMICS

> Government will seek to create conditions in which industry and trade may develop and prosper. . . . I would like to call your particular attention to the keen desire of the Government of Pakistan to associate individual initiative and private enterprise at every stage of industrialization. . . . Commerce and Trade are the very lifeblood of the nation. I can no more visualize a Pakistan without traders than I can one without cultivators and civil servants. I have no doubt that in Pakistan, traders and merchants will always be welcome and that they, in building up their own futures, will not forfeit their social responsibility for a fair and square deal to one and all, big and small.[12]

In this statement made before the businessmen at the Eighty-eighth Annual Meeting of the Karachi Chamber of Commerce in April 1948, Mohammad Ali Jinnah announced the basic economic principles that his government was to pursue. In what had been a predominantly agrarian society, industry, trade and commerce were to be vigorously pursued. In a society that, under the British, had become accustomed to paternalistic rule, the government was now to play an essentially supporting role, not actively intervening in economic matters, but helping only to create conditions conducive to the healthy growth of trade and industry. In a society that had previously been dominated so clearly by the landed interests, an equal place was now to be afforded to those who followed other pursuits. Since the state was not going to participate actively in economic decision-making, the assumption was that, with the lifting of government patronage from the agriculture sector, other parts of the economy would have at least an equal chance to flourish.

The main contours of the Jinnah regime's approach towards economic development became visible in the 1948 Industrial Policy. Under this, the government committed itself to public ownership in only three groups of industries: arms and ammunitions of war; the generation of hydroelectric power; and the manufacture and operation of railway, telephone, telegraph, and wireless equipment.[13] Given the underdeveloped state of the country's industrial sector, the private entrepreneur was not likely to move into these 'reserved spheres' for some considerable time. The reservation of these industries for development by the public sector was, therefore, an academic exercise. The British had concentrated development effort in the agricultural sector, where their paternalistic approach coincided with that of the landed aristocracy. The first Pakistani regime gave priority to the development of the industrial sector. This was in part due to the situation created by the break-up of the customs union between the two independent states of India and Pakistan and in part because of the exclusion of the landed aristocracy from the decision-making arena.[14] The neglect of the agricultural sector during this period was also due to the fact that the large landlords, not accustomed to entrepreneurial activity in a *laissez-faire* environment, were not prepared to undertake new investment. The removal of the guiding hand of the state created a situation in which they found it exceedingly difficult to function.

The institutions that supported this shift in emphasis from the development of the agricultural sector and rural areas to that of the industrial sector and urban areas included a political party, family firms and business and industrial associations. Each of these three institutions were to play an important role during this early period in Pakistan's history. Accordingly, each merits some discussion.

Under Jinnah and his successor Liaqat, the Muslim League remained a party with a strong refugee representation and, accordingly, a pronounced urban bias. The common view that the Muslim League was a party dominated by landed interests with little relevance for the people or the professions far removed from the countryside is accurate for the period 1906, when the League was founded, to 1937, when Jinnah returned to it as its president.[15] From then on, until about the mid-1940s, the Muslim League picked up the support of the urban middle classes, in particular of those Muslims who found little meaning in their role in the Indian National Congress. This attitude of alienation from Hindu politics was best exemplified by Jinnah, once proclaimed the 'ambassador of Hindu–Muslim unity',[16] and also by a number of middle-ranking leaders who were to become active in the Muslim League at the provincial and district levels. But most of these people

belonged to those parts of British India that could not be included
in the state of Pakistan. On migrating to Pakistan, they found
residence in the larger urban areas of the new country. These
refugee-dominated cities became the centres of Muslim League
activity. The landed classes of the Punjab, Sind and the Northwest Frontier – particularly the very large and important segments that had either opposed the Pakistan Movement or, at best,
had remained lukewarm towards it – remained excluded from the
Muslim League. The reaction of the countryside to this situation
conformed to the tradition that had been developed over centuries. The rural society began to realign itself behind the leaders
who had been somewhat less articulate in their opposition to the
Pakistan Movement. This process of realignment was to take six
years to complete; once completed, the landlords were prepared
to bounce back into the political arena. When they did so, they not
only overcame the urban bias of the Muslim League, but also
caused a number of changes to be incorporated into the party's
decision-making process.[17]

The view that the Muslim League was a monolithic organisation dominated by its president is true for the party of the 1940–8
period, from the time that Jinnah won the support of a large
number of prominent local leaders to the time of his death.[18] It is
not true for the League in the post-Jinnah period. Jinnah, the
Quaid-i-Azam, was simultaneously Governor-General of Pakistan, President of the Muslim League and President of the Constituent Assembly. His death resulted in a great deal of his
political power devolving on his principal lieutenant, Liaqat Ali
Khan. But Liaqat did not feel powerful enough to claim any of the
three jobs that Jinnah had held. As Prime Minister, he became the
constitutional head of the government, leaving the redefined and
therefore the largely honorific job of Governor-General to
Khwaja Nazimuddin,[19] at that time Chief Minister of the province of East Bengal. Tamizuddin Khan, another Bengali politician, became President of the Constituent Assembly, while
Choudhry Khaliquzzaman,[20] a refugee from India, became President of the Muslim League. While Liaqat established control over
the administration as the Prime Minister of a 'parliamentary
democracy', Khaliquzzaman did not surrender all political power
to the Prime Minister. Under him the President of the Muslim
League and the twenty-eight-man working committee continued
to function independently of the Prime Minister and his Cabinet

colleagues. Under Jinnah and Khaliquzzaman, the League working committee had a strong urban professional class presence,
particularly those that had migrated from India. Of the twenty-
eight members of the committee, seventeen, or over 60 per cent,
were representative of this class.[21]

Until such time as we know more about the process of decision-
making within the Muslim League during the time that a number
of important initiatives were taken about the course that Pakistan
was to follow in economic development, it seems right to conclude
from the evidence available to us at present that the party acted as
a representative of a number of social and economic groups that
were active in the refugee population. And, in acting for the
refugees, the Muslim League – and in particular, its powerful
working committee – was able to persuade the administration of
Liaqat Ali Khan to emphasise industrial development in the
private sector. This decision was to have a profound impact on
Pakistan's political development; the fact that by 1969 ten out of
the twelve largest industrial houses in the country had their
pre-independence headquarters located outside the provinces
that were to become Pakistan[22] was not lost on the groups that had
a much firmer political base *in* Pakistan, and, as I will indicate
later, contributed to the development of the Bhutto regime's
attitude towards industrial development.

The question of why Pakistan's industrial development came to
be dominated by refugee merchant-industrialists has both political and institutional answers. The political explanation has been
provided already: the new industrial entrepreneurs of Pakistan
belonged to the groups that had supported Jinnah's movement
and, after the partition of British India, had migrated to Pakistan,
mostly on the urging of the new Governor-General. But, as we saw
above, the state's attitude towards industrial development, as
reflected in the 1948 Industrial Policy statement, removed the
government's guiding hand from the industrial sector. The private sector, left to its own devices, need not have favoured one part
of it. The fact that the merchant-industrialists from among the
migrant population came to dominate Pakistan's economic life is
also to be explained in terms of institutional development. By
1948, when Pakistan launched its first drive towards industrialisation, a number of families had organised institutions that not
only made it possible for them to make a quick entry into the
industrial field, but also affected the future development of the

industrial sector. Two such institutions deserve special mention: family holding firms that provided the basis for the development of industry on conglomerate lines, and trade and industrial associations that made it possible for the new entrepreneurs to react collectively, rather than individually, to the political decision-makers.

While Hindus and Parsees dominated the first phase of India's industrial development that began in late nineteenth century,[23] the non-agricultural activity among the Muslims was limited to a few families from the west coast. These families came to specialise in trade in processed and non-processed agricultural commodities, mostly leather, cotton and foodgrains. The non-Muslim industrial entrepreneurs, by virtue of their Western education, had attained a degree of modernisation and the enterprises they founded were basically run on modern lines. However, Muslim traders and merchants continued to conduct business on traditional lines, one aspect of which were firms that depended entirely on members of the extended family, clan or community for capital, management and personnel. Accordingly, most of the large Muslim business houses were organised vertically, with the more prominent positions held by one or two families of the same clan or community and with less important members occupying the lower echelons of the firm's hierarchy. There was little outside capital invested in the enterprises. This manner of management and resource mobilisation was to develop later into a system of 'managing companies' that came to dominate much of the industrial wealth of the nation in the decade of the 1960s.

While the individual houses were organised vertically, by late 1940s a degree of horizontal co-ordination was achieved between them largely as a result of the efforts of Jinnah and his colleagues. Jinnah and his associates used the relatively modern devise of trade and merchant associations to bring the Muslim entrepreneurs together; it was under this influence that the Federation of Muslim Chambers of Commerce and Industry was organised in 1943 'to focus commercial opinion and to represent the corporate and collective view of the Muslim Commercial Community; to play a vigorous and an ever-watchful part in the political and economic life of the community'.[24] One immediate consequence of the establishment of these horizontal links between business houses was the growth of what has been described as the 'nation-building'[25] enterprises. Four companies – a bank, an insurance company, a shipping line and an airline[26] – were set up with capital and management personnel being contributed by the large business houses. In setting up these enterprises, the Muslim business houses for the first time in their history moved both resources and manpower laterally, setting up a precedence that was later to lend a conglomerate character to Pakistan's industrial development.

Jinnah's modernising impact on the trading and commercial houses, owned and managed by the Muslims, has not received notice from scholars even though it had a profound influence on the economic and political development of Pakistan. The trade associations and the chambers of commerce that he caused to be set up not only at the federal level, but also in the more important provinces of British India, and the nation-building companies that were put together under his direction, prepared the business community to exploit the situation created by the break-up in 1949 of the customs union between India and Pakistan. The dissolution of the custom union resulted in the stoppage of all trade between the two countries, producing a serious shortage of all consumer goods in Pakistan.[27] With the 1948 Industrial Policy beckoning the private entrepreneurs, the economic vacuum created by the India–Pakistan trade war brought Jinnah's business followers rushing in. Their entry produced an industrial revolution that in less than two decades was to make Pakistan self-sufficient in most industrially produced goods of common consumption.

ECONOMIC AND POLITICAL INDIGENISATION

The influence wielded by the refugees began to diminish after the assassination of Liaqat Ali Khan in 1951 and the assumption of the governor-generalship by Ghulam Mohammad in the same year. Ghulam Mohammad was not a politician; trained as a public accountant and having served a number of princely states in British India, he had been brought into the Cabinet by Liaqat as a technician in charge of finance. Once in that position he had gained considerable political power, mostly by aligning himself with the Punjab landlords, most of whom – as we saw above – had been excluded from positions of power. His training and background meant that he had no affinity with the Muslim League

politicians; his training and background did not also cultivate in
him any respect for the political institutions that Pakistan was still
in the process of developing. His summary dismissal in 1953 of the
Cabinet of Khwaja Nazimuddin, who had stepped down from
governor-generalship after Liaqat's assassination to become
Pakistan's second Prime Minister, and his dissolution of the
Constituent Assembly a year later, were clearly extra-legal acts.
Being extra-legal, they were the first assaults on the process of
political institutional development in Pakistan. Although
Ghulam Mohammad's actions were vindicated by the Federal
Court, the rather tortuous argument used by Chief Justice Munir
left little doubt that he was providing legal cover for the Governor-
General's acts in order to save the country from an even graver
constitutional crisis.

Khwaja Nazimuddin's dismissal and his replacement by an
individual relatively unknown in West Pakistani politics resulted
in a severe loss of power and prestige on the part of the Muslim
League. Mohammad Ali, the new Prime Minister, had been
hand-picked by the Governor-General; the Muslim League working committee's endorsement came after his selection had been
announced by Ghulam Mohammad. Also responsible for the
Muslim League's decline was the dissolution of the first Constituent Assembly. While agreeing that the Governor-General
had the constitutional right to dissolve the Constituent Assembly,
the Federal Court ordered that a new Assembly should be convened. When it was finally convened, it turned out to be much less
representative of the groups that had held power in the Muslim
League. The indirect election that produced the new Constituent
Assembly set in motion the process of political indigenisation
which involved loss of power by the refugee groups to those who
were natives to Pakistan. But this transfer of power was not
brought about in a situation of political tranquillity; from the time
that the Nazimuddin Cabinet was dismissed to the time that the
military intervened in Pakistan's politics – a space of only five
years – four Prime Ministers were called upon to form six different
administrations. In this period, the Muslim League was squarely
beaten in Bengal by the United Front – a coalition of diverse
groups that was put together with the main purpose of ridding
Dacca of the Muslim League – and its position of political
monopoly was seriously challenged in the Punjab with the formation of the landlord-dominated Republican Party.

The tension between the groups that supported the Muslim League and those who sought to re-enter the political arena by floating new parties resulted in a serious weakening of the legislative institutions of government. As the political parties battled with one another, the executive branch of the government, now under the firm control of the powerful Civil Service of Pakistan (CSP), came to dominate Karachi as well as the provincial capitals:

> Consequently, we are prompted to ... enquire whether, in our present state of political development, the administrative problem of law and order cannot be divorced from a democratic bed fellow called a Ministerial Government, which is so remorselessly haunted by political nightmares. But if democracy means the subordination of law and order to political ends – then Allah knoweth best and we end the report.

The quotation is from the report[28] written by the Court of Inquiry appointed by the federal government to look into the causes of the bloody anti-Ahmadiya riots that, in 1953, had resulted in scores of deaths mostly in and around Lahore. Only four years earlier, Chief Justice Munir, the president of the Court of Inquiry, as chairman of the Pay Commission, had urged the government of Liaqat Ali Khan to move talent out of public into private life since the 'correct place for our men of genius is in private enterprise and not in the humdrum career of public service where character and the desire to serve honestly for a living is more essential than outstanding talent'.[29] This view was in keeping with the philosophy of the regime of the day, which favoured a parliamentary form of government and *laissez-faire* economics. But now, with the gradual eclipse of the political power of the groups that favoured this approach, Justice Munir, too, had changed his opinion. The civil servants and the institutions that they dominated now constituted the steel frame of the administration rather than the politicians, their political parties and the legislature. Thus:

> [This inquiry] has given us an opportunity to ask our officers, on whom lies the burden of administration, to bear this burden in the traditions of the steel frame, when we saw the erect figure of a district officer in the middle of an excited procession, a soft smile on a firm mouth, determination written on his face.[30]

The passing of the administration of Khwaja Nazimuddin in 1953 not only resulted in a serious dilution in the power of legislative institutions, and of the political parties and the social groups that had dominated the Pakistan Movement, it also resulted in a fundamental change of approach as regards economic and political development. After 1953, the relatively more modernised elements in society gave way to the relatively more traditional groups. With the passing of power from urban professionals to landed interests, Pakistan's history entered into a new phase: the period of indigenisation. This period was marked by the increasing bureaucratic control of the government and a simultaneous increase in the importance of the public sector in the economic life of the country.

Although the members of the CSP had social and economic backgrounds considerably different from those of the landed interests – according to one estimate, only 13 per cent were from landed families while 64 per cent were from families with long histories of government service[31] – the two groups were able very quickly to forge a strong alliance between themselves. The CSP was the descendant of the Indian Civil Service, the Punjab component of which, under John Lawrence, had founded the paternalist school of administration. Now back in power after an interregnum that lasted for only six years, the Civil Service was prepared to go back to paternalism, to assume once again the main responsibility for managing not only the country's administration, but also the more vital parts of its economy. As we saw above, the landlords, because of their long association with the British *raj*, felt comfortable with this system of bureaucratic guidance and intervention. Accordingly, in the 1953–62 period, Pakistan moved from a parliamentary to a bureaucratic form of government and from an economy dominated by the private sector to an economy guided by the Civil Service. Accompanying this change was a change on the institutional side; political parties crumbled as parties and were reduced to loose associations of interest groups, business and merchant associations ceased to function actively as the representatives of economically vigorous groups and bureaucratic institutions gained both strength and prestige. The commonly accepted explanation that scarcity led to the large-scale intervention of government in the economy is, therefore, only partially correct. While it is true that 'the country's resources were inadequate to do all it wanted it to do, especially after the end of the Korean boom' and while it is also true that Pakistan could not achieve simultaneously the rate of growth and the degree of equity considered essential without a sharp increase in domestic and foreign resource mobilisation,[32] these problems need not have turned the decision-makers towards direct controls. That most industries in Pakistan, being at that time on the 'learning curve', were experiencing teething problems and that, with industrialisation having only recently begun, service, supply and marketing facilities were very inadequate, are also not satisfactory explanations for the exercise of government control over the economy. The objectives of rapid growth, moderate redistribution and infant industry protection could have been achieved with the government laying only a light hand on the economy. The fact that the government chose to be heavy-handed was mainly due to the re-emergence of the paternalistic bureaucrats and the landed interests as the most powerful elements in society.

The government's intervention in the economy took several forms. By far the most important of these was the reactivation of the Pakistan Industrial Development Corporation (PIDC). This corporation had been set up in 1950 during the period when the stewardship of the industrial sector was firmly in the hands of the Karachi-based refugee industrialists. Accordingly, the principal task entrusted to the PIDC was to bring industrialisation to East Bengal, Pakistan's other wing. The corporation's first major project was the Karnafuli paper mill, located in the Chittagong hill tracts of East Pakistan. With the political power of the refugees now considerably reduced, the government after 1953 began to give serious consideration to developing a new industrial entrepreneurial class that belonged to or was politically and socially close to such indigenous groups as the landlords of the Punjab and Sind and the landed interests of the Northwest Frontier. In achieving this objective, the PIDC proved to be invaluable.

The landed families of the Punjab, Sind and the Northwest Frontier, while now on the road to political rehabilitation, did not have the experience, the institutions or the liquidity to facilitate their entry into the industrial sector. The quick conversion of the refugee merchants into industrial entrepreneurs was made possible by the presence of experienced family-run organisations that could be readily adapted to manage industrial enterprises. These families also had large liquid reserves that could be ploughed into the industrial sector. The landlords of central and northern Pakistan, on the other hand, had the bulk of their wealth in physical assets that could not be easily liquidated and their lands were managed by institutional devices that, having been forged over centuries, could not be used for running modern enterprises. If they were to enter the industrial sector, they would not need the type of assistance from the government which was required by, and granted to, the country's first industrial entrepreneurs. They would need, instead, government financing, technical assistance and protection from competition: a totally different orientation in the government's attitude towards development from the one adopted in the 1947–53 period. But, as I indicated above, not an entirely new orientation: the pre-independence administrations had provided the same kind of umbrella to the development of agriculture, particularly in the newly opened canal colonies in the central parts of the Punjab. Therefore, while the landed interests did not have the resources to become successful industrialists, the bureaucrats were able to perform the role of industrial entrepreneurs. This they did not by becoming industrialists themselves but by using their experience to establish a framework in which entrepreneurship could flourish. The PIDC established such a framework.

It is significant that while the PIDC was established in 1950, it was not until 1953 that it undertook its first major operation in West Pakistan. It is also significant that in choosing the corporation's management, the post-1953 administrations did not turn to the people who had now some experience in industrial management but to the bureaucrats, mostly from the Punjab and the Frontier. Ghulam Faruque, its first chairman, has been likened to Enrico Mattei in Italy and Robert Moses in New York. He was a 'strong-willed, powerful individual who made rapid decisions, saw them carried out, and worried about government rules, procedures, or approval only afterwards, if at all'.[33] He was also from the civil bureaucracy, came from a landed background and belonged to the Northwest Frontier. There was little in common between him and the merchants who had supported Jinnah in the 1940s and spearheaded the industrial development of Pakistan in the early 1950s. The chairman hired a member of the CSP as the corporation's secretary and brought in enterprise managers quite different from those of private entrepreneurs.[34] Typically from the Punjab and the Northwest Frontier, and with such specialities as accountancy, economics and advertising, these middle-level PIDC functionaries were as different from their counterparts in private business as was their chairman from the heads of Karachi industrial houses.

With strong support from the government, the PIDC soon emerged as a major force in the industrial sector. In 1953, the beginning of the period of political and economic indigenisation, the corporation's assets totalled only $35 million or just under 7 per cent of the total for the sector. Six years later, the PIDC interests amounted to over 16 per cent of the country's industrial wealth.[35] Its share in industrial employment increased from only 3 per cent in 1953 to nearly 20 per cent in 1959 and the proportion of total industrial raw material and capital equipment imports going to it from 5 to 25 per cent. By the start of the Ayub era, the PIDC was by far the largest industrial conglomerate in the country: in terms of assets and employment more than five times that of the largest industrial house in the private sector and almost as large as the twelve largest private houses combined.[36] By using the PIDC, therefore, the government was able to dilute considerably the monopolistic power of the Karachi-based merchant-industrialists. By allowing the corporation to invest equity capital in and share in the management of private enterprises, the government was also able to introduce a number of Punjabis and Pathans, mostly from landed backgrounds, into the industrial sector. In this activity, the PIDC was helped by the Pakistan Industrial Credit and Investment Corporation (PICIC); set up in 1957, this corporation made loans and equity investment for the establishment of new enterprises and the expansion of old ones.

A comparison of the rates of return from PIDC enterprises with those in the private sector – PIDC's 'rate of profit is only about one-quarter, and the rate of return only about one-half, the rates reported by large private firms in the low profit year of 1958' – persuaded several economists to conclude that the government had made a mistake in relying so heavily on the public sector to push industrialisation.[37] This assessment, based as it is on conventional criteria which were not the basis of the government's decision to turn to the public sector in the first place, is, of course, not correct. The PIDC and such credit agencies as the PICIC were not mistakes when viewed in terms of the objectives of the political administrations: a very important reason for the establishment of these corporations was to dilute the economic power of the Karachi-based industrialists by bringing new entrepreneurs into the industrial sector, and in achieving this objective PIDC and PICIC were remarkably successful.

The accumulation of power in the hands of the civil servants did not limit the control exercised by the government to the creation of new corporations. Going back to the traditions inherited from the British *raj*, the bureaucracy in Pakistan developed a vast machinery of physical controls over all aspects of the economy. Most important of these was the control over foreign exchange, its use and allocation. The powerful Ministry of Commerce at the federal level, aided by the Chief Controller of Import and Export – two branches of the government with heavy CSP representation – took up the preparation of a 'positive import list'. Only those items could be brought into the country that were included in the list, all others must be considered banned. In this respect, the controls were similar to those that were used by the British during the war; and, as in the case of the British administrators, they gave the Pakistani bureaucracy the power to make or break industrialists. This power was used not so much to hurt the established industrialists as to favour the newcomers.

Given the return of the landed class to the political arena, we should expect a turn around in the fortunes of the agricultural sector. But the agricultural sector continued to stagnate, its rate of growth during this period being no higher than it had been when the power of decision-making rested with the urban classes. The reason for the continuing stagnation of the agricultural sector is to be found in a complex set of economic, political and social circumstances.[38] As economic men, the landlords maximised their returns within the constraints imposed by the availability of resources and the state of technology. For the big landlords, water, not land, was the real constraint and now that some political power had returned to them they used it to persuade the government to extend the already very extensive Indus irrigation system. With some increase in water thus becoming available, their typical response was 'to extend the acreage which in the past they left totally unused, rather than to increase the water applied to the acreage they were already cultivating'.[39] In doing this, the landlords behaved both as economic maximisers operating in an environment of uncertainty and also as political men. As political beings, their emphasis was on extensive rather than intensive cultivation. The more land they could bring under their control, the larger their constituency and the greater their political power. Evidence of this behaviour can be seen when one examines the charges brought by the regime of Ayub Khan against a number of politicians who held public office before the 1958 *coup d'état*. The Elective Bodies (Disqualification) Order (EBDO) was issued in August 1959, and was applied to any person who had held any public office or position, including membership of any elective body in the country, and was found guilty of misconduct while holding that office. Some 6000 persons 'laboured under the EBDO';[40] and, of all big landlords, as many as 40 per cent were charged under the provisions of the Order. Of those so charged, nearly 80 per cent were found to have used their official powers for either 'diverting to their lands a higher proportion than was allowed by law and customs of the available irrigation water', or 'for changing the scope and extent of government-sponsored irrigation schemes in such a way that a higher proportion than planned originally of new irrigation water was made available for use on their lands'.[41]

This near-monopolistic control of a scarce resource for production increased the aggregate wealth of the landlords, if not productivity of the land they cultivated. Since the productivity of the land did not increase – and in many cases declined – the overall impact on output of the political return of the landed aristocracy was at best indifferent. As we see from Table 2.2 almost all economic indices reflecting the health of the agricultural economy in 1959/60 show a deterioration as compared with that in 1949/50. The only exception is the rate of private sector investment and this may reflect not so much the political health of the landlords as the change in administration in October 1958 (see Chapter 3).

The reason behind the quick changes in political institutions that we see in this period of Pakistan's history are as complex as those that dictated some of the economic developments discussed above. It is as wrong to argue that the collapse of the Muslim League and of 'Westminster democracy' during this period was due to the political inexperience of those who now handled power[42] as it is to suggest that the bureaucratic control of the economy that was to become pervasive was due to the absence of viable economic institutions in the private sector. As indicated above, the private sector's endowment with economic institutions, while not altogether rich, was sufficient to launch the

TABLE 2.2   Performance of West Pakistan's agricultural sector

	1949/50	1959/60	1968/69
Share in Gross Provincial Product (%)	52	49	41
Per capita income in the agricultural sector (Rs)	214	197	278
Total agricultural output *per capita* (Rs)	187	171	195
Public sector investment in agriculture as a proportion of total investment (%)	2·5	2·2	4·8
Private sector investment in agriculture as a proportion of total investment (%)	2·9	3·5	–
Total food grains production *per capita* (kg)	188	151	202
Per annum rate of growth of crop production (%)	2·3	–	5·4

Source: Shahid Javed Burki, 'The Development of Pakistan's Agriculture: Some Interdisciplinary Explanation', in Robert Stevens, Hamza Alavi, Peter Bertocci (eds), *Rural Development in Bangladesh and Pakistan* (Honolulu: University of Hawaii Press, 1976), p. 291.

country on the road to rapid industrialisation. The turning away from the leadership of the private sector to that of a centralised bureaucracy was not so much due to institutional poverty as to the conflict between two groups of people, the refugees and the locals. Similarly, the shift in the course of political development was in large part due to the clash between the same groups. The process of indigenisation, which commenced with the ascent of Ghulam Mohammad to power, brought those groups the Muslim League had kept outside the political arena right into the middle of it. As the outsiders became insiders, there also occurred a corresponding change on the institutional side.

The Muslim League – initially convened as a gathering of the landed interests – was able to introduce a Westminster touch into Muslim politics largely because of the middle-class urban professionals who gained control of the party under Jinnah's stewardship. This orientation was gradually lost as the landed families began to reassert their control over the political process. The interests that the refugee leaders represented could be accommodated within the quasi-modern political party that the Muslim League had come to be during the late 1940s. The various organs of the party – the Parliamentary Board, the Council, the Working Committee, the Provincial Leagues – allowed the debate and interaction that was necessary for the protection and representation of the interests that needed 'horizontal contacts' in order to arbitrate between themselves. The vertically organised landed community had little use for these contacts at various levels; its requirement was better served by a factionalised party or by political parties that represented different factions than by an organisation such as the Muslim League of the late 1940s and early 1950s.

The fracturing of the Muslim occurred soon after Nazimuddin's dismissal by Ghulam Mohammad. Of the more important factions that were to emerge, the most powerful one was organised with the active support of the Governor-General. This faction turned to the landed aristocracy for support which, although provided with enthusiasm, was not without conditions, some implicit and others explicit. The explicit condition was the demand for a share in power, particularly at the provincial level. Accordingly, Mumtaz Daultana, the leader of the progressive wing of the Muslim League in rural Punjab, was dismissed as the Chief Minister and replaced by Sir Feroze Khan Noon, a big landlord from the district of Sargodha. In the Northwest Frontier Province, the chief ministership went to Sardar Abdur Rashid, who had the confidence of that province's landed gentry. Rashid displaced Abdul Quyum Khan, who was clearly the representative of the urban and rural middle classes not only in the Frontier, but also in national politics. Finally, in the province of Sind, the chief ministership went from M. A. Khuhro to Pirzada Abdul Sattar. While Khuhro was a large landlord, he was identified more with organisational than with landlord politics. As the Chief Minister of Sind, he had resisted the efforts of the Governor-General to intervene in political decision-making, arguing for the preservation of 'Westminster-style democracy".[43]

The implicit condition put forward by the landlords in coming to the assistance of the Muslim League was a total change in the structure of command and in the process of policy-making in the party. The landed aristocracy were aware of the fact that if the working committee, which was still in the control of the urban professionals, continued to influence decision-making, they could at best hope to achieve only a secondary role in the party. It was also clear that it would not be possible to bring about a quick change in the working committee's personnel. And, perhaps most important of all, the landlords did not feel comfortable with a process of decision-making that depended on debate, discussion and majority vote. Accordingly, the new leadership in the League rammed through procedural changes that gave a great deal of power to the national and provincial presidents, thereby effectively emasculating the secretary-generals and their working committees. The organisational changes brought about by the re-entry of the landlords into the party were important not only because they resulted in the eventual departure from the party of the more modernised elements, they were also important in helping to evolve an organisational model that was to be copied by all other important political parties in the future. While the League was virtually to disappear from Pakistan's political scene, it left an imprint on the course of political development that proved to be remarkably durable. The imprint was not that of Jinnah's organisation (1937–48) or even that of Liaqat Ali Khan's (1948–51). It was that of Ghulam Mohammad – a party with a strong central figure and a weak, even undefined, organisation structure; in which party functionaries were appointed by the central authority and not elected by the membership; in which decisions were taken to satisfy not the majority of the membership, but the most powerful faction leaders; in which efforts were made to increase political influence not by expanding and cultivating grassroot support, but by bringing in new factions; and in which the pursuit or maintenance of office rather than of ideas and ideology was the main preoccupation of the leadership. It was around this model that Iskandar Mirza, who succeeded Ghulam Mohammad as Governor-General and then became Pakistan's first constitutional President, organised his Republican Party. Ayub Khan's Pakistan Muslim League (1962–70) also followed this pattern as did the Pakistan People's Party of Zulfikar Ali Bhutto in the post-1973 period.

In addition to the weakening of the organisational structure of the Muslim League, the social realignment that occurred in Pakistan politics in the post-1953 period was to have one other significant consequence: the emergence of smaller ideological parties. The Muslim League was not only fractured into factions, some of the groups that did not feel comfortable in the new set-up left to form new parties. These were not splinter groups, as a number of political scientists would have us believe,[44] but genuine political parties that, over time, were to develop their own ideology, constituency and organisational style. While the Muslim League reappeared and disappeared on several occasions, serving the interests and responding to the whims of some national leaders, these smaller parties continued to grow in power and prestige.

The most important of them was the National Awami Party. Established first as an all-Pakistan organisation with a following in both the eastern and western wings of the country, it soon divided into three groups: the Awami League in East Pakistan, the National Awami Party (Muzaffar Group), also in East Pakistan, and the NAP (Wali Khan group) in West Pakistan. While the Awami League began to identify itself with 'provincial autonomists' in East Pakistan and the NAP-Muzaffar with socialists in the same province, the West Pakistan NAP turned its attention to the progressive elements in the countryside. As we saw above, these elements had exercised considerable influence in Muslim politics during the Pakistan Movement, when the bulk of the landed aristocracy remained loyal to the idea of a united India. However, with the return of the landlords to the political arena and their absorption into the Muslim League, the 'rural progressives' were obliged to start a party of their own. Those who stayed on in the Muslim League – a group best represented by Mumtaz Daultana – lost their following, while those who moved into the NAP were to build for themselves a strong political base, particularly in the provinces of the Northwest Frontier and Baluchistan. This conflict between rural progressives and conservatives was to have considerable significance in influencing Ayub Khan's approach to political and economic development. As I will show in Chapter 4 below, Ayub not only espoused the progressive's cause during the 1958–62 period, but also provided them with institutional means (the system of Basic Democracies) for influencing government decision-making. One reason for Ayub's fall in 1969 was that he turned away from this group at a time when it had gathered considerable political and economic strength.

The *Nizam-i-Islam* (the Islamic System) Party was born in circumstances similar to those of the NAP, although it catered for the groups at the other end of the political spectrum. The indigenisation of politics first diluted the political importance of urban professionals, while the demise of Muslim League, a little later, removed the political institution that had served them. Accordingly, in 1956 a group of urban professionals under the leadership of Chaudri Mohammad Ali – the most senior civil servant to be inherited by Pakistan from the British Indian administration, who later became the new country's fourth Prime Minister – reassembled under the conservative banner of *Nizam-i-Islam*. The party weakened during the early 1960s, when Ayub Khan managed to bring some of these groups under his wing, but re-emerged later and was reconstituted as *Tehrik-i-Istiqlal* by Air-Marshal Asghar Khan.

RISE AND FALL OF INSTITUTIONS

Pakistan's early history, therefore, is marked by the birth, development and demise of a number of political and economic institutions. None of them took root, not because Pakistani society could function only in an institutional vacuum, but because its various components did not succeed in reaching a state of equilibrium. Although Jinnah had won the partition of British India on the basis of his two-nation theory, deep social and economic fissures continued to run through the Muslim nation that he created.

The recurrent crises in Pakistan's history are the product of the clash between various interests. There was political and economic tranquillity whenever one group succeeded in dominating those that differed with it. The 1948–53 period was characterised by the domination by the urban professional classes of the political and economic system. This domination was achieved through such institutional devices as a quasi-modern political party, trade and industrial associations, family-run business houses and financial institutions. Institutions such as these never became sufficiently broad and representative to accommodate rival interests; even when this domination produced tranquillity it could only be temporary. It disappeared when the groups excluded from power found an opportunity to reassert their influence. This happened in 1953 when that powerful section of the landed aristocracy that had been excluded from the political and economic arenas returned to challenge the monopoly of the urban professionals. The conflict that ensued not only created a great deal of political confusion and contributed to a sharp slow-down in economic development, but also entirely changed the institutional structure that supported the society. The rules of the market that governed the behaviour of business, industrial and financial institutions were replaced by rules that were formulated by the now powerful bureaucracy. The broadly democratic rules of discourse and decision followed by the most important political parties gave way to the patrimonial mode of decision-making in most of the political organisations into which the parties eventually split. But these institutions were also incapable of resolving the social, economic and political tensions that remained in the society. They were also to succumb to the challenge thrown at them by the groups they could not embrace.

The picture that we get from most of the economic and political literature on Pakistan is that of a society moving aimlessly from one crisis to another. The picture that I would like to present here is not of directionless wandering but of deliberately executed moves by combatants in a ring. The moves were simple and easy to understand when they were made by a few groups and individuals; as more individuals and groups entered the arena, the moves became more subtle and the game more intense. The main purpose of this study is to understand the nature of the play; the principal function of this chapter was to set the stage for this kind of analysis.

3 The Search for a New Constituency

On 22 October 1958, responding to a call from General Mohammad Ayub Khan, Zulfikar Ali Bhutto joined Pakistan's first military government as Minister in charge of the portfolios of fuel, power and natural resources. He was then thirty-one years old. The only son of Sir Shahnawaz Bhutto, a wealthy and well-known landlord from Sind who himself had been active in politics, Zulfikar Ali had been carefully prepared for a career in politics. He was the heir to a powerful political empire that had been built by his father in central Sind. In this capacity, Zulfikar Ali Bhutto was expected to look after the interests of his family and those of other large landed aristocrats of Sind and to help the relatively backward province of Sind catch up with the more advanced parts of Pakistan. These objectives were clearly in conflict with those political goals to which he began to subscribe as a member of that small but rapidly growing class of people who can perhaps be described as Pakistan's urban intelligentsia. These objectives included a system of government based on institutions that offered political participation to a broad segment of the population, achievement of political balance between those who wielded power because of their access to sources of wealth and those who were potentially powerful because of their very large number, the right of the government to intervene when the markets failed to deliver equitably to all classes of people the additions to the wealth of a nation, and the need for the developing countries to come together and construct a new international economic order that would allow equality of opportunity to all nations and to all people.

While a number of events in Bhutto's political life and a number of actions taken by him in and out of office can be traced to this sharp conflict of interests between the social class into which he was born and the class to which he belonged intellectually, there was also another influence that should be given some weight in assessing his political behaviour. Zulfikar Ali had just entered his teens when Mohammad Ali Jinnah got the idea of Pakistan as a separate homeland for the followers of Islam in India accepted by a vast majority of the Indian Muslim community. The passage of the 'Pakistan Resolution' by the All-India Muslim League in 1940 produced a highly charged atmosphere that profoundly affected all those who breathed in it. The influence was considerably more profound for a young man whose father's house in Bombay was used as a meeting ground by a number of prominent Muslim leaders. As a teenager, Zulfikar Ali began to debate earnestly the issues that had divided the Hindu and Muslim communities of the Indian sub-continent.[1] This experience left a deep impression on Bhutto and influenced his approach towards India in general and towards the 'problems' of Kashmir and Bengali secessionists in particular.

The tension between these influences became apparent as Bhutto gained political experience. Entry into Ayub Khan's Cabinet was Bhutto's first venture into active politics. He was brought in as a Sindhi and as a representative of the landed aristocracy – two constituencies that his heritage obliged him to serve. However, once in the Cabinet, Bhutto began to cultivate a new political base for himself. In doing so, he gradually turned towards the left of the political spectrum. This move was to prove significant for many reasons. Its most important consequence was that the left in Pakistani politics acquired a leader of great political skill and dynamism.

The fact that the big landlords in the provinces that were to be carved out of British India to form West Pakistan had initially opposed the idea of a separate Muslim homeland created a leadership vacuum, and thereby provided several progressive elements in the intelligentsia with an opportunity to play an important role in Muslim separatist politics. The manifestoes of the Punjab Muslim League for the elections of 1940 and 1946 had strong socialist overtones. Danyal Lateefi, one of the more prominent leaders from urban Punjab, had his programme of fundamental social reform endorsed by Jinnah.[2] But Jinnah's support for the socialists proved to be short-lived. As the control of the highly successful civil disobedience movement, launched in 1946 by the left in the cities of the Punjab to force out of office the landlord-dominated, anti-Muslim League government of Sir Khizar Hayat, was gradually taken over by such younger members of the landed aristocracy as Mian Mumtaz Daultana and Mamdot, Jinnah turned his attention away from the urban socialists to the established but relatively more progressive elements belonging to the rural aristocracy. To the great disappointment of the urban socialists, the mantle of intellectual leadership within the Punjab Muslim League passed from Lateefi to Daultana.

With the emergence of Pakistan as an independent state, the focus of political activity shifted from the struggle between urban socialists and rural progressives to that between progressives and conservatives in the countryside. Deeply disappointed by this development, some of the urban socialists attempted to gain power by extra-legal means. The 1951 'Rawalpindi conspiracy'[3] was an attempt by a group of radical army officers and their civilian supporters to overthrow the government of Prime Minister Liaqat Ali Khan. The leaders of the conspiracy were apprehended before they could move against the administration and, after a trial that lasted for eighteen months, received long jail sentences. While the incarceration of these leaders further demoralised the progressive forces, the assumption of political power by General Ayub Khan in 1958 dealt a blow from which they took more than a decade to recover.

Ayub saw the Rawalpindi conspiracy in terms of exploitation by the leftist elements of a group of officers who were unhappy with Liaqat Ali Khan's handling of the Kashmir problem, as well as with his own selection as the first Pakistani commander-in-chief of the armed forces. General Akbar Khan, the leader of the conspiracy, was one of the senior officers not happy with the Ayub appointment. They felt that Ayub had distinguished himself neither as the commander of the border force that had been deployed to prevent rioting between Muslims and non-Muslims at the time of the partition of the Indian sub-continent nor as the General Commanding Officer of the armed forces stationed in East Bengal. They regarded his selection as motivated by political rather than professional considerations. While Ayub Khan, as the commander-in-chief of the armed forces, was able to cleanse the army of the officers hostile to him, he could do little about the politicians and intellectuals who had lent their support to the Rawalpindi conspiracy. The opportunity came in 1958 when Ayub became the President. Within a few weeks of assuming power, his government had destroyed the few remaining bases of leftist support. Progressive Papers Ltd, a highly successful publishing house that owned the *Pakistan Times* and *Imroze*, was brought under government control; the National Awami Party, a conglomeration of several leftists groups, was dissolved; a number of labour leaders sympathetic to the left were incarcerated; all political activity in educational institutions was banned; and some senior civil servants with family or ideological ties to prominent leaders of the left were retired from public service. By 1962, when Ayub loosened the control of the military over political life, the left found itself leaderless and in total disarray.[4] When Bhutto left Ayub Khan's government in 1967, he found little prospect of going back to the constituency that he had been called upon to serve in 1958. The left could not have hoped for a better opportunity. It turned to Bhutto. No other politician could match his dynamism or his rhetoric or his record as the only progressive element in a government that had rapidly turned conservative.

Bhutto's performance first as Minister in Charge of Fuel, Power and Natural Resources and later as Foreign Minister endeared him to socialists of all hues. In the first capacity he helped to ease the tension between Russia and the government of Ayub Khan. An oil exploration agreement, signed between the two governments in 1961, was the first indication of the change in Russian attitude towards Pakistan since Khrushchev's open support of India in the Kashmir dispute. As Foreign Minister, he cultivated a special relationship between Pakistan and China. However, as I will discuss later (see Chapter 6), the left soon discovered that being progressive in foreign affairs did not necessarily mean being progressive in domestic policy.

As the left gathered around Bhutto under the banner of the Pakistan People's Party (PPP), a number of circumstances led to the erosion of Ayub Khan's political power. Bhutto was the only politician who was able to grasp the nature of the factors that contributed to Ayub's fall. In a political campaign executed with a skill that no other politician in West Pakistan could match, Bhutto was not only able to disassociate himself completely from the regime that he had served for nine years but succeeded in cultivating for himself a constituency that provided him with an entirely new political base.

THE FALL OF AYUB

On 25 March 1969, after eleven and a half years in power, Field-Marshal Ayub Khan surrendered the presidency to General Yahya Khan, the commander-in-chief of the armed forces. A number of factors contributed to the collapse of Pakistan's first military regime. Among these the more important causes were Ayub Khan's near-fatal illness in the spring of 1968, a growing perception that the military regime had failed in its declared objective of setting Pakistan on the road to sustained and largely self-supporting economic growth, and Zulfikar Ali Bhutto's relentless opposition to Ayub Khan's leadership and the system of government that he had established.[5] None of these factors alone would have dislodged Ayub; together they created a situation that the rapidly aging military dictator found very difficult to tackle with his customary finesse. A serious pulmonary embolism that immobilised the President for eight weeks pointed to a grave weakness in the political system over which he presided. It raised the question of the succession, which had not been seriously examined by Ayub or any of his close associates. The fact that power was transferred temporarily to a cabal of civil servants rather than to the speaker of the national legislature who, according to the Constitution of 1962, was the designated successor showed that Ayub did not have the kind of commitment to his system that he demanded from the people. What Ayub's illness proved was not only his own fragility, but also that of the political structure that he had constructed. People's attention therefore turned quickly from the issue of succession to that of restructuring the political system. The President's recovery from illness did nothing to stem the tide; there was a very rapid erosion of Ayub Khan's political power in the twelve-month period between March 1968 and 25 March 1969, when he resigned from office.

Even if Ayub had not withdrawn for a time from active politics as a result of his illness, the movement that was to lead to his political fall would still have taken place. Its underlying causes ran much deeper than the political uncertainty created by his absence from office. Under Ayub, Pakistan had been taken through a period of economic and social change that was unprecedented in its history. The administration recognised only the positive aspects of this great change – such aggregate indices as the growth of the national product, the increase in the country's industrial wealth and the increase in the output of food. Only Bhutto seems to have understood that rapid modernisation in a society such as Pakistan's could also prove to be very unsettling for large segments of the population. He gave recognition to these negative aspects of change and initiated a political movement aimed at articulating the fears of those social groups who did not perceive themselves as being the beneficiaries of Ayub Khan's 'revolution'.[6]

In many ways, the regime's propaganda machinery did little justice to its performance; the main achievement of the administration of Ayub Khan was not only an impressive rate of economic growth, but also a massive restructuring of society. Had the government fully comprehended the nature of the change that it had instituted, it might possibly have been able to absorb the shocks that were produced. As it is, the reaction to the developments that, in official parlance, constituted the 'Ayub revolution' were mostly unexpected. Being unexpected, they could not be contained.

Perhaps the most important political development of the period was the regime's aggressive support for the process of indigenisation that had begun in the mid-1950s. As discussed in Chapter 2 above, the groups that, initially, had been either hostile or indifferent to the idea of Pakistan began coming back into the political arena after the collapse of the Muslim League. However, the social groups that had earlier controlled the political and economic processes did not entirely lose out; what evolved during the 1953–8 period was a coalition of Karachi-based interests and the landed aristocracy of Sind and the Punjab. Under Ayub Khan the power of indigenisation was quickened and the merchant-industrialists of Karachi and southern Sind saw a further decline in their process. Also to suffer, however, were the big landlords, largely because they had succeeded in combining their interests with those of the groups that had been active in the period immediately following independence.[7]

Ayub Khan had little in common with the leadership groups that he displaced. He was a Pathan from the relatively backward district of Hazara in the Northwest Frontier Province (NWFP). His family, although rural-based, did not own much land; most of its members were either in the army or in the professions. In other words, Ayub Khan's social and economic background prepared him to lead a new class into the decision-making arena. His rise to power exemplified the emergence of the rural middle classes as a powerful interest group in Pakistan's politics.

Using the cover of martial law (1958–62), Ayub Khan adopted a number of economic measures that were directed not only at improving the state of the economy, but also at reducing the power of the interest groups that could pose a challenge to him. Among the prime targets were the landed aristocracy and the

Karachi-based merchant-industrialists. The land reforms of 1959 introduced ceilings on the landlord's right to own rural property. Although the ceilings were liberal, the reforms delivered an important message to the landlords: that the government would not be reluctant to use its power once again to further curtail the economic 'rights' of the landed community. The important consequence of this measure was not so much the amount of land that was actually obtained for transfer to the landless – only 2·3 million of the 49 million acres of farmland were directly affected – but that, over the ten-year period, between 1959 and 1969, over one-fifth of the land under the control of the landed aristocracy passed out of their control.[8] Of the 10 million acres of land that the landed aristocracy gave up, mostly through sale, the bulk went to the middle-sized farmers.

A number of measures reduced the control of the Karachi merchant-industrialists over the industrial sector. By far the most important of these was the Bonus Voucher System that provided easy access to foreign exchange for importing industrial machinery and raw material.[9] The BVS replaced the system under which foreign exchange was available mostly to those who earned it through exports. The government also instituted a tax incentive scheme under which generous concessions were given to those entrepreneurs who invested in the relatively less developed parts of the country. An important consequence of these measures was the quick industrialisation of the Punjab, made possible to a significant degree by the entry into the industrial sector of hundreds of small entrepreneurs. The greater number of this new breed of industrialists had their social origin in the rural middle class.

Although Ayub did not accept the far-reaching administrative reforms that were suggested to him and his predecessors by several experts,[10] he took a number of steps to curtail the power of the bureaucracy. The main objective was once again a political one: to contain the influence of the groups who had either wielded a great deal of power before his own political ascent or could pose a threat to him. In the late 1950s, Pakistan's civil bureaucracy was dominated by the urban professionals who had migrated from India at the time of partition. Ayub's approach to them was similar to that which he adopted towards the landlords: the 1959 Presidential Order, by compulsorily retiring thirty-seven senior civil servants, delivered the important message that the bureaucracy could no longer look towards constitutional guarantees and protection. It was now entirely beholden to the will of the new regime. The next step was to reduce the influence of the bureaucracy over the economic life of the country. This was done by dismantling the elaborate system of controls that had been created in the 1953–8 period since independence and which, as the economy passed through a series of crises, became increasingly more complicated.

Together these policies had a very favourable impact on the country's economy. Redistribution of land from the large to middle-sized farmers and subsidies on inputs used by agriculture revitalised that sector and produced Pakistan's 'green revolution'. By easing bureaucratic controls on private economic decision-making, the regime also created an environment for the rapid development of the industrial sector. Therefore, while these policies had powerful political objectives, in contributing to rapid economic growth they also helped to legitimise the Ayub rule. After all, economic development was the *raison d'être* for the *coup d'état* of Ayub Khan.[11]

The rate of economic growth picked up sharply soon after the assumption of political power by Ayub Khan. The performance of West Pakistan (present-day Pakistan) was even better (see Table 3.1); as against an estimated[12] rate of growth of 2·7 per cent per annum in the gross domestic product in the 1950s, the rate of increase in national wealth was nearly four per cent higher during the first half of the 1960s. During the 1960s, gross domestic product increased at the rate of over 7·2 per cent per annum. Since population grew by just over 3 per cent during this period, the increase in incomes per head was of the order of 4·2 per cent per annum.

Ayub Khan saw this performance as ample justification for his intervention in the political life of the country. Not only was the economy doing twice as well as in the pre-martial law period, its rate of growth during the 1960s was nearly three times that of the neighbouring countries of South Asia.[13] These indices of performance mesmerised the administration and its supporters. About the time that the government launched its 'Decade of Development' celebration, the international community also seemed to have reached the conclusion that Pakistan had discovered a way out of the vicious circle of poverty.[14] The model of development pursued by the Ayub region was recommended to other nations

TABLE 3.1   Rate of economic progress (percentages)

Rates of growth of:	1949/50 to 1959/60	1959/60 to 1964/65	1964/65[1] to 1969/70	1969/70 to 1970/75
Gross Domestic Product	2·7	6·6	7·9	3·0
Population	2·4	3·0	3·1	3·0
Per capita income	0·3	3·6	4·8	0·0

[1] The rate of increase in *per capita* income during this period was probably lower than that during the previous five years. The higher estimate here is on account of the inclusion of the value added in mass media, transport, communication and storage sector to West Pakistan's GDP. In the previous periods these sectors were counted separately and not included in the product of East or West Pakistan.

Source: The estimates for 1949/50 to 1959/60 have been computed by the author. The remaining estimates are from Government of Pakistan, *Pakistan Economic Survey 1974–75* (Islamabad: Finance Division, 1977), Table 5 in the Statistical Annex.

that found themselves in the type of situation that the military dictator had inherited from the politician in 1958.

But this aura of success soon evaporated. Within six months of the celebration by the administration of ten years of the 'Ayub revolution', Ayub Khan was out of power; his constitution was abrogated, his political system dismantled, and the country placed in the midst of a political crisis that was to lead to its break-up into two independent states.

Among the factors that contributed to Ayub's fall were his administration's insensitivity to the growing frustration of those who, having made great economic progress during this period, had not been fully accommodated within the political system. Also frustrated were those groups of people who had been by-passed by both economic and political progress. The fact that these 'political have-nots' had never actively participated in the political life of the country made it all the more difficult for the regime to handle their demands. Once these demands were articulated, the regime found itself without the experience or the institutions to deal with them. To understand the social, political and economic origins of the movement that first displaced Ayub Khan, and, two years later, put Zulfikar Ali Bhutto in power and another six years later resulted in the fall of Bhutto, it is useful to describe briefly Ayub's political initiatives and how they were to result eventually in the creation of a state of economic and political disequilibrium in the society.

In establishing a constituency for himself, Ayub Khan deliberately shifted the focus of power from the groups that had come to dominate Pakistan's politics since independence to those whose weight in society, in terms of their number and aggregate wealth, made them potentially powerful. Middle-class landowners, the urban middle classes and the intelligentsia of the Punjab and NWFP were the prime candidates for this favoured treatment. But, as discussed above, the favours bestowed on these groups were primarily of an economic nature. As the middle-class landowners saw an increase in the share of their wealth in the countryside and as several middle-class families of the Punjab and NWFP became prominent in the industrial sector and, finally, as the urban intelligentsia found a greater role to play in both civil and military bureaucracies, these groups found that there was no matching advance for them on the political side. In creating the system of Basic Democracies (BDs),[15] Ayub Khan took an important initiative in providing an institutional base for helping the rural and urban middle classes to articulate their wishes and aspirations. The BD system also served as a two-way channel of communication between the regime and the constituency it was cultivating and there is reason to believe that, had the system been allowed to evolve, the political tranquillity that marked the early part of the Ayub era would have been maintained even beyond 1967/68. But the BD system was not allowed to take root. In 1964, when the second elections to the system were held, Ayub, in an effort to further broaden his political base, admitted the landed aristocracy and the Karachi-based merchant industrialists into his political party.[16] The price charged by these groups for offering their support was a diminution in the role of the BDs. The cost that the regime had to bear for picking up this additional support was the rapid disillusionment of the middle classes with the system and with Ayub's political intentions. When their economic situation also began to turn sour – as it did beginning with 1967 – these classes began to turn their attention away from Ayub to his rival, Zulfikar Ali Bhutto. In moving from one political camp to another, these groups received support from those that had been totally excluded from the Ayubian system.

As a group, industrial labour suffered the most from the

regime's economic policies. This was for a number of reasons, three of which deserve some mention. First, policies that allowed the import of agricultural machinery at a rate of exchange considerably below the market rate and those that permitted farmers liberal access to cheap credit for obtaining agricultural equipment, caused a large-scale displacement of labour from the countryside. According to one study, each tractor replaced about twelve farm workers;[17] since in the 1960s, the tractor population increased by 80,000, this form of mechanisation alone may have resulted in the loss of nearly 1 million rural jobs. Another study found that a vast majority of displaced landless workers tended to migrate to major cities.[18] Even if half of the workers displaced by agricultural mechanisation migrated to cities in search of jobs – the evidence suggests that their proportion may have been considerably larger[19] – this would have resulted in more than doubling of the labour force in the major cities.

Second, while large-scale rural-city migration added considerably to the employment problem in the cities, the government's policies did very little to encourage the absorption of labour into modern sector enterprises. These included an over-priced rupee and a good deal of emphasis on the production of goods that required capital-intensive industries. The result of these policies was that Pakistan's industry achieved one of the highest capital-labour ratios in the developing world[20] at the time when demographic pressure and large-scale mechanisation of the agriculture sector produced a rate of rural-urban migration that was also about the highest amongst the poor nations.

Third, and finally, the government discouraged unionisation; for some key industries the regime used its emergency powers, acquired at the time of the 1965 war with India, to ban collective bargaining in several key industries. This approach towards development – termed 'urban bias' in a recent analysis of the continued impoverishment of a vast mass of people in the Third World[21] – resulted not only in depriving the rural landless workers of the fruits of rapid economic growth, but also adversely affected industrial workers. In this respect, the fate of factory workers in Ayub's Pakistan was different from those of the workers in other developing countries that also experienced rapid industrial growth. In Pakistan, the sharp increase in the output of the industrial sector was accompanied by a decline in the real wages of the workers. As I will indicate presently, this neglect of industrial labour by the regime was to have a profound political impact.

Another aspect of Ayub's economic policies that was also to affect political development was the approach towards social sectors. Concerned mostly with increasing the national product at as rapid a rate as possible and with delivering economic benefits to present and potential supporters, the regime tended to give a low priority to the development of the sectors of education and health. When the Ayub era came to close, there was only one doctor for 24,200 rural people, one of the lowest ratios in the world. Only 30 per cent of the 15–19 age cohort had completed primary school and only 14 per cent of the entire population could be classified as literate. These indices meant that Pakistan at that time had the poorest health care and lowest rate of literacy of a country at its stage of development. This neglect of the social sectors in general, and of the education sector in particular, was to have grave political consequences.

Not only did the regime not provide sufficient resources for the development of the country's human resource, the little attention that it gave to human development was mis-directed. There were 500 times as many students in the universities as in primary schools as compared with the more successful educational systems of countries such as Korea and Malaysia. The little spread that there was of literacy amongst the poor was confined to formal education rather than to the type of education that would have prepared them for the job market. Consequently, by the middle of the 1960s, there was a greater proportion of unemployed among the literate workers than among those who had not attended school. Within the literate segment of the population, the rate of unemployment increased in proportion to the number of years of schooling.[22]

Given the objectives of economic and political development pursued by the regime, there should be nothing very surprising about the social origins of the people that participated in the anti-Ayub movement or the parts of the country in which it fermented for a year. In a study carried out and published soon after the fall of Ayub Khan, I showed that the political agitation that was to overthrow him started not in the autumn of 1968 in the major cities of West Pakistan but in the summer of 1967 in a large number of towns in the province of the Punjab.[23] In this agitation all the disadvantaged groups within the population – industrial

labour, unemployed college graduates and urban professionals –
were to play a prominent role. In their effort to dislodge Ayub,
these groups were joined by those who had initially benefited from
the regime's policies.

While severe and recurrent droughts in the mid-1960s brought
to a virtual halt the rapid advance of the agriculture sector that
had taken place under Ayub, the 1965 military confrontation with
India had an equally adverse impact on the urban economy.
Middle-sized landlords and small urban professionals and
businessmen – the classes that Ayub had cultivated earlier as his
constituency – felt the impact of this economic down-turn much
more severely than other segments of society. What the regime's
law enforcement agencies interpreted as random acts of political
violence in a number of small towns all over the Punjab were, in
fact, the beginnings of a movement that, a year later, was to engulf
the entire nation. At the spearhead of the movement were the
middle classes. Bhutto, dismissed from the Cabinet by Ayub
Khan in the summer of 1967, saw an opportunity for himself in the
mounting discontent in the semi-urban parts of the Punjab. On
leaving office, he undertook an extensive tour of the province,
meeting rural town lawyers and businessmen in hundreds of
katcheries (courthouses) and market places around the province.
Thus was laid the foundation of the movement that was to topple
Ayub Khan from power.

Once Bhutto had assumed stewardship of the movement, its
centre of activity shifted to the large cities. There, industrial
labour, the urban unemployed and the students joined in. The
agitation now had the following of all those groups that had failed
to find a place in Ayub Khan's political system. The principal
objective of the movement, therefore, became the dissolution of
the system and its replacement by one that would allow political
participation by the less privileged groups of the society. Bhutto
had a full share in the first part of this objective. It was obvious to
him that, having abandoned the constituency that he had inherited from his father, he could regain political power only by
finding a new basis of support for himself. Led by Bhutto, the
urban masses broke through into the political arena. By January
1969 the movement had spread to East Pakistan, where it assumed a strong secessionist overtone. By March, it was apparent
that the multiplicity of new and conflicting demands could not be
reconciled within the framework of the Ayub system. The system

could not take the load, and on 25 March, Ayub left office, to be replaced by Yahya Khan, the commander-in-chief of the armed forces.

THE ELECTION OF 1970

Although the proclamation from the military headquarters in Rawalpindi, announcing the country's return to *general* martial law for the second time in its history, did not differ much in its wording from the one issued by Ayub Khan on 7 October 1958, there was one very important change in the diagnosis that was offered of the rapidly deteriorating political situation. In 1958, Ayub Khan had put the blame on squabbling politicians who ran a system that did not 'suit the genius of the people of Pakistan'.[24] In 1969, Yahya identified a system that did not fully represent *all* the people as being responsible for political turmoil.[25] Since the diagnoses differed, the solutions had also to differ. In several pronouncements after assuming power, Ayub Khan told the country that some kind of 'restricted', 'guided' or 'basic' democracy suited the country much more than the 'no-holds barred types of systems run by those who had slavishly copied Westminster'.[26] Yahya Khan promised a return to the very systems that his predecessor had condemned and disregarded. Ayub Khan had used the power of the military to provide a guiding hand for Pakistan's democracy; Yahya Khan used the same source of power in an attempt to return the country to unfettered democracy. According to Yahya's programme of political reconstruction, once all the pitfalls had been removed in order to smoothe the ride back to democracy, the military was no longer to have a political role to play.

But the objective of getting the armed forces back into the barracks was not shared by all of Yahya Khan's colleagues. At least one of them – Air Marshal Nur Khan, who gained political prominence first as a member of the four-man military governing council that was set up by Yahya Khan as his Cabinet and then as the Governor of West Pakistan – set about rectifying the more glaring omissions in the development policy pursued by the Ayub regime. Within a period of six months, Nur Khan had persuaded his associates to promulgate wide-ranging labour and educational reforms. The fact that Nur Khan was attempting to cultivate the

very groups that had sustained the anti-Ayub movement and the
fact that those middle-rank officers from the armed forces who
were not content to play a passive role looked towards Nur Khan
for leadership were not lost either on President Yahya or on
Bhutto. Yahya first removed Nur Khan from the Military Council
and sent him to West Pakistan as Governor and later dismissed
him from the governorship. While the President was consolidat-
ing his power within the military, Bhutto began to organise a
political base for himself.

On quitting Ayub Khan's government, Bhutto had first tried to
organise a radical wing within the Pakistan Muslim League, the
ruling party. Had Bhutto succeeded in this effort, he would have
continued to serve the two constituencies to which he laid claim –
one as a result of heredity and the other on account of persuasion –
within one political organisation. This effort was blocked by
Malik Khuda Bux Bucha, the then secretary-general of the party
and the acknowledged spokesman of one of Bhutto's constituencies, the landed aristocracy. Having been abandoned by the
landlords, Bhutto turned towards the left.

As discussed above, the pro-Russia and the pro-China policies
that he successively pursued as a member of the Ayub Cabinet
had been noticed by the left; his stewardship of the under-
privileged groups during the anti-Ayub movement endeared him
further to the socialists. The left needed him as much as he needed
them. The socialists remained disorganised and badly splintered,
with no agreed programme or plan of political action. But the
success of the mass movement that displaced Ayub from power
gave great hope to the various groups that had participated in it;
beginning with 1969, the main theme of much of the leftists'
literature changed from polemics to practical politics.[27]

Although Bhutto succeeded in gathering together the more
important leftist factions into the PPP, the differences between
them were never fully resolved and, as I will discuss later in this
work, the disputes between the various groups were to result later
in the virtual eclipse of the socialists by the conservatives in the
party.

The groups that came together under the PPP umbrella included the 'traditional left',[28] which recognised the poet Faiz
Ahmad Faiz, the poet-painter-publisher Mohammad Hanif
Ramay and the lawyer-poet Khurshid Hasan Meer as leaders,
pursuing the objective of a kind of socialist renaissance; the 'rural

left' under the leadership of Sheikh Mohammad Rashid, following the aim of ultimate collectivisation of all rural property; 'socialist industrial labour', with Mirza Ibrahim and Miraj Mohammad Khan as their main spokesmen, who aimed to bring under workers' control the country's industrial wealth, and the urban 'ultra left', with Mubashir Hasan as their principal leader, who aimed at a complete restructuring of both the economy and the political system. This great difference in objectives was reflected in the means advocated for achieving them. Mubashir Hasan envisaged a new political and economic order rising from the ashes of the old one. Miraj Mohammad and Mirza Ibrahim believed in controlled violence for bringing about change. They and their followers had learnt the very effective use of '*gherao*' for getting the more radical labour demands accepted by managers. Sheikh Rashid believed in evolutionary transformation in which farmers' co-operatives would ultimately evolve into agricultural communes. The Punjab poets – Faiz, Ramay and Meer – believed in the power of ideas to transform both the mind and society. They sought to use religion as the purveyor of a socialist humanist doctrine.[29]

While all of these groups had considerable influence on some segment or other of the society, none of them was well organised. The traditional left, the rural socialists and the ultra left, all had their base in central Punjab – mainly in the cities of Lahore and in the country around it. Only the socialist industrial workers operated from outside the Punjab, from the cities of Karachi and Hyderabad. Given this concentration of support in a few areas and given the state of disarray, it is not surprising that, after having launched Bhutto from a platform of 'Islamic socialism', the left could exercise only a marginal influence on his political thinking and economic policies.

As a political party, the PPP was launched on 1 December 1970 when its founding members gathered at the Lahore residence of Mubashir Hasan. Zulfikar Ali Bhutto was chosen as the chairman and a number of members were commissioned to produce the party's 'Foundation Papers'.[30] Ten of these papers, written and published in 1970 and 1971, carried the PPP's message to the people. There was no ambiguity about the ideological nature of the programme that the PPP leadership put together. The main elements of the programme were described in *Foundation Document No 4*.[31] According to this a PPP government, if ever formed, would nationalise all basic industries and the financial and banking institutions that had helped their growth in the private sector. Iron and steel, heavy engineering, machine tools, chemicals and petrochemicals, shipbuilding, armaments, automobiles, the gas and oil industries, mining, the electricity generating and distributing industries, shipping, the railways and air and road transport were defined as being 'basic' to the economy. Three-fifths of the total assets in these enterprises were in the hands of the families that had ushered in Pakistan's first industrial revolution. And three-fifths was controlled by those industrialists who had gained economic power during the Ayub period.[32] Under the control of the state, these enterprises would bring about an equitable distribution of the wealth of the nation rather than keep it concentrated in the hands of a few families. The list of basic industries, the promise that they would be brought under public management and the suggestion that direct government intervention of this type was the only way of ensuring redistribution of wealth reflected the influence of such ultra-leftists in the party as Mubashir Hasan and J. A. Rahim. However, the less radical urban intellectuals also left their imprint on the *Foundation Document*. It was promised that a PPP government would stop well short of a total nationalisation of the industrial sector. Private participation in the industrial development of the country was to be encouraged. The fact that the industries left in the care of the private sector were those engaged in the production of basic goods and provision of basic services to the people suggest that the party ideologues were interested not so much in the objectives to be achieved by the PPP brand of socialism as in the means by which the government could extend its control over vital sectors of the economy. As I will discuss later, this confusion between objectives and instruments of policy was one of the factors that contributed to the disillusionment of the people with the Islamic socialism proposed by the PPP.

The Party's programme for agriculture, the other important productive sector of the economy, was considerably less ideological. The rural socialists under Rashid did not have the kind of influence wielded by such other founding members as Mubashir Hasan, J. A. Rahim and Hanif Ramay. Accordingly, the party proposed only a marginal readjustment in the ceilings on holdings that Ayub Khan's land reform had established in 1959. The small farmers were promised additional credit for investment and production purposes, while the landless peasants were to be ensured full remuneration for their efforts.

The efforts promised in the social sectors were spelled out in great detail. Recognising that one of the problems of Ayubian economics was the relatively low priority given to health, education and urban transport, the *Foundation Document* pledged a determined effort to improve the environment in which the poor people lived in the rural and urban areas. This was to be done by providing urban workers and peasants free access to basic education and basic health facilities, by allowing a considerably larger flow of resources into urban public transport; by building sports and recreational facilities in cities, towns and villages that the poor could use; and by developing a new 'mass culture' in which all classes of people could participate.

The PPP manifesto[33] for the election of 1970 followed, with two differences, the same ideological line as the *Foundation Documents*. The differences were important, for they reflected political reality as perceived by Bhutto, the party's chairman. The manifesto made a strong effort to reconcile 'the spirit of Islam' with socialism, arguing that the PPP was working for the establishment not of a secular socialist order but of a system that would closely follow the tenets of Islam. In emphasising this link between Islam and socialism, Bhutto seemed impressed with what seemed to him as a resurgence of religious sentiment in the country. To him *Jamaat-i-Islami* appeared as his most important competitor and he was not prepared to surrender some political advantage to this fundamentalist party on the ground that his own PPP was a secular organisation with a secular programme.

The other important difference in the approach adopted in the manifesto as compared with the *Foundation Document* concerned the treatment of the agricultural sector. Having collected the progressive elements under the PPP umbrella, Bhutto was anxious to regain at least a part of his old constituency: the landed aristocracy. Accordingly, even the very moderate reformist programme proposed in the *Foundation Document* was further diluted. In addition, the manifesto promised a considerable amount of government support to the development of the agricultural sector.

In the area of foreign policy, the manifesto continued the violently anti-India stance with which Bhutto had come to be identified both within and outside Pakistan. By now the familiar accusation of Ayub Khan's 'Tashkent sell-out' was repeated. Also repeated was the promise of an intensified struggle against India to bring Kashmir into Pakistan. It is clear that Bhutto wanted to keep alive the image that he had established in the public mind of a figure prepared to sacrifice all in order to preserve the 'idea of Pakistan'.

The election campaign began on 7 January 1970, and lasted for over eleven months. During the campaign, Bhutto was constantly on the move. By the time the people were to go to the polls, he had developed a style of rhetoric, adopted a language and cultivated a stage presence that accorded perfectly with his manifesto. The emphasis that he was to place on style and charisma was done for good reasons, for the PPP did not have the type of access to the majority of the voters that other traditional parties possessed.

The traditional means of campaigning in Pakistan has been to rely upon established leadership drawn, generally, from landed families or sacred elites (which might well be the same group). The Unionist Party in the pre-Pakistan days, the Muslim League factions in the 1951 Punjab elections and the Republican Party which governed in West Pakistan prior to Ayub's take-over were essentially *patron* parties.[34] These parties were characterised by linkages among rural notables; they used these notables and their vote banks to run up majorities in constituencies that were little more than bailiwicks controlled by the squirearchy. Additionally, the rural elite often had religious roles as well as landed-gentry roles (e.g. as *pirs* or *sajjada nashins*) and could reinforce their feudal position with the trappings of religion. Even if they held no religious position themselves, they could often draw upon support from the local professional religious leadership – in the Punjab, the *mullahs*. Together, the landed aristocracy with their traditional following and the *mullahs* with their adherents, frequently coupled with some degree of governmental interference, could ensure victory. In the elections of 1970, however, the government maintained a policy of non-interference, if for no other reason than it felt that the desired result could be obtained in a free-for-all contest, i.e. that no party would be able to assume command in the election and the brokerage role of the incumbent regime would be crucial and acceptable.[35]

The various Muslim League factions and the other parties went about the business of campaigning in a traditional fashion in the rural areas – i.e. using the rural elites, and often the 'Islam in danger' slogans, the latter hardly changed from the Muslim

League manifesto of 1936. The PPP, however, took a different line.

The party's programme was hardly designed to appeal to the traditional rural elite and *mullahs*, and thus that avenue of campaigning was very largely closed to the PPP, despite a few in both groups who, possibly for opportunistic reasons, joined the party. Students are receptive to appeals for change, although they are often uncertain of the direction they wish to take; but when the charismatic personality of Bhutto and his heroic (in their eyes) stand against Ayub and Tashkent was added, they were willing followers and missionaries of his programme. This active and energetic group, aided by the closing of schools and colleges in the final stages of the campaign, fanned into the countryside and into the less affluent sections of the cities and found willing ears among those who themselves were experiencing change and wished to see it continue and accelerate. Students alone could not do the job, but they were reinforced by active journalists, by lawyers who played a key part in the initial drive against Ayub, and – most of all – by Bhutto himself, who seemed tireless in his peregrinations in search of votes. The PPP, denied the use of traditional means, thus developed new means to reach those voters, both rural and urban, who looked for major social and economic changes, albeit in a general Islamic context.

The Yahya regime's impartiality in the elections also influenced its results. The administration seemed to have convinced itself that the best way of bringing about the result that would ensure a powerful role for itself was to be even-handed towards all parties. The political scene in Pakistan was sufficiently confused at that time to convince the generals that no single party would triumph. With the seats split among a number of parties, the regime could honestly and diligently play the role of political broker. It has been argued, perhaps with some justification, that it was this motive that led Yahya to end the system of parity between East and West Pakistan.[36] This system had been evolved as the basis for the Constitutions of 1956 and 1962; under it, the two provinces shared an equal number of seats in the national legislature. By giving more seats to East Pakistan and by withdrawing the traditional government support from them, the Yahya regime expected to dilute the weight of such West Pakistan-based political interest groups as the landed aristocracy and the merchant-industrialists, counting, at the same time, on a fragmented vote in the east wing. The regimes even-handedness, therefore, helped the new groups that the PPP wanted to usher into the political arena. The response from these groups surprised Bhutto as well as the administration: of the 132 seats allocated to West Pakistan, the PPP won 81, or 61 per cent of the total (Table 3.2). It received only one-third of the votes cast but the large number of parties contesting the seats ensured victory to the PPP candidates. A number of them were returned to the National Assembly with less than a majority of the votes polled.

The PPP polled strongest in those urban and rural areas which had been undergoing rapid modernisation.[37] In stagnant areas, even though they might be at a higher level of development, the PPP generally did less well; and the older Muslim Leagues, the Islamic parties or independents fared better. However, these statements must be made with some reservation, as the personality of Bhutto and the secular programme of the PPP were often, but not always, sufficient to overcome traditional leadership. For example, it took a Noon on the PPP ticket to defeat the 'official' Noon-Tiwana clan candidate in a Sargodha seat; and in Multan the acceptance of a PPP ticket by Sadiq Husain Qureshi, a wealthy landlord, combined PPP appeal with traditional appeal. A third element in the PPP package (Bhutto himself and the secular topics being the other two) may also have swayed some voters. This was Bhutto's early assertion of a 1000-year confrontation with India. However, this theme was muted during the later stages of the campaign; it appears that it might have been more effective for refugee voters, and that it overlapped with equally ardent slogans from the older political groupings. It was Bhutto's personality and the secular demands that distinguished the PPP most clearly from its rivals. As these were part and parcel of the same phenomenon, they were the principal bases for voting behaviour. The style of the campaign, the PPP's use of charismatic leadership and non-traditional messengers, radically changed the nature of electioneering in Pakistan and the course of the country's political, economic and social development.

TABLE 3.2 Pakistan National Assembly Elections, 1970–1

Party	Punjab seats	Sind seats	NWFP seats	Baluchistan seats	W. Pakistan seats	W. Pakistan %	E. Pakistan seats	E. Pakistan %	Total seats	Total %
AL	–	–	–	–	–	–	160	98·8	160	53·3
PPP	62	18	1	–	81	58·7	–	–	81	27·0
NAP	–	1	3	3	6	4·3	–	–	6	2·0
PML(Q)	1	1	7	–	9	6·5	–	–	9	3·0
PML(C)	2	–	–	–	2	1·4	–	–	2	0·7
CML	7	–	–	–	7	5·1	–	–	7	2·3
PDP	–	–	–	–	–	–	1	0·6	1	0·3
JUP	4	3	6	1	7	5·1	–	–	7	2·3
JUI	1	2	1	–	7	5·1	–	–	7	2·3
JI	1	3	7	–	4	2·9	–	–	4	1·3
IND	5				15	10·9	1	0·6	16	5·3
Total	82	27	25	4	138	100·0	162	100·0	300	100·0

Note: For West Pakistan, the arrangement of the parties in this table is according to their ideological position. Pakistan People's Party (PPP) under Bhutto and National Awami Party (NAP) and Wali Khan were on the left of the political spectrum while the three Muslim Leagues, PML(Q), PML(C) and CML, under Abdul Quyum Khan, Pir of Pagaro and Daultana respectively, belonged to the centre. On the right were the three religious parties: Jamiatul Ulemai Pakistan (JUP) under Maulana Hazarvi [JU(H)], Jamiatul Ulemai Islam (JUI) under Maulana Mufti Mahmud and Jamaat-i-Islami (JI) under Maulana Maudoodi.

Source: Craig Baxter, 'Pakistan Votes, 1970', *Asian Survey,* XI, March 1971, p. 211.

4 Rise to Power

The fact that the results of the 1970 elections surprised the military regime as well as the political participants should be explained not in terms of the failure of the vast intelligence machinery at the disposal of the government in correctly predicting the mood of the people. Judging from Yahya Khan's massive intervention in the political life of the country in the period following the 1970 elections, it can be argued that the new military government would not have played a totally passive role in the pre-election period had it believed that the elections would lead to such a clear polarisation of Pakistani politics. Nor can the surprise caused by the results of the elections be explained in terms of the lack of political acumen on the part of the political parties that took part in them. It was not so much lack of acumen but the underdeveloped nature of the political institutions that made it so difficult for them to reflect the aspirations and frustrations of the people. It is also very likely that, had some of the old style politicians correctly gauged the mood of the people, they would have combined their efforts and challenged Bhutto and the PPP. The overwhelming victory of Mujibur Rahman shifted the focus of political activity from West Pakistan to Dacca. With Mujibur Rahman's Awami League having captured all but two of the 168 seats alloted to East Pakistan and with Bhutto in command of a comfortable majority in the western province, Yahya Khan and his generals could not expect to play the role of political brokers that they had envisaged. Mujib's stand on political autonomy hardened after the results of the elections were announced and Bhutto, after enthusiastically accepting the role of 'sole representative of the people of West Pakistan', began to develop a strategy to block East Pakistan's rapid move towards independence.

A West Pakistan politician of the traditional mould would have found a way of dealing with Mujibur Rahman and his demand for provincial autonomy. The Awami League's objectives were not very different from those of the Muslim League in the 1940s.

Jinnah had raised the demand for Pakistan on the ground that the Muslim community could not expect fair treatment in a political system dominated by the Hindus. Mujib's 'Six Points' were a programme for restructuring the Pakistani political and economic system so that the people of East Pakistan – the poorer of the two provinces – could function without being discriminated against. The passions that Mujib's campaign aroused could therefore be understood by those leaders from West Pakistan who had participated in the Pakistan movement. But Bhutto and his followers found little in common with Mujib and his supporters. The PPP had built its constituency on the basis of a programme that emphasised economic and social rewards for the underprivileged segments of the society. The Awami League's 'Six Points Plan' promised the Bengali middle class political benefits if they loosened their links with West Pakistan. This deep difference explains both Bhutto's frustration with Mujib as well as his intransigence in dealing with him.

Bhutto's intransigence notwithstanding – or according to some because of it[1] – East Pakistan's march towards secession could not be slowed. On 7 March 1972, in response to Yahya Khan's postponement of the first meeting of the newly elected National Assembly, Mujib and his party assumed the administrative control of the province. Eighteen days later, on 25 March, Yahya Khan opted for a military solution to the deepening political crisis. The military found the Bengalis well prepared to resist. The result was of an exceptionally bloody civil war that lasted for more than eight months. By early November, a stalemate was reached. The army was able to re-establish control over all major urban areas, while the countryside remained with the guerrillas. On 23 November, the Indian army moved into East Pakistan to help the Bengali nationalists. By 14 December, the Indians had reached the outskirts of Dacca; two days later, on the morning of 16 December, General Abdullah Niazi, commander of the Pakistan army, laid down his arms before General Aurora of the Indian invading force.[2]

The surrender was unconditional and, from the point of view of the Pakistani army, particularly those engaged in battle on the western front, very humiliating:

The Pakistan Eastern Command agree to surrender all Pakistan Armed Forces in BANGLADESH to Lieutenant-General JAGJIT SINGH AURORA, General Officer Commanding in Chief of the Indian and BANGLADESH forces in the Eastern Theatre. This surrender includes all Pakistan land, air and naval forces and also all para-military forces and civil armed forces. Those forces will lay down their arms and surrender at the places where they are currently located at the nearest regular troops under the command of Lieutenant-General JAGJIT SINGH AURORA.

... The Pakistan Eastern Command shall come under the orders of Lieutenant-General JAGJIT SINGH AURORA as soon as this instrument has been signed. Disobedience of orders will be regarded as a breach of the surrender terms and will be dealt with in accordance with the accepted laws and usages of war.[3]

The Pakistan army felt humilated on account of both the circumstances and the terms of surrender. The Indian army had moved straight to Dacca without overcoming the units of the Pakistan army in a number of cantonments near the border. This rapid thrust at Dacca demoralised the high command but did not reduce the confidence of the troops of the Pakistan army that were engaging the enemy outside. It was these units that had earlier pacified the Bengali guerrillas. The sudden capitulation by General Niazi caught these units by surprise. This explains the separate stipulation about their surrender to the Indian army in the document signed by Generals Aurora and Niazi.

The surrender document treated the Mukti Bahini, the Bengali guerrilla force, on an equal footing with the Indian army. This fact, too, was resented by the Pakistani armed forces. The Pakistani officers took considerable pride in the fact that in the period between April and November 1971 they had succeeded in pushing the guerrillas out of all major centres of population. In fact, according to their point of view, it was this success that prompted the Indian army to launch a direct attack into East Pakistan. The middle-level officers who commanded the field units were therefore upset not only by the manner in which the campaign was handled, but also by the way in which the generals left the battlefield.

The surrender of the Pakistan army occurred while Bhutto was at the United Nations pleading for the country's case before the Security Council. The news of the surrender seemed to have caught him by surprise. His response was a highly emotional one:

he tore up the cease-fire Resolution that had been sponsored by Poland and stalked out of the chamber, vowing never to return to the United Nations. The UN Security Council scene, televised the same evening in Pakistan, generated a great deal of good-will for Bhutto in the country. During the last days of Yahya Khan's administration, the generals in Rawalpindi had begun to turn to him not only for advice, but also for projecting Pakistan's case to the outside world. By accepting this role and by heading two missions, one to China and the other to the United Nations, Bhutto could be said to have lent his support to the Yahya regime. However, after the fall of Dacca, Bhutto was anxious to establish some distance between himself and the generals. By walking out of the Security Council he managed to disassociate himself completely from the regime that he had travelled to New York to represent. For the second time in less than three years, Bhutto was to gain advantage from the collapse of a military regime.

Bhutto returned to Pakistan on 20 December to be sworn in on the same evening as President and Chief Martial Law Administrator. His ascent to power was made possible by a combination of three separate events: the 1970 elections from which he was to emerge as the most popular political leader in West Pakistan, the growing disillusionment of a broad segment of the society with the military's ability to alleviate the conditions that generated armed intervention in politics in the first place, and development of serious tensions between the generals and second-level command in the armed forces. The first of these three factors was discussed in detail in Chapter 3; a discussion of the second and third follows.

THE MILITARY'S FAILURE

The hour had struck. The moment so long delayed had finally arrived. The responsibility could no longer be put off. It was the 4th of October 1958, and as I settled down in my railway saloon I knew that an era was coming to an end. I was going to Karachi where an agonizing prolonged political farce was drawing to a close. A few days earlier President Iskandar Mirza had conveyed to me that the whole situation was becoming intolerable and that he had decided to act.[4]

This statement by Ayub Khan in his *Political Autobiography* is significant for several reasons. The hour struck because the politicians and their parties were engaged in what seemed to be an endless game of musical chairs. Watching the 'political farce', Ayub Khan and his army associates could not avoid what they considered to be their responsibility: to bring to an end the era of chaotic democratic politics and introduce in its place a period of controlled political tranquillity. Having decided to act, Ayub Khan moved to Karachi at a leisurely pace. The leader of Pakistan's first military *coup* took more than twenty-four hours to cover the distance between army headquarters at Rawalpindi and the seat of government nearly 1000 miles away at Karachi. For Ayub Khan's coup, the element of surprise was not a decisive factor. He knew that the armed forces stood behind him to a man and the politicians had neither the will nor the resources to challenge him. He arrived in Karachi on 5 October and set in motion the mechanics of a coup that two days later resulted in the ousting of Feroze Khan Noon as Prime Minister. The principal motive behind the assumption of power was to provide the people with a system of government that 'suited their genius'. The military could accomplish this task for the simple reason that, in its view, discipline and order were needed for the flowering of the political genius of the Pakistani people. It should be noted that in October 1958 Ayub Khan was not concerned with the economic stagnation that prevailed in the country. Neither then, nor ten years later when he wrote his autobiography, did Ayub consider economic development to be the initial reason for the political change that he was to promote and bring about. And yet, in the public's mind the success of the Ayubian system was not to be gauged in terms of the creation of an atmosphere of political tranquillity. Extreme political disorder was the main reason for Ayub Khan's *coup d'état* but, in the minds of the people, political disorder as such had little meaning. It was symptomatic of a number of economic and social problems and, by actively intervening in the political life of the country, Ayub Khan *seemed* to have assumed responsibility for solving them.

Therefore, what Ayub Khan saw as his 'responsibility' as head of the armed forces was not interpreted by the people to apply to a limited set of circumstances. His assumption of political control suggested an open-ended commitment to solve all problems; accordingly, his *coup d'état* became a 'revolution'. While the people may have been prepared to tolerate failure in some areas on the part of the politicians, the military regime, in order to legitimise its rule, had to continuously demonstrate its ability to solve problems. A change in the nature of the problems did not diminish this expectation. There is no better illustration of this problem than the regime's handling of the problems of economic stagnation and nation building.

As I discussed in Chapter 2 above, a number of policies initiated by the regime resulted in Pakistan achieving a rate of growth in its national product that was unprecedented in its history and twice as high as that of the other countries in the South Asian sub-continent. But by mid-1967 there was widespread disillusionment with the economic performance of the regime. In 1960, when the planners sat down to write the second five-year plan, their main concern was with the persisting stagnation of the economy. The first five-year plan, meant to cover the 1955–60 period, was released in 1958, the delay caused largely by the failure of the politicians to agree on its basic objectives. The politicians' replacement by the military regime did away with the need to build a political consensus around economic objectives. Cautioning that the process of growth they were going to initiate was both brutal and sordid and arguing that there existed a functional justification for inequality of income if this raised production for all and not consumption for a few,[5] the Pakistani planners, assisted by a number of experts from abroad, launched the second five-year plan (1960–5). The results were spectacular and Pakistan very quickly became a high-growth developing country. This performance received a great deal of praise and resulted in the adoption by the regime of growth as the *raison d'être* of the 'Ayub revolution'. This change in objectives, from establishing political order to generating a high rate of economic growth, confirmed the initial perception of the people of the problem-solving nature of the regime and their open-ended expectation regarding its performance.

During this period, Pakistan pursued what can be described as a classical model of development. Accumulation of capital became the main strategic variable and the propensity to save and capital/output ratio became the basic equipment of development planners and aid officials. The notion that capital was scarce and savings difficult to raise in poor countries was qualified by pointing to the opportunities of attracting it from abroad and by encouraging its accumulation in the hands of those who supposedly had a low marginal inclination to consume.[6] Accordingly, foreign capital flowed into Pakistan and a large proportion of it went to the people who, being already rich, could be expected to save a good part of the resulting increment in wealth. These savings were ploughed back into investment – a process, which was soon to be termed the 'busy-bee route' to development.[7]

While the Pakistani entrepreneurs were busy saving a sizeable proportion of their incomes in order to plough them back into productive investments, doubts began to be expressed about the equity of this process of development. From being seen primarily as a matter of economic growth and secondarily as a problem of securing the social changes necessarily associated with economic growth, development came to be perceived, in a number of influential intellectual quarters, as a process also requiring direct intervention by the government so as to improve the economic welfare of *all* people. It was a Pakistani member of this new 'priesthood of development planners' who first pointed out that the development process initiated by the regime had resulted in a tremendous concentration of wealth in the hands of a few families. Mahbub ul Haq, the regime's Chief Economist, in a speech delivered at Karachi in April 1968, estimated that only twenty-two family groups controlled at that time about two-thirds of the industrial assets, 80 per cent of banking and 70 per cent of insurance in Pakistan.[8] Haq regarded this concentration of wealth as a direct consequence of the political and economic system as it evolved under Ayub Khan:

> What Pakistan badly needs today is to broaden the base of its economic and political powers; to evolve a development strategy that reaches out to the bulk of the population; to innovate a new life style which is more consistent with its own poverty and its present stage of development. This is not going to be easy because, in the past, modernization was foisted on a basically feudalistic structure in which political participation was often denied, [the] growth of responsible institution stifled and free speech curbed, and where all economic and political powers gravitated towards a small minority. *There is not much that can be done to save development from being warped in favor of a privileged few in a system like this unless the basic premises of the system are changed* [italics added].[9]

This pronouncement by the Chief Economist was to have a profound impact on the course of the country's political development. It was seen as a severe condemnation by an important functionary of the system, of the way the system had worked and of its failure to deliver the returns from high economic growth to a broad segment of the society. It mattered little that distributive justice was not a regime objective either in the second (1960–5) or in the third (1965–70) five-year development plans. Nor did it matter that the regime that was being blamed for 'making the poor poorer' [10] was not a military administration but a political entity that represented a number of powerful non-military interests. What mattered was that the manner of Ayub Khan's intervention in the country's political life and the open-ended problem-solving commitment that he seemed to convey to the people had generated expectations that the regime was seen not to fulfil. What mattered also was the impression in the public's mind that the regime was in power not because of a broad political consensus, but on account of the not altogether invisible presence of the armed forces. A combination of these perceptions and impressions led to the widespread belief that the military regime had failed in its economic task.

The perception of the regime's commitment to create a Pakistani nation out of a number of diverse communities was the result of both its problem-solving approach as well as its explicitly stated objective of removing divisiveness in the society. One of the first acts of the administration was to set up the Bureau of National Reconstruction under Brigadier F. R. Khan, one of the four senior army officers who had accompanied Ayub into the political arena. The bureau's appointed task was to 'weld the Pakistani people into a nation that, in a united way, would pursue the ideals of its founder, *Quaid-i-Azam*, Mohammad Ali Jinnah'. [11]

According to one point of view, [12] the fact that the task of nation-building proved to be much more difficult in Pakistan than in other countries of South Asia is to be explained in part by the policies adopted by the British towards various ethnic communities. The British, advancing into India from the east and from the south, met little military or political opposition. The natives were prepared not only to be subjugated but also to adopt the ways of the conqueror. The modernisation of India proved remarkably easy until the British entered the north-west. Here, in what were later to be called the provinces of the Northwest Frontier, Baluchistan and Sind the British encountered military as well as social and cultural resistance. When this resistance could not be overcome, the new rulers adopted a different approach: they allowed the northern tribes to be governed by their own institutions and their own traditions as long as they did not cause a great deal of trouble to the *raj*.[13] Or to take another point of view, Indian society and the various communities within it 'slept for centuries, even millenia, under their despotic superstructures, until the incursion of the West awoke them'.[14] But the West's incursion did not affect all communities; it allowed some of them to slumber on. No matter which interpretation we take, it seems right to suggest that the essentially polyarchial nature of Pakistani society manifested itself as a result of the British *raj*. The Pakistan of today was carved out of those parts of British India in which a number of ethnic groups had not merged their separate identity into a single Indian nation.

Mohammad Ali Jinnah's theory of two nations based on religion – one Muslim the other non-Muslim – may have succeeded in moulding Pakistan's disparate ethnic communities into a single nation. But Jinnah, having founded Pakistan, was not prepared to turn it into a theocratic state. For him, 'Mussulmans ceased to be Mussulmans and Hindus ceased to be Hindus, not in the sense of religion, of course, but for conducting the affairs of the state'. However, Jinnah was soon to find out that with the establishment of the state of Pakistan, Bengalis did not cease to be Bengalis and Punjabis did not cease to be Punjabis. His suggestion, made to a Bengali audience, that Pakistan should adopt Urdu as the national language was received with great hostility. This was within a year of independence, when the enthusiasm generated by the struggle for the creation of a separate Muslim state had not fully died down.

The fissiparous tendencies within the new nation of Pakistan contributed to the very slow process of constitution-making. The process was begun in 1948. While the Objectives Resolution was passed in 1949, according to which the authority of the state of Pakistan was to be exercised within 'the limits prescribed by Almighty Allah', return to Islam was not sufficient to elicit agreement on basic constitutional principles. It was to take another five years for the Basic Principles committee to prepare a report and get it approved by the parent Constituent Assembly.

Another two years elapsed before Pakistan acquired a constitution built on the principle of parity between its two wings: the more populous eastern province was to have the same representation in all the organs of the federal government as the western province. To make the principle of parity work, the four provinces of the Punjab, Sind, Northwest Frontier and Baluchistan had to be merged in the 'One Unit' of West Pakistan. Although it took years to write the Constitution, the document that finally won the approval of the Constituent Assembly in early 1956 and was promulgated on 23 March of that year, was based on consensus between the various Pakistani 'nationalities'.[15] This consensus was never to be achieved again in the context of a united Pakistan. By abrogating the 1956 Constitution, Ayub Khan was to set back the process of nation-building.

Under Ayub Khan, the military's approach towards nation-building involved the use of force and authority to bring together the disparate communities. Ayub was disappointed when the Constitution Commission appointed by him did not recommend the setting up of a strong central authority. The Commission's report was set aside by the regime and a special sub-committee of the Cabinet was asked to prepare the draft of a new constitution. The committee's draft, quickly approved by Ayub Khan, was promulgated in March 1962, as Pakistan's Second Constitution.[16] There was one basic difference between this and the Constitution of 1956. Whereas in 1956 lawmakers sought to overcome the problem of national integration by establishing a federation in which a considerable amount of power devolved to the two federating units, in 1962 the regime created a strong centre empowered to use all the means that were put at its disposal to preserve national unity. In 1956, the Constituent Assembly had opted for the 'bottom-up' approach towards nation-building, hoping that, under the direction of a central authority, some common socio-cultural and economic ground could be cultivated for the people living in different provinces. One of the assumptions behind the 1956 formula was that religion could be used to unite the people of Pakistan in the same way that it had united them during pre-independence times. The country was, accordingly, to be called the Islamic Republic of Pakistan. In 1962 religion took a back seat and economic cultural and social development received emphasis. The new Constitution charged the Planning Commission with removing economic disparities

between different regions while the Bureau of National Reconstruction was charged with evolving a new culture and a new
political idiom for a unified Pakistani society.

But the regime was to discover after a decade of strenuous effort
that economic development and hybrid culture cannot bring
together diverse communities and, in fact, are poor substitutes for
religion. Passions rather than 'interests' provide a much better
cementing force for nation-building.[17]

One important lesson that General Yahya Khan and his
associates learned from the process that was to result ultimately in
the demise of Ayub Khan's regime was that a viable Pakistani
nation could not be built on the basis of shared economic and
cultural objectives. While Yahya's administration allowed the
preparation of the fourth five-year plan, meant for the 1970–5
period, to drag on, it began an attempt to bring back religion into
politics. The Legal Framework Order, promulgated in mid-1969
to guide the politicians and their parties back to democratic and
representative government gave a prominent place to religion.
Even after the regime gave up its political efforts to keep East
Pakistan within the union and resorted to force, the military
administration in Dacca continued to use religion to bring back
the 'Bengali miscreants' – a phrase widely used to describe
Bengali nationalists – into the Pakistani fold. Yahya's failure,
coming so soon after the failure of Ayub Khan to create a 'just and
equitable society',[18] confirmed in the minds of the people that the
military regime was no better at solving Pakistan's problems than
the civilian leadership it had displaced. The instrument of martial
law used so effectively by the military regime under Azam Khan
in 1953 to restore law and order in the Punjab following the
bloody anti-Ahmadiya movement and again in 1958–62 under
Ayub Khan to bring political and economic tranquillity to the
country was now thoroughly discredited. Even the military recognised their failure and were prepared to turn to Bhutto for
leadership.

BHUTTO'S RISE

Given the fact that Bhutto had won an impressive victory in the
elections of 1970 and given the fact that a military junta had failed
to keep Pakistan united, it is not surprising that a powerful
segment within the army, composed mostly of middle-rank offic-

ers, turned against the senior command and demanded the restoration of civilian rule in the country. Although no authoritative accounts are available of the stormy meeting held at the General Headquarters at Rawalpindi on 20 December 1971, it is widely known that a number of colonels and brigadiers were able to resist successfully the attempt by the generals to re-establish their control over what was left of Pakistan.[19] The vehemence of this opposition and the manner in which it was articulated – the Pakistan army, like all other armies following the British tradition, did not allow open debate between officers of different ranks – came as a total surprise to the senior military officers who had wielded power in the Yahya administration. General Hamid Khan, Yahya Khan's chief of staff, was shouted down by the audience and a number of the middle-level field commanders threatened to move their battalions and brigades to Rawalpindi if the administration of the country was not handed over to the civilians. The rebel officers also made it clear that Bhutto was the civilian they had in mind to succeed Yahya as President.

It was more than just his success at the 1970 polls that had endeared Bhutto to the middle-level army officers. Frustrated twice by the Indian army – once in 1965 when the Pakistani advance into Kashmir was beaten back and then in 1971 when 3000 square miles of territory in West Pakistan was captured by the Indians – there was now widespread resentment among these officers against the generals:

> The macabre events of 1971 showed clearly that the country was not prepared to meet the challenge politically, economically or militarily. The war in East Pakistan was brought on by the political chaos created by the idiocy of Yahya Khan and his advisers. The humiliating surrender at Dacca was the result of the ineptness of the high command and the commander appointed by him. It is no less than a miracle that in spite of indecisive and indifferent leadership, the lack of weapons and equipment, and the defection and treachery of Bengalis, the formations and units in the field still fought so tenaciously and acquitted themselves so well. . . . It is most unfair and unrealistic to ask soldiers, sailors and airmen to fight a war without proper weapons and equipment, a coherent political leadership, a higher defence mechanism *and proper professional leadership of the armed forces at the higher levels* [*italics added*].

This quotation from General Fazal Muqeem Khan's book, *Pakistan's Crisis in Leadership*,[20] which appeared soon after the military and political surrender of the armed forces, represented a line of thinking shared by a number of army officers. Along with General Muqeem,[21] they believed that under quality leadership the Pakistani armed forces would have acquitted themselves well, at least on the western front. The loss of territory in West Pakistan was hard to justify, especially when the Pakistanis faced a force that was numerically not much superior to their own.[22] Bhutto was aware of the fact that a number of middle-level officers in the army were unhappy with *their* senior command. While careful not to openly and publicly question the performance of the senior officers in the last two wars against India, in private he was highly critical of what he was later to describe as 'fat and flabby generals'.[23]

Having ushered in civilian rule in a situation that clearly demanded a drastic change in the form and style of government, the military were not prepared to abandon politics altogether. The initial appointments by the Bhutto administration to the top military positions – particularly the confirmation of General Gul Hasan as the commander-in-chief of the army and Air-Marshal A. Rahim Khan as the commander-in-chief of the air force – represented the group of officers who had successfully resisted the last-ditch efforts by the Yahya junta to retain control. Although instrumental in putting Bhutto in the President's house, both Gul Hasan and Rahim continued to envision some kind of active political role for the armed forces. Even after 20 December 1971 martial law continued to be in force; it is clear that during the first few months of his administration Bhutto's efforts to send the army back to the barracks did not entirely succeed. The generals had the Turkish model in mind.

Bhutto struck in March, less than three months after having assumed power. In an 'anti-*coup d'état*', Bhutto abolished the positions of commanders-in-chief for the army, navy and air force. The three armed forces were placed under the direct command of the President, who was to be advised by chiefs of staff, one for each force. Gul Hasan and Rahim lost their jobs. While these changes were being announced by the President in a radio address to the nation, Gul Hasan and Rahim were kept in 'protective custody' by Mustafa Khar and Mumtaz Ali Bhutto respectively, two of his trusted political lieutenants.

Also significant was the appointment of General Tikka Khan as the army chief of staff. In selecting him, Bhutto opted for an individual who was known to interpret the armed forces role in a 'supportive' rather than an 'overseer' sense. General Gul Hasan and Marshall Rahim would have liked to oversee the process of handing over political management from the military to the political parties; Tikka, on the other hand, committed the forces under his control to 'the loyal execution of the commands of the legally constituted government'. His past record – first as the commander of the army units deployed in the late 1960s to bring law and order back to Baluchistan and later, in 1971, to 'crush the secessionist activities of Mujibur Rahman and his Awami League in East Pakistan' – strongly suggested that Tikka Khan would have no hesitation in carrying out the dictates of the Bhutto regime.

Therefore, soon after assuming political control of the country, Bhutto was able to effectively exclude the armed forces from the processes of decision-making. It has recently been suggested that the taxonomic dichotomy between military and civilian regimes does not stand; not even in those societies in which civilian supremacy is clear. According to this point of view, the transition from military rule can be seen in one sense as a transition from one mixed civil-military system to another. The rulership groups in developing countries in particular are seen as being hybrid regimes representing military and civilian interests.[24] This description does not seem to apply to the change that occurred in Pakistan in 1971–2. As I will argue later, the transition from Yahya to Bhutto meant not only the transfer of power from the military to the civilian authorities. It also meant the introduction into the political arena of social groups and economic interests not represented in the armed forces.

THE SEARCH FOR LEGITIMACY

To dissociate himself completely from the military and the group of army officers who had placed him in power, Bhutto had to find a new and independent base for support. The search for legitimacy started the day he assumed power as civilian head of a military regime. He could have gone to the people soon after assuming power; had he chosen that option, it seems certain that he would have come back – with a new mandate. In the spring of 1972 Bhutto was a popular figure in the country; the nation had turned to him in a moment of grim crisis and his handling of the situation in the first few months in office seemed to justify the faith the people had placed in him. It was with great understanding and skill that he began to deal with the political problems created by the secession of East Pakistan. He went to the 'people's court' for more important decisions; for instance, the release of Mujibur Rahman was obtained when he sought an oral vote from a large public meeting at Karachi; similarly, the decision to incarcerate a number of wealthy businessmen was also announced at a public meeting, this time in Lahore. The summary dismissal of General Gul Hasan and Marshal Rahmin was also a popular step, as it was a clear demonstration of the fact that political power had finally passed from the armed services to civilian leaders. And, as I will discuss later, the economic loss of East Pakistan was not as great as had been anticipated: even the export sector, dependent on easy access to the markets in the eastern province, made a remarkably rapid adjustment. By the middle of 1972 Bhutto was, therefore, in a comfortable position. An appeal to the people at this stage would have been rewarded. Instead, in seeking legitimacy, he decided to follow a much more tortuous path, involving a number of difficult hurdles, some of which he was not able to overcome. Not generally prone to decisions based on whims, he opted for the second option, for, in the middle of 1972, it must have appeared to him the more easier one.

The first reason for Bhutto's decision to delay the quest for legitimacy was his anxiety to establish a political system with which he could feel more comfortable. The legal instruments that he inherited from the Yahya had a number of features with which Bhutto did not feel comfortable. The Legal Framework Order (LFO) promulgated on 30 March 1970 promised 'maximum autonomy' to the federating units and ensured 'the independence of the judiciary in the matter of dispensation of justice and enforcement of the fundamental rights' of all citizens.[25] Although the LFO did not prescribe any particular political system, it was clear that its various mandatory provisions could be made to work only in the context of a Westminster-type parliamentary set-up. The Presidential Order of 6 December 1971 that led to the appointment of Nurul Amin of East Pakistan as the Prime Minister and Zulfikar Ali Bhutto as the Deputy Prime Minister also envisaged substantial devolution of power to the provinces. As the end of a united Pakistan draw nearer, Yahya Khan and his administration came to accept the concept of a loose federation – even a confederation – as a possible solution to the country's political problems. Finally, the draft of the Constitution on which Yahya had spent his final days spelled out in detail the considerable powers that were to be transferred to the provinces. Under the proposed scheme, provinces were to have full command over their financial resources. Also implicit in this document was an 'overseer role' for the military. This constitution was to be promulgated on 20 December, the day Yahya Khan was forced to relinquish power to Zulfikar Ali Bhutto.

Bhutto, whose party had obtained a majority of the seats reserved for West Pakistan under the Legal Framework Order of 1970, who was appointed to the position of Deputy Prime Minister in a martial law government and had taken oath under a Presidential Order, and who had become the President and Chief Martial Law Administrator as a result of a mini-mutiny within the armed forces, faced a peculiar legal position. His claim to power was based on the performance of the PPP in an election held under the LFO; but, for reasons of both politics and temperament, he found the LFO's prescription for checks and balances within different parts of the government and for the sharing of power between the provinces and the central authority unacceptable. He had found a place in the Yahya administration under a Presidential Order that promised even more devolution of power to the provinces than indicated by the LFO. Finally, the army officers who forced Yahya Khan out of the President's House and brought Bhutto in, were interested in a new system in which the military would retain some political control. Bhutto saw only one way out of this dilemma: he started the process of providing the country with a new set of institutions under a new Constitution. The search for legitimacy had, therefore, to be postponed for the time it took the new institutions to take root.

In the middle of 1972, Bhutto was also not certain of the direction that public opinion would take in assessing his role in the Bangladesh crisis. Emotions on the question of Bangladesh still ran high. Seeking re-election at that time would have meant raising some awkward questions about his own role in the 1971 political crisis. Accordingly, he decided to work for the release of prisoners of war and return of the territory still held by India, hoping that success in these areas would help to remove Bangladesh as a political issue. In this assessment he was right. But he also knew that he had to move very cautiously in approaching both India and Bangladesh. After all, an important part of his political support, particularly in the province of the Punjab, was based on his programme of continuing the confrontation with India. In his first address to the nation after becoming the President of a martial law administration, he had also promised that the 'honour of the army would be vindicated'.

The end of the Bangladesh crisis found Pakistan a pariah nation, 'considered the villain among members of the international community for its role in the third Indo-Pakistani war'.[26] This gave Bhutto only a very limited space in which to manoeuvre: he had to maintain the image of inflexibility on the issue of Bangladesh at home and, at the same time, provide the international community with evidence that Pakistan was now in the hands of a responsible and responsive leadership. The refusal to recognise Bangladesh, the use of the Chinese veto to block the entry of that country into the United Nations and withdrawal from the British Commonwealth when it admitted the Bengalis were all acts designed to placate the more militant amongst his supporters. At the same time, Bhutto was sending an endless stream of messages and personal emissaries to the leaders of North America, Europe and the Middle East to persuade them that what seemed to be intransigence on his part was, in fact, a pragmatic response to political compulsions at home.[27] By the summer of 1972, he had cooled passions at home sufficiently to be able to travel to Simla, to meet Mrs Indira Gandhi. After a week of hard bargaining, she and Bhutto signed the Simla Agreement, which promised to give back to Pakistan both its prisoners and its territory in return for the acceptance by that nation of the principle of 'bilateralism' in dealing with the problems concerning South Asia. Translated, this meant that Pakistan would not seek help from foreign countries or institutions to resolve its difficulties with India and Bangladesh. The Simla Agreement, therefore, laid the foundations for the acceptance by other major powers in the area of India's dominant position in the sub-continent of South Asia. The agreement was a triumph for Mrs Gandhi; for Bhutto, although a painful but necessary exercise, it established the image of a leader who, having raised himself to power on the basis of passion, was now prepared to be pragmatic.[28]

With the Simla Agreement signed, Bhutto had closed the Bangladesh chapter. He could now turn to domestic affairs, to a restructuring of Pakistan's society and the institutions that supported and nurtured it. This restructuring was to bring about fundamental changes, some of which even he could not have anticipated. The society was transformed but it did not react passively to the changes that were instituted. The changes brought about by Bhutto are the subject of Part II of this work; the society's reaction that of Part III.

Part II

The Regime in Power, 1971–7

For one moves in a space-time so filled with visual and auditory occurrences that it is very difficult to lift an episode out of the flux of events, a fact out of the stream of feelings, a circumscribed relationship out of a fusion of multiple encounters. If, in all this, I should endow one word with a meaning which unites it all, the word is *fusion*.

Erik H. Erikson

5 Restructuring Institutions

Zulfikar Ali Bhutto's success at the polls of 1970 was due in large measure to a constituency that sought a complete overhaul of the country's political, economic and social institutions. Deeply troubled by the re-acquisition of political power by the traditional leaders during the latter power of the Ayub era, the most articulate component of the Bhutto constituency demanded 'modernisation of the Pakistan system'.[1] Although the term 'modernisation' – and *Mawashrati Taraqi*, its Urdu equivalent – was used freely by Bhutto and his supporters,[2] it was not defined very clearly. For the 'urban democrats' under Mahmud Kasuri and the 'traditional left' under Hanif Ramay, modernisation meant the restoration of parliamentary democracy and the granting of broad fundamental rights to all citizens; for the rural left under Sheikh Rashid, it meant the elimination of the landed aristocracy as an economic and political force; for 'socialist industrial labour' under Miraj Mohammad Khan, it meant a return to 'participatory democracy' in politics and 'participatory management' in industry, and for the 'ultra left' under Mubashir Hasan it meant the evolution of a political and economic system in which 'all power will rest with a dictatorship of the people'.[3] In coming to power, therefore, Bhutto brought with him a party that wanted to totally restructure the country's institutions but had not achieved a consensus on the shape the new structure was to take. The designs that were offered ranged from a Westminster-type of parliamentary democracy to a Soviet style 'dictatorship of the proletariat'. Bhutto did not let his own preferences be known to his various constituencies. In his pronouncements, he deliberately remained vague and equivocal. The impression that he sought to convey was that of 'keeping my options open';[4] a strategy that reassured his followers as well as his opponents. In the party's manifesto he had declared his support for a strong centre based on a parliamentary system, a stand that he reiterated soon after assuming power, in an airport rally at Lahore. This seemed to satisfy the 'urban democrats' and the 'traditional left', two political forces that had their base in that city. However, in a speech delivered a few days later at Karachi, the centre of the urban left, Bhutto talked at length about the advantages of a system in which 'political power would be weighted in favour of the poor and the under-privileged'. And, a month later, in a speech to a gathering at Peshawar and aimed at the people of the Northwest Frontier who were concerned about protecting the rights of smaller provinces, he spoke at length on the need for a 'genuine federal system in Pakistan – a system that would ensure, once for all that the rights of all citizens of Pakistan will be fully protected'.[5]

There were, of course, serious inconsistencies in these state-ments. A strong centre, even if run by an administration responsi-ble to a popularly elected legislature, was not compatible with broad sharing of power between the federal government and the federating units. A system weighted deliberately in favour of the poor would presumably involve something more than simple adult franchise. In fact, in some publications, Bhutto had pointed out that a straightforward parliamentary system in a situation such as Pakistan's worked only to the advantage of the propertied classes.[6] These inconsistencies did not seem to have troubled Bhutto; not only because he regarded 'consistency to be the hallmark of mediocrity', but also because he had clearly defined for himself the contours of the system that he wanted to evolve in Pakistan.

As early as 1962, when Ayub Khan was in the process of providing Pakistan with its second Constitution, Bhutto had made his own preferences known to the President and his Cabinet colleagues. In a long memorandum prepared to inform the Presi-dent and instruct his Constitution Commission, he argued for a one-party system in which the roles of the legislative and judicial branches of the government were to be completely subservient to the all-powerful central authority.[7] The party was to have a cell structure reaching down to the villages and to the *mohallas* (urban communities) in towns and cities. Once the party became fully operational it was to assume the functions performed by such service departments as education and health. Eventually all administrative and judicial services – and, possibly also the armed forces – were to draw their personnel from the party cadre. The details of the proposal drew heavily on the Soviet and

Chinese models as well as on those that were then being developed by Egypt, Tanzania and Tunisia. These ideas were not accepted by Ayub and his Constitutional Commission, a fact that Bhutto attributed to timidity rather than political sagacity.[8] Six years later, when the anti-Ayub movement began to gather momentum, Bhutto felt himself vindicated. He was of the view that, had Ayub adopted his proposed structure, it would have been impossible for those who opposed him to mount such a successful political campaign.

What is remarkable, therefore, is the lesson that he learned from history. It has been argued that, in spite of a strong sense of history, he remained totally uninfluenced by the events between 1962, when he proposed his scheme to Ayub, and 1971, when he found himself in the position to start implementing his ideas. I would suggest, however, that Bhutto did learn from history, but that the lesson that he drew conformed more to his personal predilections than to a sober analysis of Pakistan's political situation. In launching and conducting the campaign against Ayub, he freely invoked the passions and made use of the institutions that he wanted to contain and control. But this battle between the 'power of the state and the power of the street'[9] conformed to his belief in the importance of an institutional structure that would strengthen the former and not constructively channellise the latter. A number of his close followers, aware of his advice to Ayub Khan, expected nevertheless that the 1967–9 political movement would have converted him into a democrat who, when placed in power, would bring about the return of representative democratic institutions to Pakistan. He encouraged this belief because he needed the support of people like Mahmud Ali Kasuri and Hanif Ramay during the period of political uncertainty that preceded and immediately followed the change-over from military to civilian rule. Kasuri, Ramay and a number of their associates were dropped from the PPP as Bhutto proceeded with the task of institutional restructuring. When the task was finished the people who occupied positions of power and responsibility were those who, like Bhutto, felt comfortable in the political environment that was fashioned after the assumption of power by the PPP.

There are a number of easy explanations for Bhutto's preference for an authoritarian political system. The fact that he came from a backward part of the province of Sind was even more important than his feudal background in determining his political attitude. A number of persons from the landed aristocracy had played important roles in shaping Pakistan's political history. Although they had worked together to stem the tide of modernisation that the refugees brought with them from India (see Chapter 2 above), they were content to function within the framework of the quasi-representative system that they helped to evolve after 1953. The important difference between them and Bhutto was that the rural areas of Sind were socially less developed than those of central Punjab. Sind did not possess the groups that had softened the relationship between the landlord and the cultivators in the Punjab. Also, being a more primitive hydraulic society[10] than the Punjab, the institutional arrangements that governed the relationships between various groups were not as well developed as in the other province. The landed-political aristocracy of the pre-Ayub period–people such as Ghanzanfar Ali Khan of Jhelum, Feroze Khan Noon of Sargodha, Mushtaq Ahmad Gurmani of Bahawalpur, Mian Mumtaz Daultana of Multan–came from a rural society that, although vertically structured, had an important middle section occupied by rural merchants, artisans and moneylenders. In addition to playing a crucial economic role, these groups also served as political and social intermediaries between the landlords at the top and the cultivators at the bottom of the village hierarchy. The result was a complex set of linkages that connected different rural classes in relationships of give and take. The landlord, of course, was the principal beneficiary of these arrangements; his political and economic power rested on the support that the rural society provided for him. But these arrangements also bounded the areas of discretion available to him. Even when he seemed to be acting arbitrarily to outsiders – cattle-lifting is one example of such behaviour[11] – his actions, in fact, were in accordance with traditions and rules that had evolved over a long period of time.

The constraints on the Sind's landed aristocracy were not as well defined. There were essentially only two sets of people in the villages: the landlords and their *haris* (servants). The latter could be used as tillers of the soil, as artisans, as domestics; the nature of the function they performed depended not so much on rules and traditions as on the whims of the landlords.[12] Even when the non-farming activities of the servants were picked up by another class – as they were in the districts east of the Indus – this did not change the relationship between the landlord and the cultivators. The role of the Sindhi rural middle class was never institutionalised. Coming from this background, Bhutto's proclivity for authoritarianism can perhaps be understood. But it would be too simplistic to treat this as the most important explanation. There were other influences at work on him. One was his training in law and political science; another the desire to disassociate himself from the stereotype image of a Sindhi, cultivated initially by the British, but made popular when Sindhis, after the partition of the sub-continent, came into contact with refugees from India and migrants from other parts of Pakistan. A third factor, perhaps, was the desire to overcome the stigma associated with being the son of Shahnawaz Bhutto by a wife of low social origins.

The influence of Western education on Bhutto can be well understood by comparing his attitudes with those of Nawab Kalabagh who, as Governor of West Pakistan, was Ayub Khan's principal political lieutenant. The Nawab came from a social and economic background not too dissimilar from that of Bhutto. The social structure in the rural areas of his Mianwali district in many respects was similar to that of Bhutto's Larkana. Between 1960 and 1967 the Nawab governed West Pakistan with the same sense of authority as did Bhutto from 1971 to 1977. But there was one important difference: Kalabagh made no effort to institutionalise authoritarianism. In fact, he openly opposed Ayub Khan's efforts to bring back political parties into the political system. When the parties were brought back, Kalabagh decided to ignore them. While he governed West Pakistan with the help of the bureaucracy, he let his associates manage Ayub Khan's Muslim League in his province. In displaying great contempt for institutions, Kalabagh was being a better 'son of the soil' than Bhutto; Bhutto's attempt to create institutions reflected in part his Western education – political science at Berkeley and law at Oxford.

In January 1949, Bhutto left the University of Southern California to go to Berkeley. At Berkeley, he enrolled as a major in the Political Science department and adopted Professors Lipski and Kelsen as his mentors. 'It is really Hans Kelsen who gave Zulfi and me our solid moorings in democratic thought and practice,' says Piloo Mody, a childhood friend of Bhutto:

Even today there are still too many people who doubt Zulfi's sincerity in spite of his professions. Only time can tell whether

Zulfi's reading of history and constitutional law will over come the temptation of succumbing to arbitrariness and expediency.[13]

A much more important legacy of Kelsen's is to be found in Bhutto's attitude to developing a legal system for Pakistan. In his several submissions to the Pakistani courts during the period after his incarceration in July 1977, Bhutto argued on the lines of Kelsen's *General Theory of Law and State*[14] and *The Pure Theory of Law.*[15] Kelsen's reasoning is obscure, even to legal scholars, and an attempt to determine his 'true view' can lead to 'unprofitable wrangles amongst commentators similar to those which have long bedevilled Marxists and Hegelians'.[16] Accordingly, the 'view' adopted here is that of Bhutto as reflected in his writings and submissions to the courts.

Bhutto accepted Kelsen's definition of a basic norm which must exist in order to establish the 'objective validity' of a constitution and the acts performed under it. But

> the problem that leads to the theory of the basic norm . . . is how to distinguish a legal command which is considered to be objectively valid, such as the command of a revenue office to pay a certain sum of money, from a command which has the same subjective meaning but is not considered to be objectively valid, such as the command of a gangster.[17]

A legal command has the *potential* of becoming legally valid when it reflects the common objective of the citizens of a country, a recognition that the authority that is responsible for implementing the command has the force to do so. It is important, therefore,

> that the domination that characterizes the State claims to be legitimate and must actually be regarded as such by rulers and ruled. The domination is legitimate only if it takes place in accordance with a legal order whose validity is presupposed by the acting individuals.[18]

There is, therefore, a circularity in the argument: for the state to effectively enforce a legal order it must be objectively valid; but this can only be an effective law or a basic norm if the state has the means to enforce it. This circularity notwithstanding, the lesson that Bhutto learnt from Kelsen was that there is no natural law, at least when applied by a state; that there is a system of valid basic norms that become so when they are accepted by the state's citizenry; and that a system of basic norms should not only be valid, but should also be effective in the sense that the state has the means and the power to enforce it. Accordingly, when the state's authority collapses, as it did under Yahya Khan in December 1971, the system of basic norms ceased to exist, since it could no longer be enforced. Bhutto could therefore accept the transfer of power to himself from the military. But a society cannot exist in a legal vacuum, hence his anxiety to give Pakistan a new constitution. A new constitution must be objectively valid; hence, Bhutto's effort to win the support of all political parties for his system.

One final influence of Kelsen on Bhutto should be noted. Kelsen was concerned with 'unity of law' or the absence of distinction between public and private law. In devising his system, Bhutto gave a twist to Kelsen's concept of the Pure Theory of Law, which is a

universalistic viewpoint, always directed toward the whole of the legal order, sees in the private legal transaction just as much as in an administrative order an act of the state, that is, a fact of law-making attributable to the unity of legal order.[19]

The Bhutto system did not unify personal law and public law into a whole in which the one drew from the other. Instead, he created a dominant state structure in which public law and public will overwhelmed personal law and personal freedom.

Of some importance in Bhutto's make-up and in the development of his attitudes towards people and institutions was the Sindhi stereotype against which, consciously and unconsciously, he seems to have reacted. This stereotype had been created by the early British administrators, who found the Sindhi character very different from that of the Pathans, the Punjabis, the Brohis and the Baluchis. Whereas these administrators, when reporting on the people they worked with, had positive things to say about other nationalities, a somewhat less attractive picture was drawn of the Sindhi. He was not credited with the Punjabi's industry, or with the Baluchi's and the Pathan's valour or even with the neighbouring Brohi's intelligence.[20] These stereotypes appear to have influenced the British attitude towards Sindhis and their province. Whereas the British wanted to be closely involved with the administration of the Punjab and the Northwest Frontier, they governed Sind for more than half a century from the distant province of Bombay. It was only in 1906 that Sind was separated from Bombay and organised into a separate province of British India. Also, in recruiting Indians, the British army officers drew a clear distinction between what came to be called the 'martial and non-martial races', and whereas the Punjabis, Pathans and Baluchis were included in the 'martial stock', Sindhis were excluded from it. The result of this policy was that the army that Pakistan inherited from British India had very little Sindhi representation.

Bhutto was the first politician from Sind to become head of state and head of the administration in Pakistan. Mohammad Ayub Khuhro was the only Sindhi before him to occupy an important office at the national level. He had served as the Defence Minister in the Cabinet of Feroze Khan Noon; a position that led to conflict between him and Ayub Khan, who was then the army commander-in-chief. Ayub Khan's *coup d'état* brought Khurho's political career to an abrupt end.

Bhutto's rise to prominence within the Ayub government was not accomplished without overcoming the type of resistance to which politicians such as Khurho had finally succumbed. Once Bhutto moved from the relatively unimportant portfolio of Fuel, Power and Natural Resources to the more important one of Foreign Affairs, he found himself being challenged by Mohammad Shoaib, Ayub Khan's Finance Minister, and Nawab Kalabagh, the Governor of West Pakistan. Both Shoaib and Kalabagh had serious ideological differences with Bhutto. Shoaib's fiscal and financial conservatism and Kalabagh's authoritarian arbitrariness irked Bhutto who, at least within the Ayub Cabinet, represented more forward views and liberal interests. There were also differences of temperament: both Shoaib and Kalabagh were considerably older than Bhutto and less flamboyant in their behaviour. Those differences notwithstanding, Bhutto interpreted some of this opposition in provincial terms. In Ayub's administration, Kalabagh clearly represented the interests of the Punjab and Shoaib that of the Karachi-based refugee community. It appears, therefore, that Bhutto's experience in the 1960s helped to further confirm his feeling that the interests of the Sindhis and their province had to be pursued much more aggressively. This could not be done within a federal framework. In such a system, the Punjab, with nearly 60 per cent of the population, would be able to dominate the smaller provinces. This perception was totally different from that of NAP and its leader, Wali Khan, who sought safeguards for smaller provinces within a confederal framework.

Of the four important influences that may have fashioned Bhutto's personality and his attitudes, and one that is most difficult to document, substantiate and analyse is the fact that he was born into an aristocratic Muslim family from a woman of low social origins who had been converted to Islam at the time of her marriage. But accepting Erikson's hypothesis that the

> psycho-historian's choice of subject often originates in early ideas or identifications and that it may be important for him to accept as well as he can some deeper bias that can be argued out on the level of verifiable fact or faultless methodology.[21]

one could assume, without providing a cause-and-effect scenario that would be beyond scientific reproach, that some of the traits in Bhutto's character can perhaps be attributed to this trauma of birth and childhood.

Although Bhutto entered national politics in 1958, at the age of thirty-one, there was very little public information about his childhood. It was only in 1967, when Bhutto came out in opposition to Ayub, that the government-controlled press began to publish stories about his early days, most of them spent in India. But the thrust of this government-inspired propaganda was to prove that Bhutto was not a loyal Pakistani. For instance, in his reply to a question raised by a member of the Treasury benches, Khwaja Shahabuddin, Ayub Khan's Information Minister, said that an examination of documents filed by Bhutto in the Indian and Pakistani courts suggests that 'till 1958 Mr. Bhutto was claiming in Pakistan citizenship of Pakistan and in India he was claiming citizenship of India'.[22] The fact that Bhutto's mother was a convert to Islam must have been known to Ayub, who was a family friend, but was not exploited to question Bhutto's loyalty to the idea of Pakistan.

It was in 1970, when Bhutto emerged as a serious contender for the office of the Prime Minister, that the conservative press in Pakistan began to print stories about his mother. The respectable monthly *Urdu Digest,* the weekly *Zindigi* and the tabloid *Chattan* all speculated that the marriage between Sir Shahnawaz and Khurshid, Zulfikar Ali's mother, was not a regular one.[23] The *Urdu Digest* and *Zindigi* backed Maulana Maudoodi's *Jamaat-i-Islami,* the politico-religious association that had originally opposed the idea of Pakistan but had later on managed to cultivate a strong following among the urban middle class. Bhutto must have taken these stories seriously, for he allowed Maulana Kausar Niazi, a close political associate and the editor of the weekly *Shahab,* to launch a counter-attack on his opponents. Accordingly, during the summer of 1970 a lively, no-holds-barred debate was carried out by the Urdu press, with the conservatives alleging that the son of a Hindu woman could not be trusted with high office in Pakistan and with *Shahab* responding that Bhutto's childhood hero-worship of Mohammad Ali Jinnah made him into a much better Pakistani than Maulana Maudoodi who had opposed Jinnah's campaign for the creation of a separate Muslim state in the Indian sub-continent. However, in this exchange no attempt was to be made to analyse the significance of what psycho-historians would call 'the event' in shaping Bhutto's character.

The overthrow of Bhutto in March 1977 brought freedom to the press in Pakistan and one segment of it went back to tracing the deposed Prime Minister's early life. This time the emphasis was not so much on questioning Bhutto's sense of patriotism but on treating 'the event' as a childhood trauma that had produced a certain type of political man. Once again, the Urdu press came out with stories and 'new-findings', implying that

As would be expected in a Muslim household, Bhutto's mother, Begum Khurshīd Bhutto, was a more obscure figure. Some unsavoury speculation persists in elite circles about her social circumstances and the form of marriage undertaken to Sir Shahnawaz. She was evidently from a Bombay Hindu family of little means, though the marriage to Sir Shahnawaz was a regular (*nikah*) one and seems to have been durable enough as she gave her husband two daughters as well as a son. Her origins, and her station as a junior wife, appear to have placed Begum Khurshid Bhutto at a disadvantage in the *zenana* (women's apartments) politics of the Bhutto clan, as well as in the elite social circles in which the Bhuttos moved. Some of those who have known the Bhutto family suggest that the resultant insecurity of his mother's position, having communicated itself to the young Zulfikar in his formative years, accounts for the rather major sense of insecurity which seems to underlie the darker side of Bhutto's political leadership.[24]

Whether these factors – the scion of an aristocratic family from a backward part of the province of Sind; born to a woman who embraced Islam late in life; educated in two of the great liberal universities of the West but representative of a social class that remained authoritarian in outlook – helped shape Bhutto's political attitude can only be decided by psycho-historians who are prepared to treat him as a subject from the perspective of these events. My purpose here is simply to suggest that Bhutto, even to one not trained in psychoanalysis, is a complex character and that a number of his actions can be comprehended only if we recognise that the motivations that produced them were never very simple. I have here attempted to analyse some influences that may have kept Bhutto from fulfilling his promise to bring democratic institutions back to Pakistan. It is important to recognise that this promise was taken seriously by a number of people who were anxious for Pakistan to adopt a democratic base. These people were aware of Bhutto's advice to Ayub Khan, but seemed to have been convinced that he had learnt an important political lesson from the events of 1967–9. Bhutto's own pronouncements on the subject were made in great emotion and suggested sincerity of purpose. For instance, in one of the Foundation Documents of the People's Party, he wrote:

> In the name of God, who rules the entire universe, we submit that when a degenerate social order stifles the values of human decency; when opportunism and hypocrisy become part of the national character; when flattery of the rulers is identified with wisdom, honesty with foolishness; when men become apathetic and close their eyes to reality; when men of learning mislead others for personal advantage, and fountains of creativity dry up; then surely men have left the path of righteousness, and for those who do and should care, time for Jehad [crusade] has come.[25]

But the promise was not fulfilled. The crusade that Bhutto was to launch did not create the social order that he and his party had promised. Instead, after Bhutto had finished restructuring the political, bureaucratic and judicial institutions, Pakistan was left with an autocratic system which at least in the opinion of an important and articulate segment of the population continued to stifle decency, encourage opportunism and hypocrisy and turn a very large number of people from the path of creativity to that of personal advantage. In the words of Malik Ghulam Jilani, a politician who, having gained national recognition for his role in the anti-Ayub movement, was amongst one of the first Bhutto supporters to turn against him:

> Justice is no longer a matter of right. It is a matter of accident notwithstanding the elaborate judicial farce. . . . The so-called Constitution finds itself amended and mutilated the moment any court of law appears likely to grant relief to a citizen under its provisions and the courts accept amendments with obvious satisfaction. The press works as an elaborate device for circulating the printed word. Expression is stifled and dissent is frowned upon. . . . It seems to me that piqued and peeved by the criticism levelled at his Martial Law Administration, during the few months that it was allowed at all, and, above all, nettled by the frequent references made to the courts during the same period, my friend Bhutto decided to take it out not only on the country and the courts, but on the entire Parliamentary Government.[26]

And, according to Mrs Asghar Khan, the wife of another early political associate, 'with the debut of Mr Bhutto and his regime, an outrageous demonstration of vindictiveness surfaced'.[27]

The reasons for this change in Bhutto's attitude between the time he campaigned against Ayub's authoritarian system to the time when he found himself in power is to be explained in terms of both political strategy and personal taste.

PAKISTAN'S THIRD CONSTITUTION: BHUTTO'S VISIBLE HAND

Bhutto assumed the control of the government in what was essentially a constitutional vacuum. Shortly before the fall of Dacca he had been brought in as Deputy Prime Minister in a martial law administration headed by General Yahya Khan.

Although this was Pakistan's second military government, the martial law under which it governed had yet to develop any rules or systems for succession.[28] Ayub Khan's *coup d'état* had received judicial sanction under the doctrine of 'political necessity'. The implication was that resort to martial law was necessitated by events that could not be controlled by the prevailing constitutional processes. The application of this doctrine of necessity also meant that the imposition of martial law was a corrective measure, undertaken to restore equilibrium within the society. The question whether the return to equilibrium meant a return to the constitutional order that had preceded the martial law was not answered explicitly. There was only an implicit answer in that Ayub Khan had chosen to introduce a new constitution after lifting his martial law. Therefore, when, under pressure from the middle-level army officers, Yahya Khan decided to abdicate, the choice of Bhutto to succeed him was determined not by any rules or established precedence, but by the fact that he was at that time the most popular politician in the country. And, following on the precedence of Ayub Khan, Bhutto decided not to return to the constitutional system that had been put aside by Yahya Khan when he imposed martial law in March 1969. Like Ayub, Bhutto decided to restructure Pakistan's legal system. But unlike Ayub, Bhutto decided to move quickly.

Whereas Ayub waited for four years before giving the country a new Constitution, it took Bhutto only four months to lift martial law and institutionalise his regime within the context of an 'interim Constitution'. On 21 April 1972, the delegates elected in 1970 to represent West Pakistan's four provinces in the National Assembly met as the central legislative body of 'New Pakistan' and gave their approval to the interim Constitution that had been proposed by the Bhutto regime. This action by the new National Assembly re-established the viceregal system that the British had operated under the Government of India Act of 1935.[29] Bhutto, as President of the republic, was vested with the powers that the British viceroys had enjoyed under the Crown rule. In the provinces, Ministries were established that were responsible not to the provincial legislature but to the Governors. The Governors, appointed by the President, were responsible only to him and not to the legislature. The main reason for the support that Bhutto was able to get from the National Assembly for establishing such a strong, centralised government was his promise that it was an interim measure justified by the grave crisis through which the country was passing at that time.

After permitting Bhutto to function under an interim Constitution, the National Assembly busied itself with the preparation of Pakistan's third Constitution. A multi-party parliamentary committee was set up in which Bhutto's PPP, Wali Khan's NAP, Maulana Mufti Mahmud's JUI and Quyum Khan's Muslim League were represented. The committee found its task much easier than that of similar bodies set up by the First Constituent Assembly (1947–53), and the Second Constituent Assembly (1953–6). Its task was also simpler than that of the Shahabuddin Constitution Commission (1959–60) that had been entrusted by Ayub Khan with the task of constitution-making. The issues to be resolved now were not as difficult as those faced during the 1950s and 1960s. The first attempt to draft a constitutional framework for Pakistan bogged down largely on the question of the role of Islam in government. The length of time it took Ayub Khan to give the country a new legal structure arose from the problem of assuring the more populous East Pakistan a fair share in political and economic decision-making. Time and the emergence of Bangladesh as an independent country had reduced the importance of these issues. The triumph of the PPP in the election of 1970 was generally interpreted as a triumph for secularism and socialism, while the departure of Bengalis had produced a fairly homogeneous 'New Pakistan'. A consensus should have been quickly reached between the various parties in the parliament and between the various factions in the PPP had not Bhutto, at this stage, begun to argue for a system of government much more centralised and authoritarian than could be accepted even by some elements within his own party or by the 'provincial autonomists' within the parties that opposed him.

This change in attitude took some of Bhutto's supporters by surprise. Mahmud Ali Kasuri, his law minister and one of his early supporters, resigned from the Cabinet, telling Bhutto that the people of Pakistan were

> waiting to hear from you a reiteration of the pledge to introduce a federal parliamentary form of government which clearly implies that the executive is answerable to the legislature, the executive power vests in the Prime Minister and his Cabinet and where the executive is also removable by the legislature.[30]

It is possible to analyse Bhutto's motives in abandoning the position that he had taken during the anti-Ayub movement and in the campaign for the elections of 1970. The unequivocal support that he now began to give to the idea of a strong centre, dominated by a chief executive, secure from assaults by both the legislature and the judiciary, was in keeping with his character and also with the political philosophy that he developed during his tenure as a Minister in the first Ayub Cabinet. His social and economic background and, possibly, the trauma of childhood, played some role in Bhutto's demand for a political system that he could dominate. But other factors must also have had some influence: at least three of them deserve some mention.

Bhutto's approach to the problem of provincialism was completely different from that of the 'autonomists' in the opposition parties. Whereas Wali Khan and his associates saw devolution of power to the provinces as the only way to protect the rights of the smaller units, Bhutto believed that, given the weight of the Punjab (see Table 5.1 below), such an arrangement would not work in favour of other provinces. The Punjab, with 58 per cent of the population, 62 per cent of the gross domestic output, 65 per cent of foodgrain production and 52 per cent of the output of the manufacturing sector, could become politically and economically so powerful as to make the working of a central authority difficult. The difficulties would be even greater if the central government were controlled by a non-Punjabi such as Bhutto. In support of this argument, Bhutto cited the situation that was created by Mujibur Rahman in March 1971, when the latter refused to accept the 'writ of the central government' even when he was not the formal head of the administration in East Pakistan.[31]

Bhutto was also concerned about the attitude of the armed forces to Pakistan's political development and the ability of the politicians to bring the men in uniform under their control. This fear no doubt motivated his own approach towards constitution-making. Ayub Khan, an army man, could afford to function for four years in a constitutional vacuum; Bhutto, without the assured backing of the armed forces, did not feel comfortable without adequate legal authority. This explains the priority that he assigned to the process of constitution-making; it also explains to some extent his anxiety to achieve a broad political consensus in favour of the new constitution and to provide for a powerful central figure who would be able to exercise control over the

TABLE 5.1   Distribution of economic power between the provinces

	Punjab	Sind	NWFP[1]	Baluch-istan	Total
Population 1972[2] (million)	37·5	14·0	10·8	2·4	64·7
% of total	58·0	21·6	16·7	3·7	100·0
Gross Domestic Product 1972 (Rs billion)	29·9	11·2	6·5	1·3	48·9
% of total	61·1	229·0	13·3	2·7	100·0
Per capita income (Rs)	797·0	788·0	602·0	541·0	756·0
Foodgrain Output[3] (million tons)	7·8	2·4	1·2	0·2	11·6
% of total	67·2	20·7	10·3	1·7	100·0
Value of industrial output[4] (Rs billion)	3·8	1·5	0·3	0·2	5·8
% of total	65·5	25·9	5·2	3·4	100·0

[1] The data for NWFP includes the Federally Administered Tribal Areas.

[2] Population data are from the census of 1972. See Government of Pakistan, *Pakistan Economic Survey, 75–76* (Islamabad: Finance Division, 1976), Table 1, p. 3 in the Statistical Annex.

[3] Author's calculations based on the data in Government of the Punjab, *Development Statistics of the Punjab* (Lahore: Bureau of Statistics, 1976); Government of Sind, *Statistical Handbook* (Karachi: Statistical Office, 1974), Government of NWFP, *NWFP Statistics* (Peshawar: Planning Department, 1976) and Government of Pakistan, *Agricultural Statistics* (Islamabad: Ministry of Agriculture, 1975).

[4] Author's calculations from the sources in note 3 and Government of Pakistan, *Census of Manufacturing Industries* (Islamabad: Ministry of Industries, 1974).

military. It was his belief that this time the military would be reluctant to overturn a constitutional structure that had the support of most political parties and groups. He also believed that the armed forces could only be subjected to civilian control if political authority was not spread too thinly over the executive, legislative and judicial branches of the government.

Finally, the leftist elements within the PPP also seem to have influenced the switch in Bhutto's approach to constitution-making. As one of the principal figures from the left was to argue later, had Bhutto gone on to establish a people's dictatorship, he would not have faced the situation that resulted in his fall in the spring of 1977.[32] Bhutto paid heed to these councils in 1972. It was in the interest of the left to establish a strong central government, controlled, if possible, by one political party. It was only through this kind of centralisation of authority that the left could expect to bring about the social and economic changes to which it was committed.

It was under these influences that Bhutto decided to abandon his support for a parliamentary form of government and to opt for a system not too different from the authoritarian structure that Ayub Khan had built under the Constitution of 1973. The constitutional proposal that finally won the approval of all important political parties was a combination of the Westminster-type of parliamentary system and a presidential form of government. As in all systems derived from the British example, the National Assembly, although placed in a bi-cameral setting, was to have the greatest power. Its 200 seats were to be divided according to population, with the members selected on the basis of adult franchise. On the other hand, the Senate's forty seats were to be divided equally among the four provinces with the members elected by a 'combined sitting of the National and Provincial Assemblies'. The initiative for legislation in all areas was to be with the National Assembly; the Senate could delay the passage of a Bill already approved by the National Assembly but could not veto it.

There were two main departures from the Westminster model: the Constitution did not provide for the establishment of several of the standing committees which are common in systems following the British pattern and it provided safeguards for the Prime Minister that are also unusual for these systems. The Prime Minister was to be elected by a majority of the total membership of the National Assembly. Although he could be removed by a vote of no confidence, a motion aiming at such a vote had to include within the text the name of a successor. Such a motion could not be moved during the period when the Assembly was considering the Budget and, when moved without success, it could not be repeated for another six months. Mindful of the fact that his move towards a quasi-presidential system had disturbed an important element within his own party, Bhutto had the Assembly adopt a special clause according to which, during a period of ten years following the adoption of the new Constitution,

the vote of a member, elected to the National Assembly as a candidate or a nominee of a political party, cast in support of a resolution for a vote of no confidence shall be disregarded if the majority of members of that political party in the National

Assembly has cast its votes against the passing of such a resolution.[33]

Bhutto's Constitution – the fifth to be drafted in Pakistan and the third to be adopted – was only a year in the making. With the opposition attending and with 125 of the Assembly's 133 members casting their votes in favour, the constitution was adopted on 10 April 1973 in that 'atmosphere of dramatic surprise whose value Bhutto well understands and which he knows well how to contrive'.[34] The surprise was all the greater since Bhutto seemed to have gone back on his promise to let Wali Khan's NAP rule in the provinces of the NWFP and Baluchistan. Under the interim Constitution, Bhutto had allowed these two provinces to be governed by NAP; Arbab Sikander as Governor and Maulana Mufti Mahmud as Chief Minister in the NWFP and Ghaus Baksh Bizenjo and Ataullah Khan Mengal in the same positions in Baluchistan, wielded effective power in the two provinces. Although the NAP governments in the NWFP and Baluchistan carefully stayed within the prescribed boundaries of the interim constitution, it became clear to Bhutto that the presence of provincial administrations over which he could not exercise political control seriously limited his own authority. Accordingly, following the discovery of an arms cache in the Iraqi Embassy in Islamabad on 12 February, the NAP administration were dismissed. The government and the government-controlled media connected 'Iraq's attempts at gun running with the NAP's stated intention of carving out autonomous Pathan and Baluch areas within Pakistan'.[35] The removal of these administrations was a serious blow to the understanding that Bhutto had arrived at on constitutional issues with the NAP's Wali Khan and yet, within two months of this incident, the NAP cast most of the votes it controlled in the National Assembly in favour of the Constitution.

The NAP's support for the Constitution was in fact a triumph for Bhutto, the political tactician. The sixteen months of the Bhutto regime operating within the 'viceregal' framework of the interim Constitution were enough to convince the NAP leadership that some curtailment in the powers of the central authority would be better than a stalemate on the Constitution issue. This view was strengthened by the departure of the urban democrats from the PPP – an event that was interpreted as an important step towards the development of countervailing forces for checking

Bhutto's drive towards centralisation and authoritarianism. It was the NAP's belief that, with the help of the PPP dissidents, it could effectively check Bhutto provided the opposition was allowed to function effectively. Accordingly, the NAP acquiesced to the PPP constitutional proposal in order to provide a legal framework for interaction between the government and the opposition. Bhutto's choice of the 1935 Act of India as an interim Constitution and his operation of the viceregal system were, therefore, useful tactical ploys for producing the Constitution that suited both his temperament and his political philosophy.

I would hypothesise, on the basis of my analysis of the personality of Bhutto, that the opposition could have won more concessions from him on constitutional issues had it realised at that point that its support was crucial for the President. The practical significance of Kelsen's position on 'objective validity' – a position to which Bhutto subscribed – was that the rulers and *the ruled* must regard the basis of the authority as valid. In order to make the authority vested in the 1973 Constitution valid, Bhutto had to win the support of the ruled and, amongst those he was to rule, the NAP occupied a position of some prominence. Therefore, in order to lend validity to the establishment of what Kelsen calls the 'basic norm', the NAP could have exacted some more concessions from Bhutto, particularly on the processes needed to change the constitution. These concessions may have proved important in reining-in the administration that functioned for five years under the 1973 constitution. As it is, by first pressing for a presidential system and then agreeing to an indigenised form of parliamentary system, Bhutto gave the impression that the more important concessions, in the constitutional give-and-take, were made by his party. For instance:

I wanted a presidential system and they [the opposition leaders] said we will never have a presidential system. I said all right. . . . Then they said we will have a system of parliamentary democracy where the power lies with the Prime Minister. I said all right. They said that the Prime Minister cannot be removed under certain circumstances. I said all right, I accept your formula. Now they go back and say the President must have certain powers.[36]

When the Constitution was promulgated on 14 August 1973,

Bhutto had a legal system that he could use to bend other powerful institutions in the country to suit his style and his purpose. There was little that the opposition or the democratic elements within his party could do to prevent him for reshaping what he described as the instruments of state. The more important amongst these were the civil and military bureaucracies and the judicial system.

BENDING THE 'STEEL FRAME'

One of the important innovations in the 1973 Constitution was the withdrawal of 'constitutional guarantees' from the civil servants. The constitutions of 1956 and 1962 gave the civil servants recourse to courts under provisions that protected their rights when in service. A civil servant could only be removed before he reached the age of retirement if the 'hiring authority' could establish that he was not fulfilling the requirements of his position, a charge that was very difficult to sustain in a court of law. While constitutional guarantees gave an exceptional sense of security to all civil servants, when combined with the system of reservations of posts for one part of the bureaucracy, the Civil Service of Pakistan (CSP), they created what Bhutto called the 'Brahmins' of the administrative structure.[37]

Lloyd George had described the Indian Civil Service, the CSP predecessor, as a 'steel frame' that supported the intricate administrative structure erected by the British in India. After independence, both Jinnah and Liaqat continued to rely heavily on the CSP: 'the only model of government that Pakistan leaders had known was that of the British viceregal system in India under which the bureaucrats had exercised these powers . . . without any interference from politicians.'[38] After the deaths of Jinnah and Liaqat, the CSP was able to further strengthen its position. The politicians at the centre and in the provinces, while they worked out intricate jig-saw puzzles involving different political groups, were quite content to let the day-to-day administration be handled by the CSP. The situation admirably suited the CSP; it flourished and thrived in the near political vacuum in which it had been called upon to perform.

A partnership between the army and the Civil Service did not develop immediately after Ayub Khan's *coup d'état* in 1958. 'The union between the CSP and the military service was something that occurred during the course, not at the beginning of the revolutionary government'.[39] but once it did, the Ayub Khan regime acquired its distinguishing character as a bureaucratic state.[40] Accordingly, when Bhutto came to power, he found the CSP powerful and well-entrenched. Although at that time there were about 1 million persons in Pakistan's Civil Service system and only 320 members in the CSP, of the 300 senior positions – permanent secretaries in the central and provincial governments, chief secretaries of the provinces, heads of public corporations, commissioners of divisions and deputy commissioners of districts – 225 were occupied by members of the CSP. Altaf Gauhar and Fida Hasan, the principal advisers of Ayub Khan during the latter part of the 1960s, were members of the CSP, as were M. M. Ahmad, the head of the powerful Planning Commission; A. G. N. Kazi, chairman of the Water and Power Development Authority, the largest public sector corporation in the country; Anwar ul Haque, Chief Justice of the Lahore High Court, the most important of the three provincial courts; and Roedad Khan, in charge of the state-controlled radio and television services. Such concentration of power amongst a small group of people was resented by members of other services as well as by politicians. According to one long-time critic of the CSP, the service had 'nourished and supported autocratic military or dictatorial regimes, and prevented the march of democracy and promoted the continuation of British imperial rule'.[41] But the CSP refused to accept any responsibility for Pakistan's political problems. In a memorandum submitted to Yahya Khan's Pay and Services Commission, the CSP Association declared that the administrative structure had been victimised by an irresponsive, unaccountable and irresponsible political system:

> It is our contention that the solution to the problem of responsiveness, accountability, and responsibility lies not in the weakening of the bureaucratic system but in the intensification and strengthening of the representative institutions.[42]

But, while not accepting many of the criticisms levelled against it, the CSP agreed that it had accumulated a great deal of power, 'mostly because the politicians in the past have failed in their responsibility'.[43] For a number of reasons, some of them personal and some of them political, Bhutto could not afford to let such a great deal of power repose in the civil bureaucracy. He had experienced both the power of the Civil Service and its arrogance. As Minister of Foreign Affairs, Aziz Ahmed, a prominent member of the CSP, who was also the Permanent Secretary of the Ministry, helped him to re-orient Pakistan foreign policy from a total commitment to the West to a relatively neutral position between the United States, Soviet Russia and China. The military, tied as it was to the United States because of its dependence on that country for equipment, was not anxious to support a change in policy that would in any way jeopardise its lines of supply. Although, not as powerful in decision-making as the CSPs in Islamabad, the generals in Rawalpindi's General Headquarters still pulled a great deal of weight with Ayub Khan. In this, they used Ghiasuddin Ahmad, a CSP and Secretary of Defence, as go-between. With the help of Aziz Ahmed from the Ministry of Foreign Affairs and Altaf Gauhar from the Ministry of Information, Ghiasuddin Ahmad was able to allay the fears of the generals. These three civil servants were especially instrumental in opening up China and Russia as the suppliers of weapons to the armed forces.

Once Bhutto was out of power, members of the same bureaucracy were also able to demonstrate the effectiveness of a bureaucracy in frustrating a renegade politician. Not a single reference was made to Bhutto in *Friends Not Masters*, Ayub Khan's political autobiography. The book was written by the field-marshal with the help of Altaf Gauhar and his Ministry of Information. S. M. Yusuf, a CSP, the successor of Aziz Ahmed in the Foreign Ministry, helped to reorganise the Ministry so that those bureaucrats who remained loyal to Bhutto were removed from positions of any importance. Finally, the Divisional Commissioners, under orders from the CSP chief secretaries – Mauzur Elahi in Sind and Afzal Agha in the Punjab – used a combination of laws to prevent Bhutto from holding heavily attended public meetings. On assuming power in 1971, and after describing this phase in Pakistan's history as *naukarshahi* – rule by the civil servants – Bhutto incarcerated Altaf Gauhar and dismissed S. M. Yusuf, Ghiasuddin Ahmad, Afzal Agha and Manzur Elahi from the service.

But Bhutto had other motives as well for bending the steel frame. The concentration of power in the hands of the Prime Minister, made possible by the Constitution of 1973, could not be brought about as long as a powerful Civil Service continued to exercise a great deal of independent discretion. The withdrawal of constitutional guarantees and making the civil servants answerable to the head of the administration were steps taken to reduce the power of the bureaucracy. Once all the Ordinances and Acts aimed at reforming the civil administration were on the books[44] and once the CSP had been abolished, the senior civil servants could no longer act with the degree of independence that was available to them under the previous administrations. This diminution in the power of the civil bureaucracy made possible the concentration of power in the hands of the Prime Minister.

Bhutto's personal conflict with a number of civil servants and the need to limit the power of the bureaucracy to allow a greater degree of freedom to the politicians were two important reasons for the administrative reforms of 1973. A third was the ideological conflict between the senior bureaucrats and a number of influential leftists in the Bhutto government. The left wanted to bring about a fundamental change in the structure of Pakistani society. Mubashir Hasan, the Finance Minister and the left's most important spokesman, did not want Bhutto to stop at the nationalisation of basic industries and financial institutions. He wanted a much more radical reorientation of government policies, including collectivisation of agricultural land and assumption by the state of all urban property[45] (see Chapter 6). A number of civil servants opposed these policies. For instance, Qamar ul Islam, head of the Planning Commission, was openly critical of policy initiatives already taken or intended by the regime, a point of view that was also shared by B. A. Kureshi, head of the powerful Planning and Development Department of the Punjab. For the left to be able to implement its programmes it was clear that not only did the CSP have to be eliminated, but the strength of all services had also to be reduced. Mubashir Hasan and his associates had promised administrative reforms in the PPP's election manifesto, but the nature of the structure that was supposed to emerge from these changes was not clearly spelled out. The manifesto limited itself to the suggestion that a 'socialist regime will need a different structure of administration'.[46] The contours of this structure began to take shape as Mubashir Hasan and Khurshid Hasan Meer, his Cabinet colleague who was now in charge of the Ministry of Establishment, came to understand the reasons and sources of the CSP strength. One of them was the system of competitive examination that admitted only twenty-five persons every year as 'probationers' to the service; another was training in the exclusive Civil Service Academy at Lahore[47] that emphasised, along with the liberal arts, the development of 'horsemanship and similar attributes of leadership';[48] a third was assured access to senior positions at a relatively young age; and a fourth, the privilege to move between different Ministries. Accordingly, when the administrative reforms were announced, considerable emphasis was placed on opening up entry to the service to people of all ages and not just through a competitive examination conducted only for new college graduates. The reforms also introduced an 'eligibilitarian system' of training in a new and much more modest Academy for Administrative Training. The system of 'reservation of posts' was done away with, as was the system of lateral transfers between Ministries.[49] Under the new system of 'accountability to the government of the day', the regime also dismissed such critics of its economic policies as Qamar ul Islam and B. A. Kureshi.

A fourth motive behind the administrative reforms was to open positions in government to the supporters of the politician in power. The new system of 'lateral entry' was not administered by the Federal Service Commission; instead, the entrants had only to satisfy the not very rigorous admission standards set by the Establishment Division. The division, now under the charge of Viqar Ahmad, a long-time Bhutto associate, did not even go through the pretence that the recruitment process was without strong political overtones. Between 1973 and 1977, the Establishment Ministry inducted 1374 officers into government service, a number three times a large as the one that would have been possible under the old system. The opposition, of course, saw strong political motives behind the administrative reforms. According to the NAP, the government's plan would 'raise an army of stooges to help in fostering fascism and all civil servants becoming the humble servants of the ruling *vedaras* [landlords]'.[50] *Zindigi*, the influential Urdu monthly, in an issue devoted to the administrative reforms, identified more than 100 senior-level appointees as close relatives and associates of the Ministers in the central Cabinet.[51] Even the section of the press that was sympathetic to the government chose to voice some caution. In an editorial, *Dawn*, suggested the following:

The integrity and impartiality of the public services will be seriously undermined if they are not afforded due protection against political coercion and arbitrariness. The new experiment will have a chance of ushering in a healthy change only if this vital consideration is borne in mind.[52]

That the administrative structure inherited by Bhutto would not have served his political, social and economic purpose was clear to all; even the CSP had prepared itself for change. But when the change came, its content and manner of implementation surprised even those who had been suggesting for a long time that Pakistan had to reform its antiquated structure.[53] As we shall see in Part III of the book, an important impact of the reform was to weaken the ability of the Bhutto regime to effectively deliver services to the people. Like a number of other reforms, the more important consequence was quite the opposite of what had been originally intended by the regime.

In approaching some other areas of potential resistance and opposition, the regime's tactics was somewhat different from the one adopted in the case of the CSP. Despite their defeat in East Pakistan, the military remained well organised and powerful. And, because of the turbulent constitutional history of Pakistan, the courts had gained a great deal of power and prestige. But Bhutto recognised that both the military and the judiciary could seriously limit his freedom of manoeuvre. Accordingly, he set out to tame them both.

With the military the approach adopted was to move some of the more important personnel functions from General Headquarters to the Prime Minister's secretariat. An informal three-man committee made up of Bhutto, General Tikka Khan and General Imtiaz Ahmad approved all promotions and transfers above the rank of brigadier-general. Tikka Khan, as chief of staff of the army and Imtiaz as the Prime Minister's military secretary were intensely loyal to Bhutto and, accordingly, their advice was readily accepted. Once important positions had been filled in the armed forces' hierarchy, it became clear that the Prime Minister's secretariat had pursued a policy of reducing the power of the two regional groups that had dominated the Pakistani military establishment for over those decades. The first of these were the Pathans from the Northwest Frontier Province and Baluchistan; Generals Ayub Khan, Mohammad Musa, Yahya Khan and Gul Hasan – Pakistan's first four commander-in-chiefs – were all from this area, as were a large number of other officers who had held important positions during the 1950s and 1960s. The next most powerful group in the armed forces were those from the Potwar region – a region made up of the districts of Campbellpur, Rawalpindi and Jhelum in the northern parts of the Punjab. Whereas the Pathans had earned mostly 'king commissions' – being recruited by the British on the same terms as the officers who entered the Indian Army from Britain itself – the 'Potwar' officers had come up generally through the ranks. 'Coming through the ranks' meant that these officers had worked their way up the military hierarchy from the very bottom. As Pakistan's army came to be indigenised, the latter group, on account of a large and very loyal following amongst the rank-and-file, gained considerable power. General Tikka Khan was from this group, as were Generals Akbar Khan and Abdul Majid – two of the four corps commanders at the time of Bhutto's assumption of power.

Bhutto's tactic was to distribute the top military positions among officers who did not have known group loyalties. At the same time the command of the armed forces was divided functionally between three persons. Under Ayub Khan and his successors, those three functions were performed by the commander-in-chief. Under the new scheme, the chief of staff was put in charge of strategy and co-ordination between the army, navy and air force; the Prime Minister's defence adviser was made responsible for internal security and the Secretary of Defence was placed in charge of administration. Tikka Khan was replaced by General Zia ul Haq as Chief of Staff. The newly created position of Defence Adviser went to Tikka Khan and General Fazal Muqeem Khan was made the Secretary of Defence. Of these three, only Tikka was from the Potwar area, Zia and Fazal Muqeem being refugees from the Indian part of the Punjab. The reorganisation of the armed forces command structure made it possible not only to limit the power of any single individual, but also to reduce the influence of more powerful groups in the armed forces. It was Bhutto's hope that this dispersion of power and responsibility would reduce the possibility of the emergence of another Ayub or Yahya. As we shall see in Part III of the book, Bhutto was only partially successful in meeting this objective.

Had the armed forces not been discredited by the political and military events of 1969–71, it is doubtful that their leadership would have willingly accepted the administrative changes that were introduced by the Bhutto regime. Being on the defensive, they had little choice, but Bhutto, being a consummate politician, chose to sugar the bitter pill. In his first address to the Pakistani nation on assuming the presidency he had promised to rebuild the armed forces, to win back for them their 'pride and glory'. Three months later, once again in a speech to the nation, delivered after the announcement of the dismissal of General Gul Hasan, Bhutto blamed the indifferent performance of the armed forces in the past on 'fat and flabby generals'. Once he had his own team of commanders in place, he began to deliver additional resources to the military. This was the sweetening of the pill. In 1972/73, the first year of the Bhutto regime, the proportion of the national wealth going into defence expenditure increased to over 7 per cent (Table 5.2). By the mid 1970s, with half a million men in uniform, Pakistan was spending nearly one-sixteenth of its gross national product on defence.

TABLE 5.2   Defence expenditure and its share in national wealth

	Military expenditure[1]			Armed forces size[1]	
	Amount ($m)	As % of GNP	Per capita of population ($)	Number (000)	Per 1000 people
1966	330	5·7	6·2	295	5·5
1967	308	5·0	5·8	345	6·3
1968	343	5·2	6·1	350	6·2
1969	350	5·0	6·0	365	6·3
1970	372	4·8	6·2	370	6·2
1971	436	5·6	7·1	404	6·5
1972	522	6·7	8·2	350	5·5
1973	522	6·6	8·0	466	7·1
1974	572	5·7	8·5	500	7·4
1975	569	6·3	8·2	502	7·2

[1] Expenditure and armed forces size adjusted for the pre-1971 period by the exclusion of East Pakistanis.
Source: Computed from the US Arms Control and Disarmament Agency, *World Military Expenditures and Arms Transfers, 1966–1975* (Washington D.C., 1977).

A somewhat similar approach was adopted towards the judiciary. The constitution permitted some reorganisation of the courts; for instance, the Supreme Court was enlarged from a membership of five to one of seven. Its seat was moved from the politically alive city of Lahore to Rawalpindi. Rawalpindi housed not only the General Headquarters of the Armed Forces but also a number of Federal Government ministries. It was only twelve miles from Islamabad, the nation's capital. It did not have Lahore's political traditions. In coming to Rawalpindi, the Supreme Court came to an environment that was more bureaucratic and considerably less political than that of Lahore.

Through a series of amendments to the Constitution, the administration also sought to limit the power of the courts. For instance, the courts were denied jurisdiction over government decisions taken under the Defence of Pakistan Rule (DPR). The DPR enforced at the time of the 1969–71 political crisis was retained by the Bhutto regime on the ground that the country had not fully recovered from the shock of Bangladesh's separation. Continuation of DPR meant the suspension of civil liberties and fundamental rights. The attempts made by the opposition to have these rights restored by recourse to the courts did not prove fruitful, for the government moved quickly in the National Assembly to limit the courts' jurisdiction over these matters. The Constitution, promulgated on 16 August 1973, was amended during the first sitting of the National Assembly to specifically limit 'judicial discretion in areas sensitive for the integrity and solidarity of West Pakistan'.[54] In addition, the National Assembly adopted the High Treason Act, the Private Military Organisation (Abolition and Prohibition) Act and the Prevention of Anti-National Activities Ordinance, suggesting that the Constitution itself was not a strong enough legal document to counter the presence of fissiparous forces in the country. Each of these acts extended the power of the executive at the expense of the judiciary.[55]

In 1974, the Fundamental Rights provided by the Constitution were restored, but the state of emergency and the DPR, by which these rights were suspended, remained. As if there was not already a sufficient concentration of power in the executive branch, the government strengthened its coercive ability further by assuming the right to dissolve political parties whose activities were thought to be injurious. This was done by the adoption of the Suppression of Terrorist Activities (Special Courts) Ordinance in October 1974. 'What, then, is to be inferred?' asked a political commentator:

Either such legislation is unnecessary in which case its presence

in the Statute Book is, to say, the least, unfortunate, or alter-
nately, it is necessary, in which case we can only conclude that
the country's political life is still disturbed by dangerous
factionalism.[56]

Not only was the presence of these Acts on the Statute Book
unfortunate and unnecessary, but they and other measures of
reforms instituted by the regime also proved to be counterproduc-
tive. The changes in the administrative structure, the tightening
of the constitution, interference with the armed forces' command
structure and the reduction of the power of the courts were
undertaken to fulfil certain objectives. The most important of
these objectives was that of ensuring longevity for the regime. But,
as I will suggest in Part III, each of these 'reforms', in some
unexpected way, contributed to the collapse of the Bhutto government. In this chapter, I have been concerned with establishing the
principal motives for these changes; in a subsequent chapter
(Chapter 8), I will show why the regime could not have been fully
aware of the consequences of all this restructuring of Pakistan's
institutions.

Since the chapter that follows is concerned with the economic
policies pursued by the regime, it would be useful to point out here
that one important result of these policies was to enlarge the role
of the government in economic management. But this role was
expanded at a time when the administrative structure no longer
had the strength to shoulder this additional burden. The suggestion here is not that the administrative reforms were unnecessary
but that their timing, at least from the point of view of the regime's
objectives, was unfortunate.

6 Redirecting Economic Development: Management by the PPP Left

Dissatisfaction with the economic policies of the Ayub regime was the main reason for the PPP's triumph in the elections of 1970. While the PPP's electoral success played a part, it was not the most important reason for Bhutto's ascent to power in December 1971. In the election of 1970, the PPP had been supported by a number of groups who were unhappy with Ayubian economics. These groups had no role in the selection of Bhutto as Yahya Khan's successor. Accordingly, whereas some factions within the PPP remained responsive to the economic demands of their constituencies, Bhutto was quite content to assign a low priority to economic decision-making. The circumstances of Bhutto's rise to power as reported by some of his close associates suggests that he was helped by a faction in the army that was not satisfied in the areas of constitution-making and foreign affairs. Therefore, while Bhutto busied himself improving Pakistan's image abroad and providing the country with a new set of political and administrative institutions, the left within the PPP administration assumed control of economic decision-making. The left was able to assume control as it was the only faction within the party and within the new administration that had developed a programme of action. It also had the leadership that was politically acceptable to Bhutto. But the power that was wielded by this faction was far out of proportion to the political support that it could claim within the PPP constituency. This became clear as the groups that were hurt by the left's economic and social policies began to rally against it. Within less than three years of the left's management of the country's economic policies, sufficient counter-pressures had built up for Bhutto to move against his socialist Cabinet colleagues. In the new Cabinet sworn in by the Prime Minister in October 1974, the left lost several key positions. At this stage, an effort was made by the Prime Minister to depoliticise economic decision-making but this effort, for reasons that had to do a great deal with Bhutto's personality as well as with political dynamics generated by left-oriented policies, did not succeed. In the autumn of 1974, Pakistan entered into a phase of economic decision-making without constraints.

In describing the important economic changes that resulted from the policies adopted by the government during the Bhutto era, it is best to distinguish between the period during which the economy was dominated by the PPP left and the period during which no well-defined set of objectives was pursued by the policy-makers. Economic developments during the first period will be the subject of this chapter; those during the second period will be described in Chapter 7.

THE NEED TO ACT

When Zulfikar Ali Bhutto took office as President on 20 December 1971, Pakistan faced an uncertain economic future. There were a number of reasons for this but the two most important ones were the popular disenchantment with the model of development pursued during the 1960s and the situation created by the independence of Bangladesh. The mass movement launched against the regime of Ayub Khan in 1967 was in part aimed at his economic system, which was held responsible for an inequitable distribution of incomes amongst various classes of people. This aspect of Ayubian economics disturbed mostly the people of what was then West Pakistan, who in the elections of 1970 voted in favour of Bhutto's PPP. In its manifesto, the PPP had promised to create a more equitable social order. However, before the PPP got the opportunity to correct the imbalances in the economic structure, the Bengalis left the Pakistan fold. Their departure produced the situation that had been anticipated by a number of economists[1] but the consequences of which had never been very seriously analysed. There was a belief, popular among several serious scholars of the Pakistani economy, that the departure of

East Pakistan would create a serious problem for the western wing – a belief based on the assumption that West Pakistan would not be able to find an alternate market for its industrial goods and agricultural commodities.

Perceptions, even when not well founded, can be self-fulfilling. This was certainly the case with the difficulties that Pakistan was expected to face with the collapse of the Ayub regime and the partition of the country. In particular, the private sector – the sector that had exhibited a tremendous amount of dynamism during the 1960s – seemed to lose confidence in the country's economic future. The most important manifestation of this was a sharp decline in savings and investment. In 1969/70, the last relatively normal year, the nation had saved 13·3 per cent of its wealth, but this declined to only 8·4 per cent in 1971/72. Investment by private entrepreneurs declined to 5·4 per cent of the nation's output, from 8·5 per cent in 1969/70. At 5·4 per cent, private investment was just sufficient to offset the depreciation of the existing stock of machinery and capital. In other words, at the start of the Bhutto period, the people were putting enough resources into the economy to keep it going at about its present level of activity. Very little was being invested for the sake of the future.

This lack of confidence had its impact on the rate of economic growth. During the 1960s, Pakistan's gross domestic product had increased at an annual rate of nearly 7 per cent (Chapter 3, Table 3.1); from 1969/70 until 1971/72 period, it grew at the rate of only 0·5 per cent. Since the population was expanding by more than 3 per cent per year, this small increase in the nation's output meant a drop in *per capita* incomes. This was the first time in the country's economic history that it had suffered a decline in average incomes.

When the Bhutto government took office, therefore, Pakistan was passing through a period of great economic uncertainty. The regime could have removed some of this uncertainty by adopting measures designed to restore the confidence of the business community in the health of the economy. A number of such measures – drastic devaluation, compensation to the people who had lost property in East Pakistan, disciplining of the industrial labour force, etc. – were urged upon the new administration by the bureaucracy as well as by a number of important economic interests.[2] Of these the government accepted only devaluation.

The exchange reforms announced in May 1972 depreciated the value of the Pakistan rupee by 57 per cent, from US 21 cents to US 9 cents per rupee. The new rate of exchange, Rs 11 per US $, replaced the multiple exchange rates that had operated under the Bonus Voucher Scheme. At the new rate, the exporters had little difficulty in switching from the markets in East Pakistan to those in Europe, East Asia and the United States. In 1972/73, the first full year of 'New' Pakistan – Pakistan without its eastern wing – earnings from the export of merchandise were more than two and a half times that of the previous year. For the first time since the 'Korean War boom' of 1950/51, Pakistan had a trade account surplus.[3]

The export sector's performance in 1972/73 was significant for two reasons. It demonstrated that the health of the Pakistani economy was not dependent on the markets that had been lost in Bangladesh; in fact, it could now be argued that during the latter part of the 1960s the eastern wing had become an economic burden for the western wing.[4] The success of the export effort in the period following devaluation also showed that there was considerable scope for improvement in the economy if the government could adopt a set of sensible policies aimed at correcting prices and incentives that had been distorted under the bureaucratic management of the Ayub period. But such policies were dismissed as 'technocratic alternatives of little lasting value'[5] by the leftists in the regime. Instead, the regime embarked on a programme of major structural reform whose consequences were even less well understood and articulated than those resulting from the independence of Bangladesh. And, to make the picture a bit more cloudy, the administration chose to initiate changes at the time when it was also restructuring administrative institutions (Chapter 5 above). The results of this third shock to the economy were to be much more serious than those produced by the first two. Whereas, the economy recovered rapidly from the loss of the market in East Pakistan and whereas the popular perception about the inequities of the economic system did not prove to be long-lasting, some of the more important measures adopted by the Bhutto administration were to have a much more seriously damaging effect. However, the impact of the government's policies did not become visible immediately, partly because, even in 1972, some considerable strength remained in the economy. It

was only after the impact of the policies adopted by the left came
to be felt by some other important PPP constituencies that Bhutto
decided to change his economic managers.

THE ASCENT OF THE LEFT

It was more by default than design that the PPP left was able to
capture important decision-making positions in the new administration. Mubashir Hasan was one of the four socialists
included by Bhutto in his first Cabinet. While Mubashir was
made Finance Minister, J. A. Rahim was given the portfolio of
Industrial Production, Sheikh Rashid that of Health and Khurshid Hasan Meer that of Establishment. The Industrial Production division, in view of the nationalisation of a number of
important enterprises, and the Establishment Division, in view of
the politicisation of the civil bureaucracies, could have become
bases for establishing control over important areas of decision-
making. For two reasons, this did not happen. First, Bhutto felt
more comfortable with Mubashir than he did with the other
important members of his party. Elected to the National Assembly from Lahore, the capital of Punjab, Mubashir was not a real
Punjabi. He was a migrant to the province; he did not speak
Punjabi and did not have the type of following that would be
needed by a politician who wanted to challenge Bhutto, the
Sindhi chairman of the Peoples' Party. Bhutto felt safe with
Mubashir and Mubashir used his position within the administration and within the party to establish a new economic order in
Pakistan.

Second, the major beneficiary of the decision to nationalise
industries and the decision to establish a new system of administration was not Rahim and not Meer, but Mubashir Hasan. Not
only was Mubashir able to put a close associate in charge of the
'nationalisation office', the nationalised industries, because of the
cash-flow problems they were soon to face, became dependent on
the Finance Minister for their survival. And, the weakening of the
bureaucracy had the unexpected result of weakening the Planning
Commission. This, too, benefited Mubashir Hasan.

Ayub's system of economic management had devolved a considerable amount of power to the Planning Commission. The

President himself was the Commission's chairman and presided over the meetings of the National Economic Council, a committee of the central Cabinet that gave the final sanction to all economic decisions. The commission's functional head was the deputy chairman, a position that usually went to a bureaucrat in great favour with Ayub Khan. Bhutto's first appointment to head the commission was Qamar ul Islam, a senior member of the CSP. For a period, Qamar ul Islam wielded a considerable amount of influence in the area of decision-making. But his position was seriously affected by the regime's decision to restructure the Civil Service.

At the time the government decided to dissolve the CSP, Qamar ul Islam was president of its central association. As president of the CSP Association he advised the regime against any drastic reform of the administration, suggesting that the efficient working of the new economic order was contingent on the maintenance by the state of a politically independent bureaucratic system. This advice was not well received; Bhutto was determined not to tolerate any bureaucratic opposition to his administrative reforms. While his reasons for changing the administrative structure were different from those of the PPP left, both agreed that, as a part of the reform, the apolitical nature of the Planning Commission had to be abandoned. Without politicisation, the Planning Commission would remain the bastion of the bureaucracy, a place from which the recalcitrant bureaucrats could frustrate the regime's social and economic programmes. Accordingly, Qamar ul Islam was dismissed and the Planning Commission became a 'division' of the Ministry of Finance. Mubashir, the Minister of Finance, Planning and Economic Development, had now established himself as the person responsible for all economic policies. A number of young socialists from academia were brought in to help Mubashir with designing a new economic system for Pakistan. A beginning had already been made with the nationalisation of basic industries, and from that starting-point the left made steady progress, not without resistance but always with great determination. Bhutto, not well versed in economics, did not seem to have understood the full nature and scope of the changes that were being made. Some of these changes suited his political purpose, some appealed to his temperament. Accordingly, he went along with them.

THE NATIONALISATION OF INDUSTRIES AND FINANCIAL
INSTITUTIONS

In its manifesto, the PPP had promised the nationalisation of all
basic industries and financial institutions. Within one month of
assuming control of the administration, the PPP had fulfilled the
essentials of this promise. In January 1972, the government
announced a programme of nationalisation aimed at the public
'takeover' of thirty-one large firms in ten 'basic' industries. The
industries affected by this decision included iron and steel, basic
metals, heavy engineering, motor-vehicle assembly and manufacture, tractor assembly and manufacture, heavy and basic chemicals, petro-chemicals, cement and public utilities. Domestically
owned life insurance companies were also brought under the
control of the government. The programme was formulated by a
special unit set up for that purpose in the Ministry of Finance. For
producing the programme and drafting the Martial Law Orders
under which the government was to assume control over these
industries, the Finance Minister turned to Raza Kazim, a long-
time associate and a prominent leftist lawyer. There was, therefore, an unmistakable imprint of the ultra left on the nationalisation scheme. In the first instance, the government chose to assume
only the management and not the ownership of the taken-over
firms. This meant that the owners did not have to be compen-
sated. At the same time, trading in the shares of these firms in the
stock markets was banned. Workers' committees were organised
to help the managers appointed by the government to run the
firms with the aim of 'producing the maximum social benefit'.[6]

The swiftness with which the government chose to move
against industrial entrepreneurs was a manifestation of the power
of the ultra left in the PPP government as well as Bhutto's lack of
trust of large industrialists. It did not reflect the importance of
these enterprises or of the industrial sector in the country's
economy. In 1972, the large-scale industrial sector accounted for
12·8 per cent of the gross domestic product and employed only 3·4
per cent of the total labour force. Its contribution to exports was
only 8·3 per cent of the total. Nor could the sector be held
responsible for the perceived deterioration in income distribution.
The place of the sector in the country's economy therefore did not
justify the rhetoric that accompanied nationalisation. According
to Bhutto, the government's move was meant to 'eliminate, once

for all, poverty and discrimination in Pakistan',[7] and, according to his Finance Minister, it was 'intended to foster a healthy Pakistani economy'.[8] It should have been obvious that the nationalisation of industries would do neither. The persistent poverty of a large number of people in Pakistan could not be all blamed on the large-scale industrial sector; and the public sector assumption of large private enterprises was not a necessary condition for creating a healthy economy. As events were to prove, the reaction of the industrialists was more to the point. According to Ahmed Dawood, the patriarch of the second richest industrial family group in Pakistan:

> If you kill [a] cow, you have meat for one day only. But if you keep [the] cow, you have milk every day. Pakistan needs milk now.[9]

A period of great uncertainty followed nationalisation: the private enterpreneurs were confused about the real intentions of the government and the administration was not inclined to provide concrete assurances to them. The most the industrialists got out of Bhutto was the promise, given in May 1972, that they were 'at liberty to make reasonable profits as a reward for hard work' and that his regime was prepared to accept that 'private enterprises has a role to play in the economic progress of Pakistan'.[10]

Businessmen's pronouncements notwithstanding,[11] the reason for the government's reticence was not so much to keep the private industrialists guessing, as the ideological conflict between the ultra left on one side and the urban democrats on the other.[12] Although Kasuri's departure had weakened the opponents of Mubashir Hasan and his ultra leftist associates, some resistance was still left in them. Mubashir's programme was to follow on from the first spate of nationalisation with the public-sector takeover of entire industries. Banks, vegetable oil and textiles were the three 'industries' earmarked for nationalisation. But some other members of the Cabinet, in particular Abdul Hafiz Pirzada who took over the Law portfolio vacated by Kasuri, and some members of the bureaucracy who still retained influence with Bhutto, convinced the Prime Minister to go slow on socialisation. Amongst the bureaucrats, the most effective voice was that of the deputy chairman of the Planning Commission and the governor of the State Bank. Both were openly critical of the policies of the Finance Minister. In a long statement made to the press, the State Bank governor told the administration not to be too hasty with its policies aimed at restructuring the economy. Under this pressure, the regime seemed to give up its plans for the nationalisation of the banks and other sectors of industry. Accordingly, in May 1972, the State Bank of Pakistan established rules reorienting the credit policy of banks in favour of wider dispersal of bank credit. Small farmers and small industrial entrepreneurs were the immediate beneficiaries of this policy; the large industrialists also seemed to take heart from it. In the latter half of 1972, both the stock market and industrial confidence – when measured in terms of the number of loan applications made to financial institutions – recovered sharply. However, this period of peace between the administration and private industry was not to last for very long. It was disturbed for good by a set of events that could not have been anticipated by the industrialists and their supporters in the bureaucracy.

In the summer of 1973, there were floods in Pakistan for the first time in more than fifteen years. One by one all the major rivers cut through the protective embankments that had been built since the major floods of the early 1950s. While not many lives were lost – the official estimate of 200 was challenged by the opposition but no alternative figure was offered – the damage to property was extensive. Four million acres of cropland, or 10 per cent of the annually cultivated area, was inundated. Some 885,000 homes were seriously damaged; 54,000 head of livestock, including cattle, buffaloes, sheep and goats, were lost; and $38 million of damage was done to roads and other communication infrastructure. The government estimated the total loss at $800 million.[13]

The floods were severe, but the damage would have been less extensive had the various branches of the bureaucracy moved in time to help the affected areas and their inhabitants. But the bureaucracy was being reorganised that very summer (see Chapter 5); those who could have acted decisively had either been removed from office or were demoralised. Under the reforms the Chief Secretaries and the Flood Relief Commissioners of the provinces of the Punjab and Sind had lost their jobs. Without these officials to guide the administrative machinery, the bureaucratic response was slow. One manifestation of this was the inability to organise the delivery of basic items of consumption to the affected areas. In the northern areas, people had to go for days without petrol and cooking oil. The price of cooking oil trebled in the deficit areas. The situation clearly worried the government, but its response was not entirely anticipated, at least not by the business community. Under pressure from Mubashir Hasan, on 16 August Bhutto announced the nationalisation of the vegetable *ghee* (oil) industry, blaming the private businessman for 'exploiting a national crisis for personal advantage'.[14] Bhutto seemed genuinely disappointed with the business community, for he had been persuaded by Mubashir that the escalation in the price of cooking oil showed not just lack of altruism on the part of the private business sector, but it was, in fact, a deliberate attempt by the capitalist class to embarrass Pakistan's socialist regime. The Finance Minister promised that the Government would not tolerate any resistance to establish a new social order in the country.[15]

For a number of reasons the nationalisation of the vegetable oil industry was an important development. Whereas the January takeover mainly hurt the 'twenty-two families'; a good proportion of the cooking oil industry was owned by small and middle-sized entrepreneurs. Some of these people had been active PPP supporters and many others belonged to social groups that were favourably disposed towards the party. The government's encroachment into this industry, therefore, was resented by its own constituency. It generated not only resentment but also pressure for reducing the influence of the left in economic decision-making.

This nationalisation also brought the government into closer contact with cotton producers, another powerful PPP constituency. The farmers did not like the side of the government they saw as a result of this contact. The bureaucrats who took over the control of the fifty firms that had operated in this industry did not possess the expertise or the capital of the owners they had displaced. But the cotton farmers needed both. What was worse, it soon became clear that the new managers were also not very honest. A report that was to be commissioned by the government later cited a number of examples of the way in which the 'bureaucrats-managers' had sought bribes for 'lifting the farmers' produce'.[16]

The government's takeover of the vegetable oil industry also disturbed for good the uneasy truce that had been reached between Bhutto and the business community. Bhutto had broken his promise; his assurance of no further nationalisation until the elections of 1977 no longer seemed meaningful and the little confidence that the businessmen had developed in the regime was now completely gone.

In January 1974, as his 'present for the New Year to the people of Pakistan',[17] Bhutto announced the nationalisation of all private and domestically owned banks. This announcement was followed by a statement by the Finance Minister that all the pledges of the PPP in the election manifesto of the PPP had been fulfilled and the type of 'mixed economy' that the government wished to establish in Pakistan had been created.[18]

The expansion in the role of the public sector, erosion in the confidence of the business community and a sharp increase in the share of wages in industrial earnings (see below) all had a profound impact on the development of the industrial sector. By far the most important consequence of these policies was the flight of businessmen and their capital from Pakistan to countries in Africa and the Middle East. A number of industrial houses branched out into other countries – for instance, the Saigol family started operations in Tanzania, Kenya and the United Arab Emirates; the 'Service' house picked up enterprises in Saudi Arabia and Tanzania; the Haroon family began activities in New York and London – and a number of staff from the nationalised banks moved to banking institutions in the Middle East. Those businessmen who remained behind diversified into other areas: the Dawood family went into rice trading, the Fancies into deep-sea fishing; the Saigols took up construction and consultancy activities, as did the Habibullahs; and a number of small industrial houses began to invest in residential and commercial estates in Karachi and Lahore.

These movements of capital and managerial skills resulted in a sharp decline in private sector investment in manufacturing (see Table 6.1). The total amount invested by the business community in 1972/73 was only Rs 572 million ($58 million) compared to Rs 1198 million ($121 million) in 1964/65. In 1972/73, only 5·4 per cent of gross domestic product was invested in industry as against 1·5 per cent in 1964/65. In part to compensate for this decline and in part as a result of the regime's economic and political objectives (see Chapter 7 below), the public sector investment increased dramatically. During the last year of the Bhutto regime, it was six times the level that had prevailed during the Ayub period.

TABLE 6.1   Public and private manufacturing investment
(Rs million in 1959/60 constant prices)

Year	Investment		
	Private	*Public*	*Total*
The Ayub period			
1960/61 to 1964/65			
(annual average)	992	57	1069
1965/66 to 1969/70			
(annual average)	930	106	1036
1970/71	908	43	951
The Bhutto period			
1971/72	767	61	828
1972/73	572	68	640
1973/74	648	175	823
1974/75	740	154	894
1971/72 to 1975/76	682	115	797
(annual average)			

Source: Computed from Government of Pakistan *Economic Surveys* for the period 1964/65 to 1976/77.

The PPP left had used nationalisation to reduce the political and economic power that had been accumulated by a small number of industrial and financial houses. In this, it succeeded. But it did not succeed in maintaining the momentum that the manufacturing sector had picked up during the Ayub period. During the five years between 1971/72 and 1976/77, the industrial sector output grew by only 2 per cent per annum as compared to 8 per cent during the 1960s. This stagnation in the rate of growth was not so much due to nationalisation as to the priorities that were assigned to the public sector that now came to play a dominant role.[19] The public sector was made to concentrate on investments with long periods of gestation. While the private entrepreneurs waited for a change in the country's political environment, the managers of the public enterprises busied themselves with programmes that were not going to yield high returns in the near future. Both the economy and its political managers were to suffer as a consequence.

LABOUR REFORMS

A reduction in the power of the industrialists was an important reason for the nationalisation of industrial firms and financial institutions. In that sense, they were essentially 'negative measures' adopted to hurt a group whose economic and political interests were viewed as being inimical to that of the regime. Viewed from the perspective of 'helping the supporters, hurting the opponents', the comprehensive labour reforms, announced in June 1972, were amongst several 'positive' actions taken by the government during this period. But, as was to happen in a number of other cases, the impact of the measure was quite different from the one actually intended.

Organised industrial labour had played an important role in putting Ayub Khan out of office. In a number of cities, particularly in the industrial areas of Lahore and Lyallpur, the industrial workers had been also significant in getting the PPP candidates to win National and Provincial Assembly seats. Labour was an important element in the constituency of Mubashir Hasan. The PPP had won the support of some of the workers' unions on the basis of promises that included a substantial improvement in working conditions as well as a substantial increase in minimum wages. These promises also won endorsement from those elements in the party that considered labour reforms an essential step towards improving the distribution of incomes in the urban areas. Although this perception was not supported by facts – organised workers in large-scale enterprises and public employment usually obtain real wage increases while the wages of the majority of the workers do not rise because of competitive conditions in the labour market – it nevertheless strengthened the hands of those who wanted to help industrial labour. Accordingly, the labour reforms mandated large increases in both monetary and non-monetary rewards for the workers. Non-monetary benefits included contributions by the employers to pension, medical and welfare funds as well as workers' participation in some management decisions. A government report estimated the total cost to the employers for implementing these reforms at Rs 250 million or 12·5 per cent of the share of wages in the value of industrial output. The report assumed that 'this amount would be transferred from industrial profits and would not be passed on to the consumer. As such, we do not expect these reforms to result in an increase in the level of prices of industrial goods'.[20]

At the time labour reforms were announced, only a quarter of the industrial labour force worked in 'registered enterprises', so-called because they were registered by the Ministry of Labour as being responsible for following the labour legislation on the statute book. The definition used was that of the Labour Laws Ordinance of 1964, according to which labour laws were applicable to those enterprises 'that employed ten or more persons and/or used power'. Of the 2·2 million persons employed in the manufacturing sector, some 570,000 worked in these 'registered' enterprises. The reforms of 1972 changed the definition of 'registered' firms by reducing the threshold from ten to five workers, 'bringing the benefit of the reforms to another 1·2 million workers'.[21] This change in definition caught the owners of 155,000 small enterprises by surprise; it had not been included in the 1970 manifesto as one of the PPP's promises to the electorate and it had not been mentioned by any of the PPP leaders after the party came to power. As a result of the reforms, the small entrepreneurs found that they were now subject not only to the new legislation that was being introduced, but also to a number of other regulations concerning labour welfare. They also disputed the government's estimate of the cost to the industrial owners of implementing the reforms. It was argued that the costs of conforming to the new labour regulations would be much greater for small owners than for large enterprises. The smaller units were being included in the category of 'registered' enterprises for the first time and as such they would have to rebuild their factories in order to conform to the health and environmental standards prescribed in the legislations that had hitherto not applied to them. The protests that the announcement of the labour reforms drew from the small industrial owners were sufficient to take Mubashir Hasan on a tour of the affected districts in the Punjab to explain the 'real meaning of the reforms'. Mubashir visited Lalamusa, Gujarat, Wazirabad, Kamoke and Muridke – small towns along the Grant Trunk Road in which the affected industries were concentrated – and found that the PPP had been seriously hurt in the heart of its Punjab constituency. He got the message but found himself caught between two PPP constituencies. A redefinition of a registered enterprise to exclude small firms would offend industrial labour, a group whose support the left had tried hard to cultivate. However, if the full force of the new laws was applied to small enterprises, the regime would certainly lose the support of the small industrial owners. A number of PPP leaders from the Punjab had been equally assiduous in winning over this group to the PPP. The debate that ensued between the PPP leadership suggests that the economic and political repercussions of introducing the labour legislation had not been carefully considered. Mubashir Hasan remained sufficiently powerful to prevent the government's retreat, but the pressure applied by the other side was strong enough for the Labour Ministry to order its field officers to go slow in implementing the new order. One immediate consequence of the labour legislation was, therefore, to increase the control of the bureaucracy over small-scale industrial enterprises, whose owners were now at the mercy of the local labour officers.

Opposition to the labour legislation also came from an unexpected quarter. The Bhutto administration had placed the nationalised firms under the charge of a cadre of managers recruited specifically for this purpose. The first test of their performance was to show an increase in profits. If profits under nationalised industries could improve it would demonstrate that the public sector could efficiently run industrial enterprises. It would also show that the old owners had under-reported their earnings to reduce the tax that the government could collect for them. However, labour reforms were promulgated before the new managers had the time to reorganise the firms placed under their control. Also, the increase in the minimum wage and other benefits that had now to be paid to the workers affected profits. The new system of profit-sharing and worker participation in management also made it difficult to compare the performance of the managers with the original owners of the enterprise: if the government estimate cited above was correct, the nationalised firms would have to increase payments to their workers by at least 12 per cent.

Mubashir Hasan and his Ministry of Finance had been generous to the managers of government-owned enterprises during the period immediately following nationalisation. Most managers faced serious cash-flow problems; the disruption in industrial activity that had marked the 1969–71 period had drained a number of these firms of their liquid resources. The resources needed to pay back-wages to the workers and to get the industries working at normal capacity were provided from the government's revenues. This was done in part to make a success of nationalisation and in part to establish the control of the Ministry of Finance on this important part of the economy. However, the impact of labour reform on the nationalised industries had not been fully comprehended by the Finance Minister. The impact was serious enough for the managers to switch their support from Mubashir to J. A. Rahim, the Industrial Production Minister. In a memorandum prepared by his Ministry and leaked to the press, it was suggested that the PPP administration was 'not serving its main constituencies by allowing a greater share of the earnings of industrial enterprises to go to the workers they employed'.[22] The position taken by Rahim brought to the surface the differences between the two factions of the left that were represented in the Bhutto Cabinet. The surfacing of these differences made it possible for other PPP factions to move against the left.

THE NATIONALISATION OF EDUCATION

According to Article 37 of the new Constitution,

The state shall:
  (a) promote, with special care, the educational and economic interests of backward classes or areas;
  (b) remove illiteracy and provide free and compulsory secondary education within the minimum possible period;
  (c) make technical and professional education generally available and higher education equally accessible to all on the basis of merit. . . .
  (f) enable people of different areas, through education, training, agricultural and industrial development and other methods to participate fully in all forms of national activities, including employment in the service of Pakistan. . . .

Considering the state of education in the country, these were essentially long-term goals to be achieved not within a specified period of time, but 'within the minimum possible period'. The careful wording of this clause within the Constitution indicated that the government was well aware of the difficulties it would encounter in achieving free and compulsory secondary education; in using education for promoting the interests of backward areas and backward classes; and in using non-conventional education to make full and productive use of the country's large human resource. However, the fact that these promises were included in the Constitution indicates the importance the administration attached to them. It also indicates the administration's recognition of the interest of a number of its supporters in bringing about these changes in the priorities of the educational sector and its institutional structure.

In fact, the area of educational reform was considered sufficiently important for political reasons for the government to announce a policy aimed at achieving a somewhat more limited set of goals: 'Perhaps one of the most impressive aspects of the whole enterprise is the fact that the new policy was formulated and announced in a period of less than three months after Mr. Bhutto took office on December 20, 1971.'[23] The policy was announced fifteen months before the regime's long-term objectives were incorporated in the Constitution. Its principal architect was neither Bhutto nor Abdul Hafiz Pirzada, his Minister of Education, but the members of the PPP left. And, although the policy was far-reaching and all-inclusive, and although it placed special emphasis on the expansion and strengthening of technical training in a wide variety of fields, its main thrust was aimed at private schools and colleges and its principal purpose was to bring these institutions under the control of the state. This aspect of the policy was carried out expeditiously and on schedule. By 1 September 1972, some 175 private colleges were placed under the management of the provincial departments of education. Private schools, more numerous and diverse, were nationalised in a 'phased manner', with the phases lasting over a two-year period between October 1972 and September 1974. By the time the left was relieved of its more important positions in the central Cabinet, most of the educational sector had come under the direct control of the government. Only two dozen institutions – including St Mary's Academy at Rawalpindi, Burn Hall at Abbotabad, St Joseph's School and Grammar School at Karachi – remained under private control. The exempted institutions were managed by foreign missionaries: the decision not to nationalise them was consistent with the decision to restrict the nationalisation of economic and social institutions to those owned and administered by Pakistani nationals.

'Although it was rationalized on reformist and developmental grounds, the nationalization of education in Pakistan was essentially a political matter, from start to finish.'[24] The rationalisation presented in the Education Policy statement and in Bhutto's address to the nation announcing the policy included the inability of the education sector to provide the right kind of education to a rapidly growing population, the propensity of the existing institutions to emphasise university education at the expense of primary education and functional literacy, and the sector's failure to attract people of the quality and in the numbers required by a 'dynamic society'.[25] All these were valid reasons for introducing educational reforms, but the reforms that were actually implemented[26] could not have met all of these objectives. As in the case of new labour laws – and, to some extent, as also in the case of the nationalisation of firms in the industrial sector – the administration's approach towards education was motivated more by political considerations that appealed to a faction of the ruling party than by the demands of the prevailing situation.

The situation that prevailed in the education sector clearly demanded government action and intervention. At the time that the Bhutto administration took office, only 43 per cent of children of school age were enrolled in schools. This meant that some 7 million children were not attending school; of these nearly 5 million were girls. Although the 1972 census reported one-quarter of the adult population as being literate, in fact, according to some non-official surveys, only one-sixth could read and understand newspapers. A number of other indices[27] would also suggest that even for a country at its low level of development Pakistan was not paying sufficient attention to education. What was worse, even within this low level of commitment, there was a serious misallocation of resources. A third of the total expenditure in education was going into building, staffing and equipping institutes of higher learning as compared to only one-sixth in all developing nations (see Table 6.2). But these centres of advanced education were not making the best use of the resources being made available to them. For instance, a study sponsored by the University of Karachi found that only one-third of the physical and human capacity of the institution was being put to use, that 30 per cent of the classes were being cancelled 'on account of both student and teacher disinterest'; that one-quarter of the faculty was on leave while still drawing salary; and that the existing library facility – not by any means a very pretentious one – was under-utilised.[28] The cost of university education was Rs 15,000 per student per year as compared with the Rs 250 being spent on educating a child in primary school.

TABLE 6.2   Education expenditure as a percentage of
Gross Domestic Product, 1972

	Pakistan	*All developing countries*
Primary	0·6	1·7
Secondary	0·4	1·4
Higher	0·6	1·8
Functional	0·1	0·4
Total education	1·7	4·6

Source: Percentage expenditure figures for all countries except Pakistan taken
from M. Zymelman, 'Patterns of Educational Expenditures', World
Bank Staff Working Paper no. 246 (November 1976).
       Percentage expenditure figures for Pakistan calculated from figures
used by the Planning Commission for 1975.

There was, therefore, a clear case for reform of the educational sector and the regime was being pressured into action by several interested groups. There were demands for reform from teachers' associations, university students, the middle classes and the urban poor. The teachers urged the government to nationalise all educational institutions; university student associations desired greater participation in management; the middle classes, not satisfied with the quality of education being offered in both government and private schools, sought improvements in the curriculum as well as student discipline; and the poor wanted the government to make more resources available for primary and functional education. For a number of reasons, the PPP left was sympathetic to the demands of the teachers. Accordingly, it chose nationalisation of schools and colleges as the instrument for 'preparing Pakistan's educational sector for meeting the demands of a modern and dynamic society'.[29]

The clash between the left and the right in the urban areas of the Punjab – particularly the debate between *Shahab*, the Urdu journal that supported the socialist cause in the elections of 1970, and *Zindigi* and *Urdu Digest*, which favoured the religious groups – seemed to galvanise and radicalise college teachers. For the teachers, the debate was no longer abstract; the *Anjuman-i-*

Himayat-i-Islam (Trust for the Sustenance of Islam), had clashed with the West Pakistan College Teachers Association (WPCTA). The *Anjuman* was a 'venerable and mildly aristocratic institution' which ran Islamiya College, Lahore, a medical school, eleven high schools, several orphanages and a home for destitute women.[30] The WPCTA was an association of college teachers with considerable backing in the cities of Karachi, Lahore, Hyderabad and Rawalpindi. The *Anjuman* had always taken a lively interest in Punjab politics; its links with several aristocratic families in Lahore and its constitutional obligation to promote Islam had brought it to the centre of rightist politics in the capital city of Lahore. The refusal of the Ayub administration to take steps to improve the status of the teachers employed by private colleges, including those owned and operated by the *Anjuman*, brought WPCTA teachers out into the streets. In the autumn and winter of 1968, the teachers joined the political agitation against the regime of Ayub Khan and, once Ayub was out of power, they began to lend support to Bhutto's PPP. In the summer of 1970, when the PPP began to fight the parties of the right for seats in the national and provincial legislature, the *Anjuman* let it be known that it favoured the candidates of the Muslim League and other 'Islam *passand* [those who appreciate Islam] parties'. The WPCTA, being under the influence of teachers that included Eric Cyprian, a former Communist, and Manzur Ahmad, Zahur Ahmad and Muhammad Amin Mughal, all with very strong links with Lahore's 'ultra lefts', began to work for the candidates of the PPP.

The dispute between the *Anjuman* and WPCTA centred on the association's claim, voiced during the anti-Ayub agitation, that, being a national educational trust, the *Anjuman* had no right to lock out striking teachers. This lock-out action had been taken against those teachers who had actively participated in the agitation against the Ayub administration. Rather than accept the WPCTA contention, the *Anjuman* dismissed Cyprian, the Ahmad brothers and Amin Mughal. The dismissed teachers founded 'two innovative institutions, Shah Hussain College and Shah Hussain Institute, in memory of the non-conformist sixteenth century Punjabi mystic poet',[31] and joined the PPP in its fight against 'the established order, especially in the urban areas of the Punjab'.[32] The teachers of Shah Hussain College and Institute provided a considerable amount of organisational support to Mubashir

Hasan in his campaign in 1970 and helped the PPP draft its educational policy.

The *Anjuman* episode had convinced Cyprian and his associates that the rights and interests of the teachers could not be protected in a system in which 'commercial education' played an important role. The private sector was most active in higher education, for, it was at that level that 'minds were formed'[33] and profits made. Organisations such as the *Anjuman,* the Fathers of Mill Hill, London, and various American Christian missions operated mostly at the higher level, as did a number of private entrepreneurs motivated mostly by profit considerations. The share of the private sector diminished as one moved down from colleges to schools: in the late 1960s, the private share of colleges was 52 per cent, of high schools 40 and of primary schools 4 per cent.[34] But these aggregate statistics do not reflect the service the private sector was performing in the major cities of Karachi, Lahore and Rawalpindi at all levels of education. In Karachi, 57 per cent of the students attending primary schools were in private institutions; at 75 per cent, the proportion was considerably higher in Lahore. Even more important, the share of the private sector was increasing – increasing, not because of 'mind-forming' and profit motives, but because of the government's inability to provide the type of education demanded by the urban middle classes. The largest concentration of the private primary and higher schools was in such predominantly middle-class areas as the Pakistan Employees Cooperative Housing Society (PECHS) in Karachi, Gulberg and Samnabad in Lahore and the Cantonement in Rawalpindi. These schools resembled community institutions in which there was a strong involvement of the parents with teachers and managers. In terms of quality, they fell somewhere between the foreign missionary schools and the schools run by the Department of Education. A vast majority of the teachers in these schools were women from middle-class homes who found the work environment appealing to themselves and acceptable to their families. The private schools in middle-class urban neighbourhoods had provided these women with the type of opportunity to work that was not available to them in any other part of the economy. The teachers in these schools did not belong to any association and had not demanded the nationalisation of the institutions in which they worked.

By extending nationalisation to urban schools, in particular those in the major cities, the regime took a step for which there was no well-articulated demand. Nationalisation of the private urban schools was urged neither by the WPCTA nor by the Pakistan Teachers Union (PTU) which represented the school-teachers. The decision to nationalise was taken in the name of comprehensiveness and, in that respect, resembled the extension of labour laws to small manufacturing enterprises. The 'People's Government was committed to restore the dignity of teachers so that they could act as guides, preachers and mentors for the moral training of the younger generation.'[35] But the teachers in private urban schools did not feel comfortable with the new bureaucracy under which they were placed; beginning with October 1974, when this phase of nationalisation was completed, a large number of them gave up their positions.

Not only did the quality of education deteriorate in the schools that were now being controlled by the government bureaucracy, but the urban neighbourhoods could also no longer use their own resources to establish new institutions. This situation caused a great deal of frustration but the people who were affected could do little about it. The urban middle classes were not as well organ-ised as the small entrepreneurs of central Punjab and the PPP as a political institution was not sufficiently developed for the dis-pleasure of this group to be conveyed to Bhutto and his associates. Therefore, while Bhutto regarded the educational reforms as one of the finest accomplishments of his regime, dissatisfaction with them was one of the several reasons that brought the urban middle classes out in the streets in such large numbers in the 1977 agitation against his regime.

Bhutto's education policy had some success in catering for the aspirations of the urban poor. The policy called for a two-phase programme to make education free and universal for all children up to the age of fifteen. During the first phase, which began on 1 October 1972, education for all children up to the age of thirteen was made free but not compulsory. The second phase was to start two years later, when the goal of compulsory education was to be finally achieved. Free education provided some relief to those parents who were prepared to send their children to school but could not afford even the small fees that were charged by schools in the state system. But the bulk of the poor children remained out of school because their parents could not afford to pull them out of the labour force. For these families, the rate of return from education was small – according to one study it was as low as 6 per cent, reflecting the high opportunity cost of keeping children in school and the small impact schooling had on increasing productivity.[36] Accordingly, the rate of enrolment during the 1972–4 period increased by only 8 per cent per annum. At this rate and in view of a more than 3 per cent increase in population every year, the government could not have achieved the goal of universal education for children before the end of the century. These difficulties notwithstanding – as suggested above, their recognition had prompted the government to be cautious in the wording of the educational clause in the Constitution – in principle, the education reforms appealed to the poor. Even if they could not immediately make use of the offered facility, the poor were satisfied that it would be there when the need for it finally arose.

REFORMS IN THE HEALTH SECTOR

Health was another area of government neglect in which several PPP constituencies demanded action. As in the case of education, Pakistan had not done as well as other countries that were at the same stage of development. For instance, in 1972, when the PPP government was established, the rate of infant mortality was estimated at 120 per 1000 live births; the rate of mortality for children between the ages of one and five at 25 per 1000; the rate of general mortality at 14 per 1000 of the population; and life expectancy at birth of 54 years.

These indices suggest that the health standards achieved for Pakistan were not as high as those attained by countries such as India and Sri Lanka. What is more, for some groups the gap was considerably larger. Female mortality was much higher in Pakistan than in other countries of South Asia; the difference in the rate of mortality for female infants and children was large enough to suggest that in some areas female infanticide was still being practised.[37]

While these statistics indicate poor health standards, some considerable improvements had been made. For instance, such mass killers as plague and smallpox were eliminated, while a substantial reduction was made in the incidence of tuberculosis and cholera. The success of these 'single disease' control programmes had resulted in a decline in the general rate of mortality from

18 in 1951 to 14 in 1972 and increased the life expectancy at birth from 45 to 54. Since people lived a little longer, this success increased the pressure on the health system in the areas of the prevention and cure of non-lethal diseases. It was the failure to ease this and to provide an adequate coverage to the population that resulted in the pressure on the PPP administration to improve the country's health system.[38]

The constituencies for the reform of the health system were as diverse, and their motives as different, as those for changes in the system of education. Private physicians were important amongst the urban professional classes that had supported the PPP – one of them, Dr Ghulam Hussain from Rawalpindi was to occupy several important positions in the PPP Cabinets in the Punjab – and they supported a quick increase in the commitment of government resources to health. At 2·4 per cent of the gross domestic product, health expenditure in Pakistan was amongst the lowest in the developing countries. The urban middle classes were anxious to see an expansion in modern health facilities, while the urban poor wanted better access to the existing facilities. In addition to these, there were a number of other groups whose demands were somewhat more specific. For instance, industrial labour wanted the PPP administration to make employers responsible for providing medical coverage; lower-level government employers desired free medical care; and the practitioners of traditional medicine – a group that wielded considerable power in the semi-urban areas of the Punjab – urged the government to provide some form of recognition of their profession. It is important to note that the area that needed the most attention – the provision of preventive medicine for the rural population – did not have a strong constituency.

As in the case of education, the Bhutto regime announced a comprehensive public health care programme. Made public in August 1972, the programme was prepared by the Ministry of Health. Sheikh Rashid, the Health Minister, was the only 'rural socialist' in the Bhutto Cabinet; accordingly, the scheme had a strong rural bias. The scheme was developed around the Basic Health Unit (BHU) which was to serve between 8000 and 15,000 people as a sub-unit of a larger Rural Health Centre (RHC). These BHUs and RHCs were then to refer the more seriously ill to country hospitals of no more than 60 beds or to district hospitals of no more than 250 beds. In terms of vertical linkages, the scheme was not too different from the one that the government of Ayub Khan had attempted to bring into operation in the early 1960s. Its one major innovation was to make use of auxiliary health workers in place of fully trained doctors to provide basic coverage. The Ayub scheme had faltered because of the reluctance of doctors to serve in the rural areas; Sheikh Rashid, borrowing from the Chinese system of 'barefoot doctors', sought to overcome this problem by staffing BHUs and RHCs with 'auxiliary workers'.

Despite this innovation, the Health Minister found it difficult to implement the rural health component of the scheme. The political pressure behind its implementation proved to be inadequate to overcome the traditional obstacle: the reluctance of the established health bureaucracy to shift resources from urban to rural areas. Even though the scheme did not envisage the movement of a significant number of doctors to the countryside, it did assign a higher priority to rural health care. Since the overall resource allocation to the health sector was not being increased significantly, the demands of the rural sector could have been met only by sacrificing those of the towns and cities. This the regime and the urban-based ultra left were not prepared to do. Accordingly, the rural component of the People's Health Scheme survived only in the form of a pilot project that was launched in the province of the Northwest Frontier under the auspices of the central government.[39]

One part of the health programme that had a strong political backing pertained to the provision of medical care to the industrial workers. Once again, the PPP administration built on the experiment that had been initiated but then all but abandoned by the Ayub government. In 1967, the government of Pakistan had set up Employees' Social Security Institutions (ESSIs) in the provinces of the Punjab, Sind and the Northwest Frontier. The ESSIs were managed by the government but paid for by the employers as well as the workers. The benefits included coverage for sickness and injury, as well as minimal life insurance and survivors' pensions. Under the People's Health Scheme, the employees contribution to ESSIs was abolished and the entire burden was shifted on to the employers. The employers' contribution was set at 7 per cent of the total wages paid out by them as against 3·5 per cent under the scheme that had been initiated by the Ayub government. The other major change was to make more industrial workers eligible for coverage by ESSIs, an outcome that followed automatically the extension of labour legislation to small enterprises. The result was that the coverage extended by ESSIs increased from 300,000 in 1970/71 to 450,000 in 1973/74.

Another area of success of the People's Health Scheme was an increase in the number of trained physicians to come out of medical colleges in Pakistan. The government set up new medical graduate training institutions in the cities of Lyallpur (now renamed Faizalabad), Rawalpindi, Larkana and Quetta. The new colleges, along with the existing ones, trained an additional 6000 doctors during the 1972–77 period. This should have increased the stock of physicians in Pakistan to about 20,000 from 13,000 at the time that the Bhutto regime took office. But this did not happen. In 1977, Pakistan had only 11,000 medical graduates, 2000 less than in 1970. This net decline was due to the large-scale migration of doctors from Pakistan to North America and to the countries in the Middle East. This pull from the outside could have been countered somewhat by the greater domestic demand for doctors that would have resulted from an expansion of medical facilities. Instead, the government chose to adopt a bureaucratic solution to the problem: a martial law regulation was issued in early 1973 that empowered the Ministry of Health to block the exit of the trained physicians. As indicated above, this regulation did not slow down the exodus; it only succeeded in providing the urban middle classes with another reason for being unhappy with the regime.

As the data of Table 6.3 suggest, the People's Health Scheme did not result in increasing the health coverage available to the general population. The only improvement that occurred was in the number of beds available; the increase in hospital beds, largely because of the new teaching hospitals established by the government, was more than the increase in population. However, the doctor patient as well as the nurse patient ratios declined substantially during the seven-year period between 1969/70 and 1976/77.

The urban middle classes were clearly dissatisfied with the government's inability to meet their demand for an improvement in health facilities. In the case of education, the government had nationalised schools that were meeting the middle classes' requirements for quality education; in the case of health, the private institutions, catering mostly to the high-income groups and out of reach of the middle classes, were left untouched. The lack of

TABLE 6.3   Health facilities in Pakistan

		1969/70	1976/77
Doctors:	Number	13100	11000
	People per doctor	4769	6818
Nurses:	Number	4400	3200
	People per nurse	14091	23468
Hospital	Number	33000	44800
Beds:	People per bed	1879	1674

Source: For 1969/70, Government of Pakistan, *Fourth Five Year Plan, 1970–1975*
(Islamabad: Planning Commission, 1970), p. 231; and for 1976/77, Gov-
ernment of Pakistan, *The Fifth Plan, 1977–83* (Islamabad: Planning
Commission, 1977), p. 590.

symmetry in these approaches was clearly perceived by the
groups that were adversely affected and contributed towards their
disenchantment with the regime.

One other government policy was to seriously hurt the middle
classes. In May 1973, Sheikh Rashid announced a scheme of
'generic medicines' according to which the sale of most brand
name drugs was banned. Instead, the domestic drug manufacturers were told to provide retail chemists with drugs and medicines
under their generic names. The scheme's main objective was to
reduce the price of those drugs that could be produced without
patent rights. For a number of common medicines such a price
reduction was indeed achieved; a government report claimed that
the average cost to the consumers had declined by more than 60
per cent during the first six months of the scheme's operations.
Over the long-run, however, the adverse consequences of this
scheme's implementation were to outweigh the more positive
ones.[40]

Retail chemists, allowed to dispense drugs without prescription, had played a role in Pakistan's health system that was not
fully comprehended by the government. In a country with a
serious shortage of doctors, the chemists, especially in small
towns, functioned as quasi-physicians, providing diagnoses for
simple ailments as well as medicines for curing them. Diagnosis
was provided free but the patients were charged for the drugs. The
sale of drugs that were marketed under brand names yielded a
larger profit to the dispensing chemist, a profit that was reduced
considerably by the introduction of the generic medicine scheme.
Resentful of this outcome, the chemists first protested to the

government.[41] But when the government refused to accommodate them, they started a campaign to discredit the reform. Within a year of the government's announcement of the scheme, sufficient distrust had been created about the quality of generic medicine for the government to begin to remove the ban on the sale of what were termed 'brand name, life-saving medicines'. The fact that a number of well-known foreign drug manufactures closed their plants in Pakistan while a number of inexperienced local manufacturers entered the drug-making business further eroded the confidence of the people.

Nationalisation of companies in the more important 'basic industries', government takeover of the insurance and banking industries, labour reforms, establishment of public sector control over private schools and colleges and the introduction of a scheme of generic medicines are examples of measures adopted by an administration with a distinct urban bias. These measures were mostly designed by the PPP left, a faction within Bhutto's party that had a fairly well defined group of supporters. The benefits that accrued to these groups were substantial, an outcome that contributed to the political strengthening of the left. However, the political weight of the groups that benefited was not as great as that of the groups who did not benefit or, as in some cases, even suffered. Thus the combined strength of industrial labour in the large manufacturing sector, the recipients of credit from the financial institutions now under government control and college teachers was considerably less than that of the small-sized industrial entrepreneurs who had to bear the cost of labour reforms, the urban middle classes who were now denied opportunities for obtaining quality education, and the urban classes whose demand for improvement of the health system was not satisfied. The groups that had not been satisfied had also been supporters of the PPP. The left had consolidated its own position at the expense of that of other factions of the party and also at the expense of Bhutto, the party's chairman. The full political impact of the economic and social measures was not felt immediately; it became visible in the spring of 1977, when Bhutto went to the polls to seek a new mandate from the people.

THE URBAN BIAS IN ECONOMIC POLICIES

The urban bias that was reflected in the adoption of the policies discussed above was also responsible for the government's attitude towards the rural sector. The PPP left's principal interest was to ensure the supply of agricultural commodities and processed goods to its constituencies in the urban areas at 'equitable prices'. The government was prepared to intervene massively in the marketing system whenever prices rose by amounts that were considered to be 'unreasonable'.

The first such crisis occurred in the autumn of 1972 when, because of a sharp decline in the output of sugar cane, the price of refined sugar in the urban markets more than doubled in a period of less than three months. The government's embarrassment was compounded by the fact that during the spring of the same year it had permitted the sugar mills to export their surplus output. A two-market system was quickly established under which the urban consumers were permitted to purchase a part of their requirements from ration shops at heavily subsidised prices. For those whose demands were more than what the government regarded as the 'minimum daily requirement', a parallel private market was allowed to operate.

For the government the scheme could have become very costly; it could not pass a part of the burden to the sugar-cane growers or to the sugar-mill owners, for these two groups possessed a considerable amount of political power. Sugar was an important crop in the province of Sind; the Sindhi landlords, with ready access to Bhutto, would not let the government reduce the price at which the mills had to procure from the producers. The refiners could not be squeezed because a good share of the output came from the mills that were operated by the Fauji Foundation – an organisation managed by the armed forces for the welfare of the veterans. Eventually, the bulk of the burden was passed on to the not-so-poor urban consumers as a more conservative definition of the minimum daily requirement was adopted. During the height of the crisis, the private food retailers charged three times the price at which the ration shops were selling sugar to their customers. This arrangement suited the poor, who were able to meet the bulk of their requirement from the ration shops; it was not so popular with the more affluent consumers who had to rely heavily on the private market.

A less successful but somewhat more innovative approach was adopted for meeting the demands of the poor for coarse cloth at 'prices they could afford'. One consequence of the world commodity boom of 1972–4 was to increase sharply the price of raw cotton, cotton yarn and grey cloth exported by Pakistan. Because of these increases, the price of coarse cloth sold domestically more than doubled in the period between June 1973 and December 1974. To meet the situation thus created, the government stepped into the market to implement a comprehensive scheme of 'increasing the production of raw cotton and diverting a good part of it for producing the type of cloth demanded by the poor people'.[42] The scheme was designed to 'protect the consumer without harming the grower'.[43]

The government's intervention included an increase in the minimum price payable by the ginners to the growers, 'to encourage the growers to bring in more land under cotton and to use a greater amount of chemicals against pests'; the establishment of a Cotton Export Corporation under the Ministry of Commerce, so that only 'that part of our output would be exported that is not needed for meeting the domestic demand for fabrics'; an increase in export duties so that the 'profits from the trade of these vital commodities are used for increasing the welfare of the people rather than the profit of a few'; and prescription of 'grey cloth production quotas' for all textile mills so that the 'supplies needed by the poor received the highest possible priority in the production programmes of the industry'.[44] This scheme is an interesting example of a set of measures designed by the PPP left to meet its ideological and political objectives without seriously harming the political groups who were also powerful within the party. Low-income urban consumers were the intended beneficiaries – a group that the left attempted to cultivate with some success during the period it was in power. The interests of the cotton growers – large farmers in south and central Punjab and in the province of Sind – was protected by allowing them a higher level of price support. The groups that were to be squeezed included textile owners and cotton traders, both without any support within the PPP.

The 'grey cloth scheme' did not succeed in its objective, for the textile sector reacted to this type of government intervention by reducing new investments and closing down marginal units. In 1973/74, the output of cloth was only 708 million yards, which was 10 per cent less than the record level of 787 million yards achieved in 1970/71.[45] In response to this situation, Mubashir Hasan, the Finance Minister, proposed a scheme of partial nationalisation according to which all mills that were being worked by the industry at less than their full capacity were to be taken over by the government without any compensation to the owners. The contents of the proposal became known to the industrialists and the Habib Bank index of Karachi stock exchange prices suffered a decline that was unprecedented even for that turbulent market. The opposition to the regime's economic policies was now mounting. Accordingly, in October 1974, the Prime Minister brought a new Cabinet into office that excluded Mubashir Hasan; J. A. Rahim and Khurshid Hasan Meer. Mubashir's departure was 'received on the private sector with undisguised satisfaction . . . his management of the nation's financial and economic affairs has been heavily criticised.[46]

The policies described above were not, of course, designed to bring about 'fundamental changes in our economic structure'; nor were they aimed at adopting 'positive ways of dealing with the rural problems'.[47] In the 1970 election campaign, Bhutto had repeated his 'fundamental changes' and 'positive ways' promises a number of times and, in one particular pronouncement, he had been unusually explicit about the nature of the reform to be introduced:

> We cannot leave the fate of our peasantry entirely to the anarchy of private possession. There must be a bold and an imaginative agrarian programme aimed at reformation. The remaining vestiges of feudalism require to be removed. State lands will be given to the landless peasants, cooperative farming will be introduced on a voluntary basis. The small landowners will be exempted from the payment of land revenue and self-cultivation will be laid down as a principle of land policy.[48]

But Bhutto had allowed the 'remaining vestiges of feudalism' to enter the PPP in large numbers. Their political weight within the party and the administration was great enough to preclude a 'bold and an imaginative programme aimed at reformation'. A number of measures were taken, but all of them fell well short of the promises made during the election campaign as well as the rhetoric that accompanied their announcement. Amongst the initiatives taken by the PPP, the land reform were announced with a greater deal of fanfare. The reforms were described by Bhutto in a radio and television broadcast on 11 March 1972. Its most important provision was the reduction in the ceiling of holdings from 500 (laid down in the reforms of 1959) to 150 acres in the case of irrigated land and from 1000 acres to 300 acres in the case of unirrigated land. The land in excess of these ceilings was to be resumed by the state without compensation to the owners, to be transferred ultimately to the tenants, who would receive it free. The new law also provided security to the tenants; they could not be ejected except under certain conditions including using the land in a manner that would 'render it unfit for the purpose for which it was held'. Although the 1972 reforms did not change the rental arrangements in force, they shifted on to the landlord the burden of paying 'land revenue' and 'water rate'. In all these respects, the reforms took the direction that had been adopted in 1959, the only difference being that the ceilings that were prescribed were a little lower, the safeguards against the ejection of tenants somewhat more stringent and the division of production costs between the tenants and landlords a little more in favour of the tenants. However, in one important respect the Bhutto reforms differed from those of Ayub: by cancelling all land awards made by the previous regime, the PPP administration signalled clearly to the landed interests that political support from non-rural groups would not be sought by giving them land grants. The Ayub administration had used the land owned by the state to reward loyal civil and military bureaucrats and to accommodate the industrial and merchant classes who wanted to diversify into other sectors of the economy. This induction of non-rural entrepreneurs into the rural economy had promoted commercial farming in the agricultural sector. It had also upset the landed interests, who resented the intrusion of and competition from non-rural entrepreneurs.

No major structural change was expected from the reforms – 'Pakistan will continue to be a country in which a large number of cultivators will own land in small holdings, while a small number of owners will have a significant proportion of the cultivated land'[49] – and none was achieved. The landed interests – large landlords as well as the middle-sized farmers – continued to dominate the countryside economically as well as politically. For that reason, Bhutto, despite his rhetoric demanding change in the countryside, continued to receive the support of the more important landed groups.

In part because of the regime's urban bias and in part because of the absence of support from well-defined and articulate non-

landed interests in the countryside, the regime did not formulate
programmes of 'comprehensive change' of the type that were
introduced in urban areas. A number of attempts were made to
'improve the quality of rural life', but these attempts, lacking
political and bureaucratic support, did not have a substantial
impact. Thus, in the summer of 1972, Mubashir Hasan's Ministry of Finance and Planning announced a People's Works Programme that was to provide new employment opportunities to the
rural poor. A Works Programme Unit was created in the Planning
Commission and a list of 'eligible schemes' was drawn up for the
guidance of the provincial governments in funding 'local initiatives'. The programme was patterned after the Rural Works
Programme (RWP) launched by the Ayub government in 1963
but the RWP used the system of Basic Democracies for planning,
executing and maintaining village-based, small-scale projects.[50]
The Basic Democracies system was abolished by the Bhutto
government and nothing was put in its place. Without such a
system, a public works programme could not be efficiently implemented. Accordingly, although the programme remained on
the list of active projects, it received little financial or administrative support.

About the time that Mubashir's Planning Commission was
introducing the People's Works Programme, J. A. Rahim's
Ministry of Production announced a plan for the development of
'agrovilles' in the country. The East Pakistan Comilla experiment
was the main inspiration behind the agrovilles; the plan called for
the establishment of a number of small marketing and administration towns all over the countryside to perform the functions
that had been successfully entrusted to the Thana Development
Centres in Bangladesh.[51] The plan assumed the availability of
resources for building agrovilles as well as co-operation between
different government departments for co-ordinating their field
activities. Since both financial resources and interdepartmental
co-operation were in short supply, the agrovilles plan was given
up after the launching of one project – Shadab near Lahore.

The third attempt at modernising the rural sector was made
soon after the launching of the People's Works Programme by the
Planning Commission and the agrovilles plan by the Ministry of
Production. This new initiative was bureaucratic rather then poli-
tical and was taken by the Ministry of Food and Agriculture.
The Integrated Rural Development Programme was 'to stop the

polarisation of the rural society through agrarian reforms; provide institutions and to obtain the whole-hearted co-operation and participation of the rural population in development work.'[52] The first and third objectives were dependent upon the second, but the second – creating an effective and viable system of rural institutions – was never achieved. Accordingly, the IRDP, as an approach to rural development[53] was implemented only in the form of a few pilot projects.

The 1972–4 period, therefore, saw the adoption of a number of social and economic reforms by the Bhutto regime that were aimed at improving the incomes and access to public services of the groups that were considered politically important by the PPP left. Since the left was essentially urban-based, the rural areas were not affected by the structural changes introduced by the Bhutto regime during the early period. The changes that affected the urban areas included the enlarged role of the public sector in the industrial and financial sectors; industrial workers became an important political force in the country; and the government expanded its role in the sector of education. These changes affected the direction of Pakistan's political, economic and social developments. Since the changes were confined to the urban areas and since the countryside remained largely unaffected, the dynamics of the new situation were felt mostly in the towns and cities.

7 Economic Decision-making without Constraints: 1974–7

It is possible to speculate that the tensions generated by the structural reforms discussed in the previous chapter would have been contained had the process as well as the substance of decision-making not changed as drastically as it did in late 1974. The main problem with the policies adopted during the 1972–4 period was that they discriminated against a number of powerful urban groups. Politicians do what they seem to be necessary to survive; it is possible, therefore, that the left might have become responsive to the demands of the groups that had been hurt or frustrated by its handling of the economy. It is also possible that once the structural changes considered necessary by the left had been made and once the economy and the polity had been set on a new course, the left would have quickened the rate of economic growth. And, a quickening in the rate of economic expansion might have provided an opportunity for a better sharing of the national product between the established groups that the left tried to deprive in order to help those it sought to favour. An expanding economy provides a better opportunity for instituting social reforms. But a change did occur and the decision-making roles vacated by the PPP socialists came to be occupied by a group with no strong ideological orientation.

It can also be speculated that, had the pendulum swung back completely and had the departure of the left brought the established groups back to power, Pakistan would have been saved some of the economic chaos of the mid-1970s. For a variety of reasons – with Bhutto's personality and his style of decision-making, the weakening of the institutional base which had supported the Ayub system, and an increase in the left's political power amongst the groups who had benefited from its management of the economy being the more important ones – the old order could not be established. With the left no longer performing decision-making roles and with the old order unable to establish itself, whatever progress the economy made was without much purpose and without any defined direction.

NEW CENTRES OF DECISION-MAKING

After Mubashir Hasan's departure from the Cabinet, Bhutto tried to involve senior civil servants in economic decision-making. To facilitate the depoliticisation of economic management, he appointed Rana Mohammad Hanif as Mubashir Hasan's successor in the Ministry of Finance, Planning and Economic Development. Rana Hanif was a mild-mannered lawyer from Sahiwal, occupying what can be described best as the centre-right of the PPP's ideological spectrum. Urban Sahiwal, which he represented, was typical of the medium-sized cities in the Punjab in which the economy was dominated by small-scale enterprises processing agricultural output.[1] Cotton ginning and flour milling were the city's principal industries, its largest single employer being the Montgomery Biscuit Factory. The groups that had helped to radicalise politics in the larger cities of the Punjab were still not important in Sahiwal – industrial labour, college and school teachers and such urban professionals as lawyers did not have the kind of weight in the city's polity as farmers, owners and operators of small enterprises, merchants and shopkeepers. Compared with Lahore, Lyallpur and Rawalpindi, Sahiwal was a conservative town with conservative politics. Rana Hanif's appointment was therefore welcomed by the business interests, in particular by the small-town merchants and industrial entrepreneurs who had been badly hurt by some of the reforms instituted by Mubashir Hasan and the PPP left.

Other economic Ministries in the reconstituted Cabinet also went to the politicians from rightist factions. Rafi Raza was appointed to the Ministry of Production vacated by J. A. Rahim. Raza was a lawyer from Karachi with no political base of his own. His entry into the Cabinet was made possible by his election to the Senate – a body whose members were chosen by the national and provincial legislators mostly on party grounds. The Ministry of

Fuel, Power and Natural Industries went to Yusuf Khattak of the Pakistan Muslim League, a rightist party from the Northwest Frontier that had collaborated with the PPP in order to keep Wali Khan's NAP in check. Khattak was a prominent businessman from Peshawar. The Ministry of Industry was put under the charge of Feroze Kaiser, the Prime Minister's Special Adviser. Like Raza, Kaiser had no political ambition. As a certified accountant from Karachi, he was one of the group of professionals who had been brought in by Bhutto to help him administer the Prime Minister's secretariat. Agriculture was the only important Ministry that was given to the left; Sheikh Rashid, the new Agriculture Minister, remained in the Cabinet in part to placate the left and in part to balance the Punjab landed interests who were now being brought into the PPP in large numbers.

With the established groups now back in important Cabinet positions, it was Bhutto's expectation that much of the decision-making would devolve on the bureaucracy, as had happened during the latter part of the Ayub era. New appointments were made to the more important economic Ministries and the divisions of finance, planning and development were put under the charge of A. G. N. Kazi, a senior civil servant with a long and distinguished record of service. The stage was thus set for the bureaucratisation of decision-making. However, the Ayubian model could not be re-established and the bureaucracy could not perform the role expected of it. There were essentially two reasons for the bureaucracy's failure to regain power: Bhutto's personality and the drastic changes that had been made earlier in the structure of the bureaucracy.

Bhutto found it very difficult to accept the kind of discipline that Ayub Khan had imposed on himself. Under Ayub, the Planning Commission had used a variety of devices to direct public and private expenditures into high-priority sectors and projects. The economy's long-term goals were described in the Perspective Plan for the 1965–85 period. The planning framework for achieving these goals was provided in five-year plans; the first of these new-type medium-term plans was announced in June 1965 to cover the 1965–70 period. The government's appropriations for sectoral and project development expenditures were made within the framework of the five-year plan. These appropriations were included in the Annual Development Plans (ADPs). For a project to be accepted for inclusion in the

ADPs, the sponsoring agencies had to produce a feasibility report in terms of the cost-benefit methodology prescribed by the Planning Commission in its PC1 form. Development expenditures by the private sector were guided by 'investment schedules' that conformed to the goals of the Perspective Plan and the planning framework of the five-year, medium-term plans.[2]

Bhutto found the twenty-year perspective, five-year medium-term and annual development plans cumbersome devices. He was also not inclined to accept the discipline of the Planning Commission's PC1 forms and feasibility studies and industrial investment schedules. He became impatient with these instruments of planning, but, since they could not be abandoned by the bureaucracy, increasingly the more important economic decisions came to be taken without much participation by the civil servants working in the finance and development Ministries. Thus, the decisions to construct a steel mill in Karachi with Russian assistance; to build a highway on the right bank of the Indus River, connecting Karachi and the western parts of Sind with the northern areas of Pakistan; to construct a series of nuclear plants, including a plant for reprocessing nuclear fuel; to build a tunnel connecting Chitral with the Frontier Province; and to construct a sports complex with the help of the Chinese in the capital city of Islamabad – all were taken without adequate PC1 feasibility studies. These decisions differed from those taken during 1972–4 in one important way: none of them was pushed by powerful political groups and none of them would have benefited any particular political interest. And yet the motive behind each of them was political in the sense of responding to the wishes and aspirations of important groups of supporters. The motive was political because each of the large projects symbolised in some way or other Bhutto's vision of an economically independent Pakistan 'that will not be dictated to by any foreign power [and that] will not succumb to external pressures'. By undertaking projects such as these, Pakistan would never need to 'barter away its sovereignty'.[3] Each one of them was a 'grand' solution to a problem that could have been solved in less dramatic ways. However, the Prime Minister and his secretariat did not confine their intervention to large, grandiose projects. Once freed from such urgent foreign policy issues as rapprochement with India and Bangladesh, Bhutto turned his attention to improving his political base in the provinces in which his party had not been very active. He made extensive use of 'economic directives' to the provincial authorities in the Northwest Frontier Province and Baluchistan to reach the people of those two provinces.

During 1975 and 1976, Bhutto made six 'meet the people' trips to Baluchistan during which he sanctioned more than 300 health, education, water supply and housing projects. Since these projects were outside the sectoral programme of the province, a new category – 'Prime Minister's Directives' (PMDs) – was included in the development plan. PMDs were also used by Bhutto in the other provinces to fulfil the 'simple aspirations of the people of Pakistan'.[4] To monitor the PMDs, a special unit was set up in the Prime Minister's secretariat. As PMDs grew in number and as more resources were committed to them, the economic planning role of the Prime Minister's secretariat came to rival that of the Planning Commission's. As the power of the Prime Minister's secretariat increased, it also came to be used by government departments for adjudicating the differences between them. This further weakened the Planning Commission.

It might have been possible for the bureaucracy to introduce a measure of discipline in economic decision-making had it not been so thoroughly reorganised and demoralised. Under Ayub's administrative system, most of the senior civil servants belonged to the CSP, a service with a remarkable *esprit de corps*. The service tradition demanded that the differences between its members should not be allowed to stand in the way of their common interest. It was this solidarity and the ability to act in a concerted fashion that made possible the accretion of a great deal of power in the hands of a few people. These attributes also made it certain that a politician of Bhutto's temperament and independence would use all the power at his disposal to subject the civil servants to his will. This he did with remarkable skill and success. Because of this success, Bhutto found that the process of economic decision-making could not be depoliticised and bureaucratised. Even when given the opportunity to do so, the bureaucracy no longer had the confidence or the *esprit de corps* to function without guidance from the politicians. When Mubashir Hasan left the Cabinet, the responsibility for economic decision-making had to be assumed by the Prime Minister. This was the second reason for the failure of the bureaucracy to take charge and for decision-making to move from the Ministry of Finance, Planning and Development to the secretariat of the Prime Minister.

With the Prime Minister and his secretariat playing important decision-making roles in the area of economics, some other bureaucratic innovations were also introduced. The most important of these was to reorganise a part of the existing bureaucracy along project rather than functional lines. Where such a reorganisation could not be undertaken, new organisations were set up to undertake the planning and implementation of large projects. Accordingly, a number of new agencies were set up to implement the large projects that came to dominate the economic field during the 1974–7 period (see below).

The best example of the reorganisation of a functional department along project lines was the decision to set up a new 'bureaucratic division' for population planning. The failure of the ambitious family planning programme – launched in the mid-1960s with considerable expectation – to produce a visible demographic impact called for a new initiative in the area.[5] Despite the commitment of large financial and administrative resources during the 1960s, the census of 1972 indicated that the crude birth rate at about 46 births per thousand of the population was amongst the highest in the developing world. The old programme's emphasis on the delivery of contraceptives and its lack of recognition of the importance of the social and economic environment in which families were being formed were regarded as the principal reasons for its failure. In the late 1960s, therefore, the task of providing family planning services was given to the Ministry of Health and Social Welfare so that the more important influence on family formation could be dealt with simultaneously. However, in 1975 a new population planning programme was formulated and handed over to the new Population Planning Division for execution. The division was to function independently of the Health and Social Welfare Division.

A number of similar developments took place in other sectors. A new division was organised to facilitate the export of labour to the Middle East. It was to function independently of the Labour Division. The procurement and distribution of food was separated from agriculture, statistics from planning, rural development from agriculture, energy from fuel and power, culture from education. Each of the new divisions was to look after one or two important projects.

With the Planning Commission weakened, the CSP abolished and with the establishment of a number of single-purpose Depart-

ments and agencies, it became increasingly difficult to define a set
of objectives central to all economic decisions. What ensued was a
three-year period of decision-making without constraints. During
this period, the regime embarked on a number of schemes with
long periods of gestation and limited economic and political
returns. The adoption of these schemes had a number of important economic and political consequences. Since together they
claimed a large proportion of development resources, it became
difficult to adopt more innovative solutions to the country's
economic problems. Since they were long-gestation projects, it
also became difficult to plan the government's development
expenditure on a long-term basis. And since, these schemes were
adopted as grand solutions to Pakistan's economic problems, they
generated a political momentum of their own that the successor
government found very difficult to halt.

EMPHASIS ON 'GRAND' SOLUTIONS

The Karachi Steel Mill is the best example of the type of project
that received Bhutto's support on grounds that were strictly
non-economic. The plans for making Pakistan self-sufficient in
steel were first formulated in the 1950s when, with the support of
Saltzgitter Hüttenwerk, a German firm, the Pakistan Industrial
Development Corporation suggested a project based on the
Kalabagh iron ore deposits. The project was debated for more
than a decade and was finally abandoned during the 1960s when
the Ayub regime decided that there was little economic justification for going ahead with it. The Kalabagh ore was known to be of
inferior quality and the Saltzgitter process for using it was considered too outdated for a modern steel mill. However, the decision
not to proceed with the mill drew some fire from those who
thought indigenous steel-making capacity vital for the country's
economic independence. When Bhutto left the government of
Ayub Khan, he used the 'steel mill case' as an illustration of the
'regime's dependence on the industrial countries of the West'.[6] He
promised his followers a mill that would make Pakistan self-
sufficient in steel and, to get it 'I will go to any country that has the
technology and does not object to Pakistan becoming economically independent'.[7] Although the Pakistan Steel Mills Corporation was set up before the PPP assumed office, and although the

foundations for an integrated steel mill were laid by Bhutto at Pipri near Karachi in December 1973, it was not until July 1975 that the plans were finalised for a mill with a 1 million ton capacity. At that time, the government obtained credit for over $525 million from Soviet Russia, for the purchase of machinery and technology for the construction of the mill.

The proposal for the construction of a highway on the right bank of the Indus River was also put forward for the first time in the early 1950s. The initiative came from the Ministry of Defence at the time of the serious tensions between India and Pakistan. The existing link between Karachi and the northern parts of the country was considered extremely vulnerable – for a distance of about 100 miles northeast of the Sind city of Sukkur, the road ran less than fifty miles from the Indian border. A road on the right bank of the Indus was therefore considered to be of strategic importance. It would not only be further from India, there would be the added advantage of having the Indus River in between. As in the case of the steel mill, the scheme was dropped from active consideration by the Ayub regime. It was not even revived after the 1965 war with India; experience now told the defence planners that Pakistan's communication network was much more susceptible to air than to artillery assault and putting a river in between would do little to deter a modern air force.

A new justification appeared for the scheme in the summer of 1973 when the Indus, over-flowing its right bank, flooded and breached the existing highway at a number of places. As a result an enormous amount of disruption was caused, and on the grounds that 'the need for a dependable alternate road link between north and south of the country has been felt',[8] the Prime Minister announced the creation of the Indus River Highway Cell to supervise the planning, design and construction of a highway 800 miles long and estimated to cost about $500 million. No detailed economic feasibility study was sought or provided when an allocation of $2 million was made to the cell in the 1975/76 development plan. With this allocation, the new highway authority began to implement the project.

The Bhutto government's decision to go in for a series of nuclear plants was announced in early 1975. According to this, a 500 megawatt plant was to be set up at Chasma, a small town in the northern Punjab. This plant was to become operational in 1979; thereafter, starting in 1980, an additional reactor was to be commissioned every two years. The Nuclear Power Development Programme also envisaged the setting up a fuel reprocessing plant of French design with French assistance. As in the case of the Karachi Steel Mill and the Indus Highway, the decision to put the emphasis on the development of nuclear power for meeting the country's energy requirement was another reflection of Bhutto's penchant for 'grand solutions'.

In 1975, when the Bhutto regime decided to meet the country's 'energy gap' by installing a dozen nuclear reactors over a twenty-five-year period, Pakistan's energy output per head of the population was far less than the average for the developing world: 32 megawatts *per capita* as against 290 for all developing countries. With the 1975 population at 71 million, the energy gap was therefore of the order of 20,590 megawatts.[9] The increase in the price of imported oil – in 1974/75 Pakistan spent \$385 million on petroleum imports as against \$66 million in the previous year – and problems with the Tarbela Dam were good reasons for the government to start looking at alternative sources of energy. Given the country's large hydroelectric and natural gas potential – in 1975 Pakistan's natural gas reserves were estimated at 16·74 trillion cubic feet[10] and the hydroelectric potential of the Indus gorge alone at 30,000 megawatts[11] – a careful examination of the alternative sources could not justify such a large commitment for the development of nuclear power. According to one estimate, the power obtained from the small Gomal Dam project, producing 135 megawatts, was much cheaper in terms of both initial capital and maintenance costs than that provided by the 137 megawatt Karachi Nuclear Power Project.[12] The economics of larger hydroelectric power projects was even better. Therefore, the decision to emphasise nuclear development was not taken on entirely rational economic grounds. India's entry into the nuclear club was apparently a strong motivating factor.[13] Long before coming to power, Bhutto had declared his opposition to Pakistan's acceptance of nuclear non-proliferation arguing that the country's 'position is entirely different because, for us, the nuclear threat is real and immediate'.[14]

Lowari Tunnel was the fourth large project to be included in the portfolio developed by the Prime Minister's secretariat. Once again, the project was aimed at meeting a need that had been felt for a number of years: to connect the 'northern areas' with the rest of Pakistan. And, once again, the main reason for including the project was political rather than economic.

The northern areas were made up of the states of Chitral, Dir and Swat. The British did not merge these 'princely states' with the Northwest Frontier Province and they continued to enjoy a great deal of administrative autonomy. In return for accepting the sovereignty of the British *raj*, the hereditary rulers of the states were allowed to use indigenous fiscal, administrative and political systems. Even after independence the states did not lose their autonomy; various Pakistan governments continued to treat the states as being 'less settled' than the settled districts of the Northwest Frontier. Under Bhutto, however, the government changed this policy: the princes were pensioned off and the states of Chitral, Dir and Swat were merged with the settled districts.

One reason for this change in the government's policy towards the administration of the northern areas was to dilute the strength of Wali Khan's NAP in the Frontier Province. The NAP, the main opposition party to Bhutto's PPP, was strong in the 'settled districts'. It was in these districts that Abdul Ghaffar Khan (Wali Khan's father) and his *khudai-kidmatgars* (God's helpers) had built a strong political base for themselves by siding with the local peasants and workers in their struggle against the landlords and merchants. The PPP was on the point of becoming strong in the princely states: during the 1968—9 anti-Ayub movement and during the 1970 election campaign, Bhutto had introduced the 'oppressed people of the northern areas'[15] to the socialist programme of the PPP. By bringing the northern areas into the Frontier Province, Bhutto felt that he could introduce his party and his platform into the province that had continued to resist his political overtures. Accordingly, the states were brought into the Frontier Province and an intensive development programme was initiated there to consolidate further the PPP's position amongst the people. The Lowari Pass Tunnel Project was one dramatic way of showing to the people of the northern areas the type of benefits that would accrue to them in return for supporting the PPP and its chairman. When completed, at a cost of over $200 million, the tunnel was to provide an all-weather link with the rest of Pakistan for the people of Chitral. Although, without such a road, the people remained snow-bound during the winter, lack of communication with the plains was not one of the major problems of the people of Chitral. Like other people living in the northern areas, their main problem was insufficient opportunities for productive employment, which in turn contributed to inadequate nutrition, high rates of mortality and fertility and a very low level of literacy. Bhutto's promise to provide jobs and to meet the basic needs of the people had won some support for the PPP in Chitral and other princely states during the 1970 election campaign. While the people waited for the fulfilment of this promise, the Lowari Pass Tunnel claimed the bulk of the resources that could be spared for the development of the northern areas. The allocation of $2·5 million made to the Lowari Tunnel directorate from the Annual Development Programme of 1974/75 was three times the commitment to all other development schemes.

The Z. A. Bhutto Institute of Sports and Culture, which included a Chinese-assisted sports complex at Islamabad, is one more example of a large-scale, long-gestation project that was given high priority by the government on essentially political grounds. The motives behind the setting up of this institute and its related facilities were as complex as those which resulted in the commitment of government resources to other large projects. During the 1968−9 anti-Ayub campaign, Bhutto had discovered the importance of developing a political rapport between himself and the people. Ayub, the archtypical Sandhurst-trained army officer, unable to communicate with the people largely because his style, language and manners were foreign to them failed to build a mass following for himself. Bhutto proved to be much more flexible in style, manner and language. As the campaign against Ayub gathered momentum, Bhutto found that it was not only the PPP's attractive political platform that was attracting large crowds to his meeting. The crowds also came to his meetings to see a politician who did not belong to the traditional political mould. Jinnah, Liaqat and Ayub were politicians who did not seem to feel the need for populist politics. They 'talked down' to the people. Bhutto took a different route to political success. He succeeded in portraying himself as their man, not only speaking their language, but also partaking of their culture. He had turned local culture and his ability to adapt to it into a great political asset.

During the 1970 election campaign, Bhutto's identification with the masses increased largely because of the adept use of cultural symbols to which the people could respond. He was now telling the audiences that there were two Bhuttos: one who resided in his own body and the other who lived in each one of them:

> They and he were thus united in an unbreakable bond and made inseparable. He declares that, being human, he is

capable of making mistakes, but that if he makes any, he will own up to them and seek the peoples' forgiveness; he will take off his hat and place it at their feet [a gesture of humility in Pakistani culture, after which the one who is unforgiving is the more blameworthy].[16]

The lessons learnt from these campaigns were not forgotten by Bhutto once he had attained political power. He was a populist; he had overthrown a powerful military dictator by getting close to the people, by first understanding and then articulating in their own idiom their needs and aspirations. Once in power, Bhutto attempted to strengthen his bond with the people by making use of their symbols, their culture, their language and their music. However, what had been intended as a programme aimed at developing Pakistan's 'native cultures' soon mushroomed into an expensive plan for the setting up of national institutes of sports, culture, folklore and heritage. In quick succession, the government approved the setting up of the National Council of the Arts, the National Institute of Folklore and Heritage, the National Academy of Performing Arts and the National Dance and Song Ensemble. The Z. A. Bhutto Sports and Cultural Institute was founded to co-ordinate and promote all cultural activities. The Prime Minister's name was lent to the Institute to 'emphasize his close relations with the ordinary people of Pakistan'.[17] A loan was obtained from China to build a large sports complex at Islamabad – a complex that would promote 'sports and culture not only within Pakistan but also within all countries of the Third World'.[18] Plans were announced to hold a number of Third World athletic and sports events. These events, it was hoped, would 'underline the central role that Pakistan was playing under Prime Minister Bhutto for bringing together the countries of the Third World'.[19] What had started as a programme to bring the 'ordinary people of Pakistan' into contact with those who led them changed into a programme with political objectives that had little meaning for the poor people. The government rhetoric that accompanied the launching of this $100 million programme of investment in sports and culture was no longer aimed at the ordinary people. It was now aimed primarily at gaining access to the Third World fora for Pakistan. This access had been denied to Pakistan on account of its formal military links with the United States. Pakistan's membership of SEATO and CENTO had been the reason for not asking Bhutto to participate in the Third World Summit held at

Colombo in 1976. Bhutto's subsequent call for a summit of Third World leaders won little support from the developing countries. Thus frustrated, the Prime Minister chose sports and culture as one of the ways of gaining acceptance among the Third World countries.[20]

The Karachi Steel Mill, the Indus Highway, the Nuclear Power Development Programme, the Lowari Pass Tunnel, the Z. A. Bhutto Sports and Culture Institute were examples of economic decisions taken for essentially non-economic reasons. The Prime Minister's penchant for grand – sometimes ultimate – solutions and the bureaucracy's inability to prevent their adoption were the main reasons for the priority assigned by his administration to these expensive programmes. One important consequence of this type of decision-making without constraints was that the sectors that needed development resources and that could have helped the country out of a number of its economic difficulties did not receive the attention they deserved. Agriculture was one such sector. Bhutto's rural background, his continuing interest in the welfare of the farming class, and the departure of the urban-based PPP left from the Cabinet had raised the expectation that his government would help the agricultural sector to grow rapidly. The regime did not disappoint its growing rural constituency. In the 1974–7 period, the focus of the government's attention shifted towards the countryside and a number of measures were adopted to aid the agriculture sector. But these efforts, fairly strenuous at times, yielded little largely because they were aimed at the relatively less efficient part of the agriculture sector. The more dynamic part – the part that was responsible for the Green Revolution during the 1960s – was neglected by the regime. This neglect was to prove politically very costly.

TREATMENT OF THE AGRICULTURAL SECTOR

With the PPP left having been made to surrender decision-making to Bhutto and the Prime Minister's secretariat, and with the Prime Minister's continuing interest in developing the rural economy and the landed interests having been inducted back into important positions, the rural sector should have expected favourable treatment from the administration that took office in October 1974. The way Bhutto restructured the Cabinet and moved the senior civil servants around seemed to indicate that the reorganised administration was being equipped to restore balance between the priorities assigned to the urban and rural sectors. The left in the PPP had exhibited a definite bias towards the urban areas, particularly towards the large cities in the provinces of the Punjab and Sind. The new Cabinet was expected to tilt in favour of the countryside and, to some extent, in favour also of the large number of towns in the Punjab and Sind that in many ways supported the agricultural sector of the two provinces.

Khuda Bux Bucha was the person who was to bring about this change in the government's priorities. Bucha, a retired bureaucrat who had entered politics during the last years of the Ayub era, was now appointed by Bhutto to help shift the focus of the regime's economic policies from urban development to the promotion of the agricultural sector. Threatened by the growing disillusionment with the government's policies amongst the liberal elements in Pakistan's political system and the modern elements in its economy, Ayub had turned towards the established forces for political and economic support. Bhutto's difficulties with the left and the departure of the left from the Cabinet in October 1974 had placed him in a situation that resembled Ayub's after 1965. Accordingly, Bucha was brought in to consolidate the Prime Minister's support amongst the landlords. In return for the support that they were very willing to give to the Prime Minister, the large landlords expected to be suitably rewarded. Suitable rewards were no longer those sought traditionally by the farmers – subsidies for the inputs they used and higher prices for the surpluses they produced. For, such rewards would not have benefited only the large landlords; they would have brought greater benefits to the more productive and efficient middle-sized farmers who had been cultivated by Ayub Khan as his own political constituency in the countryside. The favours granted to this class of farmers by the Ayub regime made it possible for them to bring the Green Revolution to Pakistan. The success of the Green Revolution made the middle-sized farmers economically prosperous and politically powerful. When the landed aristocracy were brought back into the political arena by Ayub Khan, one of their more important demands was that the further growth of the economic and political power of the middle peasantry should be curbed. But events moved very fast in the late 1960s and Ayub Khan's regime was not able to restore the balance between these two groups of the farming community. Restoration of this balance, therefore, was one of the important objectives of the series of policies that were initiated by the Bhutto regime. But the middle peasantry were now too well entrenched in the rural economic and political systems to be easily replaced by the landed aristocracy. Accordingly, several initiatives taken by the government relating to prices and subsidies, mechanisation, the ownership of agro-industries and the restructuring of local institutions created a great deal of political tension in the countryside. These policies contributed as much to the 1977 fall of Bhutto as did the economic measures adopted during the 1972–4 period to affect changes in the urban society.

Pakistan has a long history of encouraging farmers to expand output by providing them with subsidies on the inputs they use and by ensuring that the price of their output would not fall below a certain level. The use of these instruments for achieving production aims has been well analysed.[21] What has not been studied is their use of obtaining political objectives; for strengthening, that is to say, the economic and political power of the rural groups that could influence decision-making. In order to reflect on the dynamics of decision-making in this area, it is necessary to disaggregate the available data and to use the indices that portray more closely the political motives that were involved.

Viewing the entire Bhutto period from the perspective of agricultural incentives, we get a picture that does not support the hypothesis being presented here. For, according to the available data,[22] 1973/74 marks a high point in the 'parity ratio', the ratio between agricultural and non-agricultural prices. This means that in the history of Pakistan's agriculture terms of trade were more favourable to agriculture in 1973/74 than they were in any previous year. However, it was suggested above that the urban-based PPP left was still powerful at that time and that its attitude towards the countryside was at best that of benign neglect. The same set of data indicates a sharp deterioration in the agriculture terms of trade during the post-1974 period, when the landed interests were installed once again in important decision-making roles. According to one study, '1974–75 and 1975–76 mark consecutive years of decline that result in one of the most unfavourable ratios to be found in the entire 20 years for which the price index has been calculated.'[23]

However, disaggregation of the price data according to different crops, when combined with the prices that the farmers had to pay for the inputs they used for growing these crops and with the procurement policies adopted by the government, suggests that the regime's approach towards the agricultural sector was motivated to some considerable extent by the decision-makers' preference for certain constituencies. As the decision-makers changed during this period, so did agricultural policies.

Ayub Khan's land reforms and his structure of Basic Democracies brought about a number of changes in the agricultural production system, including the division of the farming community into three categories. The large landlords came to specialise in the production of such cash crops as cotton, sugar cane, and oil seeds, using the seed varieties that did not need much application of chemical fertilisers. The middle-sized farmers, with better access to modern inputs, concentrated on the production of wheat and rice, using the high-yielding varieties of seed. The small farmers, with very little access to modern inputs or the credits with which to buy them, continued to produce foodgrains for on-farm consumption. If they grew wheat and rice they used old seed varieties rather than those that would have required large applications of chemical fertiliser and water.

The PPP left, with its urban bias, was anxious to provide abundant food to city dwellers at subsidised prices. Accordingly, it pursued a policy of high procurement prices to obtain as much surplus for the farming sector as possible and making it available to the urban consumers at a large subsidy. The difference between procurement and ration-shop price was financed by the government. But the high procurement price the government was prepared to pay for foodgrains did not have a significant impact on the farmers' output. A high price of output translates into an incentive for the producer only when the cost of the inputs that he uses does not increase proportionately. However, in 1973/74, at the height of the PPP left's power, the real cost of purchasing inputs by farmers growing wheat was more than double that during the 1960s. Between 1962/63 and 1964/65, the real cost of purchasing input had declined by 38 per cent, a fact that, no doubt, contributed to the wide-scale adoption of the new high-yielding seed technology. The doubling of costs between the mid-1960s and the late 1970s worked as a disincentive and contributed to the stagnation of agriculture during the Bhutto period.

In 1972–4, the regime's policies changed. Responding to the pressure from the landlords who had now joined Bhutto, the administration changed its approach towards the agricultural sector. The sector was no longer assigned a low priority; instead, under Bhutto's direction, an incentive structure was adopted to favour one category of farmers. However, the beneficiaries of the change in approach were not the more dynamic middle-class farmers who had brought Pakistan its Green Revolution but the large landlords specialising in cash crops. The changes in the prices of inputs and outputs during this period took away the incentive that the price and subsidy policies had provided to the middle-class farmers during the Ayub period. The fortunes of the large-scale cotton growers in the southern districts of the Punjab and northern districts of Sind moved in the opposite direction. For them, the real cost declined by 46 per cent between 1970/71, the year when they reached their peak, and 1975/76, when the Bhutto regime's policies favouring the landed interests began to have an impact.

The government's approach to mechanisation also reflects the desire to favour larger farmers. I have already referred to the farm mechanisation policies adopted by the Ayub government during the late 1960s. These policies resulted in the importation of a large number of tractors which, in turn, caused the displacement from the land of a large number of workers. Their displacement and migration to cities contributed to the political destabilisation that marked the last two years of the Ayub era. The exchange reforms of 1972, which resulted in a substantial reduction in the value of the Pakistani rupee, caused significant increases in the domestic price of all imported equipment, including farm machinery. However, a series of measures adopted in 1974/75 reduced the purchase price of tractors once again, as well as the cost of maintaining them and other farm equipment. These measures included the expansion in the role of the government-controlled Agriculture Development Bank in making available credit on easy terms for the purchase of machinery; the establishment of a network of government-operated service centres for the mainte-nance of farm machinery, with the farmers charged only a fraction of the cost of servicing the equipment; and the grant of a substan-tial subsidy on the diesel fuel used for the machinery. The effect of this promotion of mechanisation was much the same as in the Ayub period: it helped the landlords to displace tenants and sharecroppers with hired workers even though the tenants had legal rights on the land they cultivated.

The state's decision to assume the management of some 4000 agro-industries helped the large landlords to overcome the challenge of the middle-sized farmers and middle-class rural entrepreneurs. The decision announced by Bhutto in July 1976 surprised the business community. It had been expected that with the departure of the PPP left from the administration, the government would no longer be interested in expanding the industrial role of the public sector. However, this nationalisation decision differed from those taken during 1972–4, when the motivation had been mostly ideological. Although political, the motives this time were not ideological. In this respect, the decision was not too dissimilar from those that resulted in the incorporation of several large projects into the development programme. The Prime Minister in a long television and radio address to the nation explained the decision in terms of reducing the profits gleaned by the middle men and also in terms of the quality of wheat flour and cleaned rice that was being made available to the urban consumers. There was no doubt about the poor quality of wheat flour and milled rice that were being supplied by the traders to the consumers: according to a report commissioned by the government from a private consultant,

> the farmer supplies a higher quality [of foodgrains to the millers but] at some stage dust, weed, seeds and other foreign matter, and even damaged wheat from the old stocks, is added before making deliveries to the purchase centers. There are allegations that influence, if not pressure, is exercised on food officials to accept wheat which is not up to the prescribed standard.[24]

There is also no doubt that the Prime Minister was influenced by the analysis of this well-documented report of a private consultant. But the real significance of the decision to nationalise the wheat flour, rice-milling and cotton-milling industries was not that the government was responding to a popular demand. The real political and economic significance of this measure was that it resulted in the vertical integration of the agricultural sector in the sense that the landed aristocracy now had a share not only in producing a sizable part of the output traded in the market, but also in the marketing, processing and distribution of this output.

For historical reasons, trade in foodgrains in the areas that were now in Pakistan had remained in the hands of either a non-farming class of *arthis* or had been taken over by the commercial farmers who had played such a significant role in developing the agricultural sector during the Ayub period. In the period before partition, the large sized farmers producing for the market had concentrated their attention on production. The marketing and processing of agricultural crops was generally in the hands of 'non-agricultural castes', mostly Hindus and Sikhs. With the departure of the Hindu and Sikh *arthis* in 1947, the large landlords could have assumed control over marketing and processing, but their stand against the creation of Pakistan as an independent state had seriously weakened their position once that state was created. In the period following partition and independence, the politically powerful class of refugees brought in their own people to take over and manage the agro-industries that had been left behind by the non-Muslims. Accordingly, even after 1947, agriculture continued to be dominated by two economic and political groups: large landlords who were indigenous to the areas that now constituted Pakistan, and settlers from India who took over the control of the processing industries that had been left behind by Hindus and Sikhs.

Although the process of indigenisation that gained considerable momentum during the Ayub period brought back the large landlords into the political and economic arenas, they were not able to dislodge the grain merchants and agro-industrialists. In fact, taking advantage of the land market that had developed in the early 1960s after the rural properties abandoned by the non-Muslims were finally settled in favour of the refugees from India, a large number of merchants and petty rural industrialists also became farmers. Their commercial experience as well as easy access to lines of credit made it possible for them to become important members of the new class of agricultural entrepreneurs that emerged under Ayub. It was this class that was most affected by the 'agrarian reform measure of July 1976'. By directly intervening in these industries, the government dislodged the merchants and brought in the large landlords and their representatives to manage the 4000 nationalised enterprises. Of the 4000 new managers, nearly three-quarters had close links with the large landlords who had now become prominent in the PPP.[25] With one stroke of the nationalisation pen, the regime had succeeded in vertically integrating the more important economic functions in the country's agricultural sector.

It did not take very long for the political repercussions of this intervention by the regime to be felt by the Prime Minister. Not unlike the small urban businessmen who had been hurt by Mubashir Hasan's labour reforms, the grain traders and agro-industrialists were also strong PPP supporters. Support to Bhutto and his political party was given by these two groups for much the same reason. The PPP's socialist philosophy and its initial re-cruitment of support from amongst weaker economic groups promised these groups protection against encroachment by those they feared most: large industrialists and large landlords. How-ever, the support of these groups was lost when it became clear that the regime was prepared to sacrifice their interests in cul-tivating the support of some other elements in the political society.

In addition to implementing economic policies that discrimi-nated against the urban and rural middle classes, it also became apparent that the regime's programme of political reconstruction was also biased against them. Ayub Khan had courted the middle classes by creating the system of Basic Democracies, a system in which these classes found more than adequate representation. Bhutto dissolved the local councils that formed the BD system. With their dissolution the middle classes, including the small-town industrialists and rural merchants, lost the opportunity for influencing decision-making. The BD system had been used very effectively by groups such as these for obtaining government support and benefits for themselves. This could no longer be done.

A cell structure was built into the PPP in order to make the party more representative of the people it was supposed to represent. In 1975, the party was thoroughly reorganised; a network of village and *mohalla* (urban community) cells was spread horizontally to catch the rapidly politicising segments of the population. The village and *mohalla* cells were put under the control of district parties and district parties were placed under the control of provincial parties. A national executive committee was set up to co-ordinate the activities of the cells and other sub-units of the party. This structure, therefore, did not differ a great deal from the BD system; like the local councils of the BD system, the party was also given a multi-tiered and pyramidal shape. The important difference was that the village and *mohalla* cells were not provided with the degree of autonomy that was allowed to the union councils, the lowest tier of the BD system. District units became the most important constituents of the PPP system and the leadership of these was captured by the established groups. Of the fifty-two district parties that were set up after the reorganisation, the chairmanship of thirty-two was claimed by large landlords, prosperous lawyers and large industrialists. Bhutto's populist rhetoric, combined with an organisational structure in which the established social and economic groups exerted considerable influence, eventually resulted in a political coalition between the rich and the poor. This restructuring of the political system was to have a much deeper impact on the growth of the agricultural sector. The PPP-dominated political system excluded and thereby demoralised the progressive farmers who had been exceptionally active during the 1960s. Their demoralisation, coupled with that of the large- and small-scale industrial sectors was to result later in total stagnation in the growth of the nation's product. As suggested earlier, a growing economy can accommodate change and, to some extent, cope with political discontent. In a situation of economic discontent, political discontent acquires a more sinister meaning. This was to happen during the last few months of the Bhutto regime.

ECONOMIC CONSEQUENCES OF THE REGIME'S POLITICAL PRIORITIES

The departure of the left, the eclipse of the Planning Commission by the Prime Minister's secretariat as the focal point for economic decisions and the Prime Minister's unwillingness to accept a certain amount of discipline in reaching policy decisions created an atmosphere of uncertainty in which both the private and the public sectors found it difficult to function. Had the left remained in control, it would have provided the country with the bureaucratic machinery that was needed to operate the enlarged and rapidly growing public sector. Had the reforms of the bureaucracy and its later politicisation not demoralised 'the Planning Commission and other parts of the 'development bureaucracy' so thoroughly, it is possible that, even after the left's exit from the Cabinet, some control over economic decision-making would have remained. Instead, the combination of a political figure who refused to be disciplined, a bureaucracy that had neither the power to enforce discipline nor the ability to contain the damage that was being done by decisions arrived at in an *ad hoc* manner and a political system that could not aggregate conflicting interests produced a situation in which the economy could no longer function efficiently.

It is, of course, impossible to ascertain the exact influence of these decisions on the health of the economy. But it can be said with some confidence that their overall impact was negative. The Prime Minister's fascination with grand solutions to the country's economic problems and the political system's inability to apportion benefits between various competing groups resulted in a development programme that the country could not afford. The large, long-gestation, ambitious projects that emerged from the Prime Minister's secretariat were included in the development programme that had also to provide resources for hundreds of small projects aimed at winning the political support of several diverse groups. Accordingly, investment in the public sector nearly tripled between 1974 and 1977, from Rs 6700 million to Rs 18,203 million. At the same time, and again largely on account of the failure of the political system to mobilise resources for development in the amounts required to achieve the regime's political priorities, savings did not increase in step with the level of investment (see Table 7.1). The result was that the country's dependence on foreign capital flows increased enormously. This affected the burden of debt. By the time the Bhutto administration left office, Pakistan's debt burden had increased to $7 billion. This was equivalent to nearly 6 per cent of its national wealth. The servicing of this debt, not counting the debt relief the country had obtained earlier, needed 44 per cent of its merchandise exports – at that time, one of the highest debt service ratios in the developing world.

The emphasis on large projects meant that the country could expect to benefit from this investment effort only after a long period of time. And the neglect of the middle-sized farmers, small industrialists and small merchants – three groups that had in the past lent a great deal of dynamism to the Pakistani economy – meant that even those sectors failed to perform at their historical level. Accordingly, the rate of growth of the economy deteriorated sharply after 1974; during the 1974–7 period, the economy grew at a rate of only 2·7 per cent per annum, or 0·3 per cent less than the rate of population growth. In other words, in 1977 income per head of the population was lower than it had been in 1974.

But aggregate economic indices such as the rate of growth in

TABLE 7.1   Financing investment, 1974–7

	1974		1977	
	Rs million	*% of GDP*	*Rs million*	*% of GDP*
Gross fixed investment				
Public	6774	7·9	18187	12·5
Private	3840	4·5	7950	5·5
Total	10614	12·3	26137	18·0
Gross savings				
Public	6157	7·1	13271	9·1
Private	−131	−0·1	2910	2·0
Total	6026	7·0	16181	11·1
Resource Gap	4588	5·3	9956	6·9

Source: Computed from the data provided by the Planning Division, Government of Pakistan.

national product, the contribution to this growth of various sectors of the economy, the rates of saving and investment and the growth of these rates, and the burden of debt in terms of the proportion of exports needed to service it are of little help in understanding the way people react to the changes in their economic environment. Put in a historical perspective, as has been done in Table 7.2, what these indices show is that the performance of the economy during the 1970s was much poorer than in the 1960s. In some respects it was even worse than in the 1950s. But these numbers cannot be used to link the poor performance of the economy during the 1970s with the policies that were adopted by the Bhutto regime. In fact, a strong case can be made that the rapid growth of the economy during the Ayub period was the result of the adoption of easy solutions to the country's problems. These easy solutions had an immediate beneficial impact on the economy over the short-run but they also complicated further such structural problems as the low productivity of a large part of the agricultural sector, the excessive concentration of investment in import-substituting industries, neglect in developing the economy's considerable export potential, the failure to develop the large human resource available to the country and the inability to bring under control a very high rate of population growth. According to this interpretation, the Ayub government exploited easy options, leaving a number of very hard problems to be tackled by later governments. Attempts were made by the Bhutto administration to address these problems; given the fact that difficult structural changes cause disruptions over the short-run, the poor performance of the economy during the early 1970s should be attributed to this rather than to the type of economic management that has been described in this chapter.

TABLE 7.2   Real growth rates (percentages)

	1949/50–1959/60	1959/60–1969/70	1969/70–1976/77
GDP at factor cost	3·1	6·8	3·0
Population	2·5	2·9	3·0
GDP *per capita*	0·6	3·8	0·0
Agriculture	1·6	5·0	1·7
Industry[1]	7·8	9·9	1·6
Services	4·0	4·4	4·1

[1] Includes manufacturing, mining and quarrying.
Source: Computed from the data provided by the Planning Division, Government of Pakistan.

There are, of course, elements of truth in this argument but a similar case can also be made for the options available to the Bhutto administration. All the 'easy options' had not been exhausted during the Ayub period; Bhutto and his administration could have adopted some of them in order to ease the impact on the economy of the structural changes that they introduced. Industrial production need not have stagnated the way it did had nationalisation of some of the private enterprises been carried out on the basis of a well-developed and well-thought-out plan. The adverse effects on industrial output that are inevitable when a major structural reform is undertaken would have been less severe had the small-scale enterprises been allowed to fill a part of the gap. It was not so much the pursuit of a particular ideology that was the cause of so much economic disruption but the failure to plan and co-ordinate the various government initiatives.

While the establishment of a linkage between policies and outcome would have to await the availability of more information and data, what is important is to understand that the people's reaction to economic developments is based not so much on the facts of a situation but on how they perceive it. As was pointed out above (Chapter 4), the anti-Ayub movement of the late 1960s was based on the perception of some influential political groups that their interests had been willfully ignored by the regime. Similarly, the movement against Bhutto was fuelled by the perception of some powerful groups that the government had deliberately moved against them. While there is now some evidence to suggest that Ayub's economic programme did not lead to a deterioration of income distribution,[26] for the present the evidence from the Bhutto period indicates that the groups that were to agitate against him did in fact suffer economically, socially and politically. It is this type of evidence that is useful in understanding the political consequences of economic change.

POLITICAL CONSEQUENCES OF ECONOMIC CHANGE

The economic impact of the political choices made by the Bhutto regime have been examined. This final section, by providing a brief analysis of the political consequences of economic developments during the same period, completes the circle. It also sets the stage for the third part of the book, which describes the fall of Bhutto.

Pakistan has a very poor statistical base upon which to pronounce any meaningful judgement on the question of trends in income distribution. Most of the studies cited in this book use sources that have data covering very small samples of populations. In addition, the data from the several surveys of households are not strictly comparable. Nevertheless, the judgements about changes in income distribution, made by professional economists as well as politicians, have been significant in the country's political history. It is not surprising, therefore, that changes in income distribution during the Bhutto period were an important subject of debate, especially after 1975 when the PPP began to prepare itself for new elections.

Evidence on the distribution of incomes appears to indicate that income distribution worsened during the Bhutto period. This appears to have happened for several reasons, some of which can be attributed to the policies pursued by the government. Perhaps the most important reason for the deterioration in income distribution was the decline in the share in total wealth of the middle classes – the classes that were made up of such groups as the middle-sized farmers, small industrialists, small merchants and government employees. The government policies that affected the share of these groups in the country's wealth included the extension of labour laws to small industrial and business enterprises, automatic adjustment of industrial wages to keep in line with increases in prices, discrimination in favour of the large farmers in the granting of production incentives and investment credit, the provision of price support for the production of the crops in which the large farmers specialised, the encouragement provided to the unskilled workers to migrate to the Middle East and the decision not to provide cost-of-living compensation to government workers. These policies had a profound impact on relative incomes. For instance, whereas the real agricultural incomes stagnated, the real wages of agricultural workers increased substantially;[27] whereas real wages in industry declined during the 1960s, they increased substantially in the early 1970s;[28] and, whereas there was a substantial decline in the real salaries of all government employees, the reductions were much more severe at the upper end of the government salary structure.[29] The large-scale emigration of unskilled workers from Pakistan to the countries in the Middle East and a dramatic increase in their remittances to their families back in Pakistan added to the incomes of the low-income groups but also indirectly affected the incomes of the middle classes. Migration no doubt contributed to increasing the wages of unskilled workers in both rural and urban sectors and affected adversely the incomes of the middle-class rural and urban entrepreneurs. For these entrepreneurs, unskilled wages were a larger share of total earnings than for large farmers and large industrialists, the two latter classes being much more dependent on capital-intensive means of production.

There is little doubt, therefore, that the middle classes were worse-off as a result of the economic policies adopted during the Bhutto period. They also suffered political and social deprivation. After several changes in its structure, the PPP emerged as a political party in which the power of such old-established groups as large landlords and such new groups as industrial workers and peasants was much in evidence. The middle classes had been by and large excluded from the party's decision-making positions.

The reduction in the power of the middle-class-dominated civil bureaucracy further eroded their power. After the left had left the PPP administration, there were few ideological reasons for discriminating against the middle classes. The administration need not have played politics as a zero-sum game. A number of groups that were alienated could have been retained within the PPP fold. There was, for instance, no need to frustrate small businessmen in urban areas in order to bring industrial labour on board. The conflict between these two groups was not as sharp as between workers and the owners of large-scale industrial enterprises. The choice between the large and middle-sized farmers was a more difficult one, but the latter did not have to be alienated so thoroughly in order to win the political support of the former. Even if the regime had to reconstitute the coalition that made up the PPP by jettisoning some groups in order to pick new ones, it would have been politically wise to bring about the changes that this regrouping entailed in a situation that was not further complicated by economic uncertainty, especially when that uncertainty was produced by avoidable government policies. As it is, the brisk changes in the political situation occurred at the time when the economy began to respond negatively to a number of the regime's policies. It was in this environment that Bhutto chose to go to the people for a new mandate.

Part III

The Fall from Power

Convergent and parallel trajectories far outnumber divergent trajectories in cultural evolution. Most people are conformists. History repeats itself in countless acts of individual obedience to cultural rule and pattern, and individual wills seldom prevail in matters requiring radical alteration of deeply conditioned beliefs and practices.

Marvin Harris

8 Preparing for Elections in 1977

Zulfikar Ali Bhutto's fall from power came swiftly and unexpectedly. On 7 January 1977 he announced the dates for the national and provincial elections. The national poll was to be held on 7 March 1977 and the provincial elections three days later. In both elections, the Pakistan People's Party won impressive victories in three of the four provinces of the country. The opposition had campaigned vigorously for the national election, and if the attendance at public meetings was any indication of support, it could expect to win many more seats to the National and Provincial Assemblies than it had done in 1970. The opposition, therefore, found it difficult to accept the results when they were announced by the Election Commission; charging that Bhutto and his associates had massively rigged the elections, they opened a campaign against the government that quickly gained momentum. Only a month after the Prime Minister, with great confidence, made his victory speech the army was battling with protesting mobs in all the major cities. Unable to control the mounting violence, Bhutto was forced to impose military rule in the principal urban areas, thus inviting the armed forces into the political arena. On 5 July 1977, the Prime Minister was toppled from power by a *coup d'état* led by General Zia ul Haq, the army chief of staff.

Bhutto's fall from power, therefore, occurred much more rapidly than that of Ayub Khan. The anti-Ayub campaign took more than a year to mature and another year to pick up the ferocity that the anti-Bhutto movement managed to acquire within a space of only four months. What brought about Bhutto's swift fall from power? The *Washington Post*, in an editorial, provided an explanation that many people then appeared to accept: 'To the extent that his troubles arose from personal hubris rather than the economic and social conditions that tend to overwhelm the political leadership of most poor countries, there is hope for Pakistan.'[1] There can be little doubt that in Bhutto's case, exaggerated pride and great self-confidence resulted in retribution, but can these leadership attributes be separated from the economic and social conditions 'that tend to overwhelm the political leadership of most poor countries'? The answer to this question has to be in the negative. One of the main themes of Part II of this book was that several important decisions taken by Bhutto's administration in many ways contributed to the difficult social and economic situation that prevailed in the country when he decided to seek a new mandate from the people. The main theme of this part of the book is that in these conditions it was politically unwise for Bhutto to go back to the polls. This is a judgement that benefits only in part from hindsight. For, it can be argued – as I will presently argue – that an astute politician should have been able to judge that the political situation that prevailed in Pakistan was highly uncertain; being uncertain, it was highly volatile. Astute politicians do not take decisions in uncertain conditions. Why is it, therefore, that Bhutto, one of the shrewdest political figures of his day, should have decided to risk his entire political career by calling for a general election in a potentially difficult situation? Once again, the answer to this question will have to be a complex one. It will draw upon Bhutto's personality and how it influenced both the style and content of decision-making; on the dynamics produced by the political, economic and social changes introduced by the Prime Minister and his party in the period following their assumption of power in December 1971; and on the failure of the institutions fully to inform Bhutto of the way in which his reforms and changes had been received by several important groups within Pakistani society. In other words, the explanation to be provided in this part of the book is similar to the one given in the previous part in which decision-making during the Bhutto period was explained in terms of the motives of the decision-makers. In this, I will review first the state of Bhutto's mind at the time that he decided to call a general election, providing an assessment of the reasons why he felt confident at that time about his political future, and giving as well the reasons why he should have been less sanguine. The second section will present an analysis of the change that had occurred in Bhutto's constituency and how this constituency differed from the one that gave his People's Party an impressive victory in the elections of 1970 and brought him to power a year later. The third section deals with the new coalition of social and economic groups that Bhutto brought into the PPP to fight the 1977 elections. This chapter will therefore set the stage for Chapter 9, which provides a brief overview of the events that led to the fall of Bhutto on 5 July 1977.

THE DECISION TO SEEK A NEW MANDATE

In January 1977, Bhutto gave the impression of being in full command of the political situation in Pakistan, able and willing to take decisions that could hurt even parts of his own constituency. For instance, on 5 January, he celebrated his forty-ninth birthday[2] by surprising his landlord supporters with his second land reforms, which reduced private holdings to 100 acres of irrigated and 200 acres of unirrigated land. Although, the announcement of the new ceiling on land holdings appeared to signal another change in the political course the Prime Minister was following, once again there was not a whimper of protest from the landed community that now supported him enthusiastically. The absence of protest from the landlords was another indication of the fact that few people were prepared to challenge Bhutto. The land reform decision was also another illustration of Bhutto's approach towards political management: those sudden shifts in policies 'enabled him to remind the public how fully the nation's politics turned on his will and whim'.[3] There can be no doubt that he felt confident of another resounding victory at the polls when he announced the decision to hold the first general election under the Constitution of 1973. He went to the polls 'a confident man, a strong man, arrogant in his exercise of power',[4] and fully convinced that Pakistan did not have a leader of equal determination to challenge him, let alone remove him. In January 1977, Pakistan did not seem to have a viable alternative to Bhutto or his People's Party.

There were, of course, good reasons for the confidence that Bhutto exuded in the winter of 1976–7 and which prompted him to seek another mandate. A number of sudden and unanticipated changes in the neighbouring South Asian countries influenced this decision, as did several domestic developments that the Prime Minister interpreted as having improved his standing with his *new* constituency. Mujibur Rahman's assassination, followed by a series of military coups, quickly transformed the political situation in Bangladesh. The concentration of power in the hands of Mrs Gandhi's central government that resulted from constitutional changes introduced by her under the 'Emergency' made the Indian political situation resemble that of Pakistan. With the military in full control in Bangladesh and with the Indians being subjected to the rigours of emergency rule, Pakistan no longer seemed a deviant case in the political development of South Asia. Bhutto's announcement of 7 January that elections would be held two months later made Pakistan look politically more mature than its neighbours, a development that was not lost upon the new Democratic government of President Carter in Washington.[5]

But it was not only the political developments in South Asia that persuaded Bhutto to call elections. He was fully aware of the fact that, once the problems created by the separation of East Pakistan had been solved, the attention of the people would turn very quickly towards the domestic policies pursued by his regime. And he was also aware of the fact that his party's management of the economy and polity had resulted in the reappearance of the crisis of 'legitimacy and participation' that had marked much of Pakistan's history. After winning political power, the PPP had entered into a 'phase of decay';[6] the movement that Bhutto had launched in 1969 had 'failed to convert itself into a party'.[7] In the process, the Prime Minister's own popularity had suffered a great deal, a fact that he recognised by avoiding large political rallies of the type that punctuated his progress from political oblivion in 1967 to ascent to power in 1971. In 1972, his first full year in power, Bhutto addressed thirteen mammoth public meetings, at which he announced to the people such major decisions as Mujibur Rahman's release from jail and the setting up of a judicial commission to investigate the circumstances that led to the 1971 civil war. Six similar meetings were held in 1973 to announce such important developments as the decision to go to Simla to meet Mrs Gandhi, the agreement that was reached with India concerning the return of Pakistani territory and of the prisoners captured by India, and the financial and political support that Pakistan had begun to receive from its Muslim neighbours in the Middle East. In 1974, the Prime Minister addressed only one large public meeting, while most of 1975 was devoted to visiting a very large number of villages and small towns. This practice of avoiding large public gatherings in major cities in favour of several meetings in towns and villages was continued in 1976. Bhutto was now reacting to a decline in urban support, as well as attempting to build a new constituency for himself in rural Pakistan.

However, by the close of 1976, he began to think that he could once again broaden the base of his political support by appealing once again to urban groups. A number of economic, political and social developments seemed to suggest that the phase of PPP decay might well be over and that the party may be able to provide an umbrella under which several diverse political groups could gather once again as they had done in 1970.

In early 1977, the economic situation seemed very encouraging. The rate of inflation which averaged 25 per cent per annum from 1972/73 to 1974/75 had declined to a mere 6 per cent in 1975. After a number of years of stagnation, agricultural output had increased significantly: the wheat harvest in the spring of 1976 set a new record of 8·6 million tons. Largely on account of the good performance of the agricultural sector, the rate of GNP increase also picked up from the sluggish 2 per cent growth of the period 1971/72 to 1974/75 to nearly 4 per cent during the 1974/75 to 1975/76. The large number of skilled and semi-skilled workers who had migrated to the oil-rich countries in the Middle East since 1973 had now begun to remit their earnings to their families back in Pakistan. In the financial year ending 30 June 1976, those remittances amounted to $500 million or nearly one-third of the total foreign exchange earnings of Pakistan. Most of this went to a few districts in Northern Punjab and Western Frontier Province that had contributed the bulk of the migrants to the Middle East. The Prime Minister was, of course, not oblivious of the political significance of this sudden surge in the prosperity of these areas, especially since the PPP had managed to gain little support in them in the elections of 1970. Three times during 1975/76 he visited the villages and towns in these districts, reminding the people that they owed 'their good fortune to the shrewd foreign and economic policies pursued by his regime'.[8] As 1976 came to a close, the economic situation looked propitious to Bhutto and provided him with some good reason for rushing into another election.

A leadership conscious of the long-term impact of the structural changes that it had introduced would have reached a different conclusion. It would not have been swayed by the good performance by the economy during one year. As it turned out, 1976 proved to be an exceptional year in which good weather and a favourable international climate had overcome the difficulties the economy was facing on account of the structural changes to which it had been subjected. The indices that the government had relied upon to form a favourable judgement about the health of the economy simply masked a number of severe problems that it faced. A different set of numbers showing the trends in the rate and direction of investment; the inability of the large and growing public sector to generate from within the resources required for investment; the persistence of high levels of deficit financing; the deterioration in the ratio of capital to output; the high rate of unemployment, especially among the educated; the failure of the rate of fertility to decline from high levels despite heavy investment by the state in family planning programmes, etc. – these would all have provided the Prime Minister with a different picture of the economy. Not only was the economy facing a number of structural difficulties, it also had to cope with a series of unanticipated setbacks. Three large government-owned cement factories had to shut down because of mechanical problems, resulting in a decline of 5 per cent in the output of cement. This affected the construction industry: the price of cement increased by more than 50 per cent in a year, forcing a number of large construction companies to suspend their operations and lay-off workers. The potential of the large earth-filled dam on the Indus at Tarbela was not being fully realised because of the differences between the provinces of the Punjab and Sind on a formula for distributing the water in the Tarbela reservoir. Some 2·5 million acre-feet of water – more than a quarter of the addition made to Tarbela to the irrigation system – was lost to the Arabian Sea in 1976. The dam itself continued to face problems; two of its tunnels were damaged in 1974 but the repairs carried out did not prove to be entirely adequate. The problems that resulted from the government nationalisation of 'agrarian businesses'; the problems being faced by the textile industry, the largest single employer in the manufacturing sector; the shortage of cement and the resulting problems in the construction industry; and the failure of Tarbela to deliver the planned supplies of water and power could be expected to affect the economy. The economy had performed well in 1976; it was not expected to do well in 1977, the year chosen by

Bhutto for going back to the polls for a fresh mandate. This turned out to be a correct expectation: the main indices of economic performance, announced by the government on 30 June 1977, only five days before the military assumed power, showed that 1976/77 was the worst of Bhutto's six years (see Table 8.1). The output of the industrial sector declined by 1 per cent. There was a 3 per cent decrease in the rate of growth of the output of the services sector, a sector that had been remarkably buoyant during the first half of the 1970s. Agriculture's recovery from the 1974/75 slump also slackened, with the rate of growth in output down to 3·3 per cent compared to 4·5 per cent during the previous year. The net result was that in 1976/77 the gross domestic product was less than one percentage point higher than the previous year. Since the population had grown by 3 per cent, average income had declined by more than 2 per cent.

TABLE 8.1   Growth rates at constant 1959/60 factor cost (annual rate %)

	1970/71–1971/72	1971/72–1972/73	1972/73–1973/74	1973/74–1974/75	1974/75–1975/76	1975/76–1976/77
GDP	0·95	7·03	6·84	1·94	3·80	0·83
Agriculture	3·47	1·67	4·18	−2·12	4·45	3·26
Industry	−1·86	9·45	6·63	−0·59	0·18	−0·91
Services	5·05	5·23	5·45	5·65	5·74	−2·94

Source: Computed from Government of Pakistan, *Pakistan Economic Survey, 1976–77* (Islamabad: Finance Division, 1977), Table 5, pp. 10–11, Statistical Annex.

For a government seeking a new mandate from the people, the downward trend that the economy resumed after 1976 was, of course, politically significant. Even more significant was the fact that a number of important groups had lost confidence in the economy's future or the regime's ability to manage it. The extremely adverse reaction to the government's nationalisation of wheat, rice and cotton processing units had surprised Bhutto; while the move had been supported by the landlords, it had caused a great deal of resentment among the small business interests. The grain millers and cotton ginners were an important source of production capital for the farmers, especially those with smallholdings. In fact, the very poor cotton crop of 1976 – with output down by more than one-third compared to previous years

– could be attributed in part to the nationalisation of the processing units. The sharp reduction in the output of lint cotton and the failure of the textile owners to modernise their units caused a deep recession in the textile industry. For the first time in the industry's history, there was a decline in the number of workers hired. Also for the first time in the textile industry's history, the output of cloth and yarn declined – that of cloth from 550 to 440 million square metres – causing a serious upward pressure on the price of a basic commodity. The government's emphasis on large-scale projects had diverted resources from those that could have helped to absorb labour from the growing pool of unemployed. Small businessmen, middle-class farmers, industrial labour, the urban unemployed and urban poor had all supported Bhutto and the PPP in 1970. Now they found themselves being badly hurt by the regime's economic policies; some by the rise in prices of basic consumer goods, some by the inability of the economy to provide the jobs they needed and for which they had trained, some by a sharp erosion in the profits they managed to obtain from their modest enterprises. With the exception of the urban poor, all the other groups were to join first the Pakistan National Alliance (PNA), the organisation that was to spread its umbrella over nine opposition parties, and later to support the movement that eventually sent Bhutto out of power.

This wide gap between Bhutto's perception of the state of the economy and economic reality was due in large measure to the institutional collapse that occurred during the latter part of his rule. The analytical capability that was created in several parts of the government during the Ayub period was quickly dissipated under Bhutto. As discussed in Chapter 7 above, the style of economic management adopted by the Prime Minister during the 1974–6 period, reduced the role of the Planning Commission as well as its capacity to offer advice to the political decision-makers. It should also be recalled that in the late 1960s the Planning Commission's Chief Economist had warned Ayub of the problems that his model of development had created for the economy and the society. No similar warning was issued to Bhutto when he was about to take the most important decision of his political career.

Institutional failure was also responsible for the distorted signals Bhutto received from the political area. As on the economic side, he could draw comfort from a number of developments that seemed to indicate that he might have consolidated his position among some powerful political groups. The departure of the left from the Cabinet and later from the party had weakened considerably the Prime Minister's position in most of the large urban centres, particularly in the provinces of Sind and the Punjab. Bhutto attempted to compensate for this loss by winning the admiration and possibly also the support of several important groups in the small towns and villages. In this effort he was helped by the remarkable wave of prosperity that spread through a large number of villages in Northern Pakistan when a massive capital flow from the Middle East began to produce an economic impact. The economic situation in the large cities was considerably less comfortable, a fact that began to be successfully exploited for political advantage by the left. Mubashir Hasan now began to organise the left into a new 'socialist bloc', not so much to oppose Bhutto, but to save him 'from the corrupting influence of the reactionaries who are now wanting to climb onto the PPP bandwagon'.[9]

Bhutto reacted by appealing to a sentiment that he knew had considerable hold over large sections of the urban population. In the spring of 1976, he convened a meeting of the heads of state of the Muslim world. The meeting was held at Lahore, the centre of leftist politics in Pakistan and, from Bhutto's point of view, it was a remarkable success. Not only did his domestic and foreign policies receive endorsement from the monarchs of the Arab world, they also won praise from such Arab radicals as Gaddafi of Libya and Mohammad Assad of Syria. The Islamic Summit was followed by an invitation to the Imams of the mosques at Medina and Ka'ba – the two holiest places of Islam – to visit Pakistan: 'The dignitaries visited, led prayers, and warmed the hearts of the faithful in major cities.'[10] Later the government sponsored an international conference on the life and work of the Prophet Mohammad. This catering to Islamic sentiment was expected to generate support for Bhutto and the 'new' PPP; it was also expected to balance the erosion in the Prime Minister's political base that occurred after he lost the support of the PPP left.

Recognising that the support of college and university students would be crucial for the success of any effort by the ultra left to regain power, Bhutto made a number of attempts to cultivate the students. Those attempts included a programme of 'cultural education'[11] in some of the more important educational institutions as well as the co-option of a number of student leaders by the

Ministry of Education and Culture to 'provide the right political content to the emerging educational priorities of the regime'.[12] The fact that the campuses remained quiet during 1975 and 1976 seemed to suggest that Bhutto had succeeded in preventing a coalition from emerging between the students and the ultra left.

A number of other developments also seemed to have strengthened Bhutto's political position. The 'dissidents' in Baluchistan had been contained by the army; the National Awami Party, the political group that had been most effective in opposing Bhutto, had been dissolved after the Supreme Court's decision that it represented a threat to Pakistan's integrity; the efforts of two groups in the Punjab – the rightists under Mustafa Khar and the urban socialites under Hanif Ramay – to challenge the Prime Minister in the Punjab had been successfully thwarted; the feuding landlords in the province of Sind had been made to accept the discipline of the PPP; and, from Bhutto's perspective by far the most important development, the entrance into the political arena of the Pir of Pagaro, the respected religious leader of Sind,[13] did not seem to have eroded the Prime Minister's base of support in the villages of his home province.

The jettisoning of the socialists, the attempts to separate the ultra left from the students, the dissolution of the National Awami Party and the incarceration of most of its important leaders, and Bhutto's break with such close associates as Mustafa Khar and Haneef Ramay were all important events that occurred within a short period of two years. He could not have been certain about the impact of these developments, especially when he did not have the institutions that could provide him with adequate feedback. The cell structure that was being created within the PPP to take the place of the system of local government that had been created by Ayub Khan was still not operational. Quick changes in party personnel at the district level had produced a great deal of confusion about the direction the PPP was now taking.

While the political situation seemed sufficiently placid on the surface for the Prime Minister to risk another election, it was full of uncertainties that needed time to be resolved. Bhutto was in the process of completely changing his constituency. While the strength of the old constituency had been tested in 1970, that of the new one was totally unknown. And yet, Bhutto decided to go to the polls much earlier than required by the Constitution of 1973. The content as well as the tone of the scores of speeches that he delivered all over the country in the year preceding the election suggest that he was seeking a new mandate from the people to 'rebuild Pakistan's economic, political and social institutions on new foundations: foundations that were to be fashioned from materials available locally and not from those imported from the outside':[14]

In 1970, I promised you democracy. In 1973, I gave you democracy. You asked for participation at all levels of decision-making. I provided you with that opportunity. I not only asked you to participate in the decisions I took, I also asked your permission when I took the decisions that affected all of us. You allowed me to send Mujibur Rahman home; you permitted me to go to Simla to discuss peace with Madame Gandhi; you let me go to the countries of the Middle East to seek their help in our hour of need. You and I have trusted each other, worked together. We understand each other. But there are people in this country that don't approve of our association. These people have attempted to put obstacles in our way; to stop us from building a new Pakistan. They can do this because we have allowed them to do so. Should we continue to permit them this freedom? Mustn't we change the rules of the game so that our progress towards a new and dynamic Pakistan is not continuously thwarted.[15]

This speech, delivered at Charsadda, a small town in the North-west Frontier Province, contained an important message. The message was repeated in a number of other addresses, all delivered before small audiences in small towns and villages all over Pakistan. Bhutto was not satisfied with the economy's response to the changes that he had introduced in its management, structure and direction of growth;[16] he was not happy with the small-power status to which Pakistan had been reduced even amongst the countries of the Third World;[17] and he was not content with the political system that still made it possible for the groups in opposition to question both his purpose and his method.[18] Despite the heavy commitment of resources by the public sector to a number of ambitious industrial and infrastructural projects, Pakistan remained economically backward even by the standards of the Third World. Its industrial capacity and social infrastructure were much inferior to those of neighbouring India and Iran.

The rapid pace of economic modernisation that Bhutto witnessed during his many trips to the Middle East made him acutely aware of the secondary position to which Pakistan had been reduced in its part of the world. Seeing all this, Bhutto came to the conclusion that the country needed a new set of political and economic institutions that would help it to keep pace with its neighbours.

But the Prime Minister fully recognised that he was now embarking on a path that was completely different from the one he and his associates had advocated in 1970. The PPP manifesto for the elections of 1970 promised to reintroduce democratic institutions into Pakistan in which the people's 'voice will be heard at all levels of the government'.[19] The speeches by Bhutto and his colleagues repeatedly referred to the concentration of power that had occurred during the Ayub period. From this the people, in particular the middle classes, understood that the PPP was committed to the restoration of democracy in the country of the type that had been promised by the British in 1935 and practised by the Indians ever since 1947. However, after the PPP came to power and the debate over the new constitutional structure for Pakistan started once again,

> Mr. Bhutto's preferences for 'vice-royal system' or 'presidential dictatorship' [became] well known. . . . His political opponents, particularly the chief of the National Awami Party, Wali Khan, accused him of having 'dictatorial powers'. Mr. Bhutto, according to Wali, wanted both a '21-gun salute' and 'powers of a Prime Minister'.[20]

But, as discussed in the earlier chapters, the 1973 Constitution was accepted by the opposition only after Bhutto had agreed to temper the quasi-presidential system that he wanted to introduce by including some semblance of control by the national assembly on the exercise of power by the Prime Minister.

Bhutto's speeches in the year preceding the elections of March 1977 indicated that he was not satisfied with the Constitution of 1973 and the constraints that it imposed on the executive. The Charsadda speech quoted above is a good reflection of his unhappiness with the system that he himself had helped to create in 1973. In later speeches he was to elaborate upon its deficiencies, sometimes referring to the systems being operated in other countries as illustrations of the rewards that Pakistan could not obtain from its own. Thus, in Sibi, a small town in Baluchistan, Bhutto talked about the

> tremendous advance made in the countries in the Middle East and in the countries in the Pacific because the administrations there were free to act without being inhibited by a handful of people of the type who have used the excuse of parliamentary democracy to stop me, my administration and my people from making similar progress in Pakistan.[21]

In a speech at Pattoki, an agricultural market town fifty miles from Lahore, the Prime Minister held the opposition responsible for Pakistan's economic and social backwardness: 'We have remained backward because we have had to preserve the civil and legal rights of a small minority in Pakistan at the cost of advancing the economic conditions of the vast majority of its people.'[22] And at Khairpur, a small town of less than 20,000 in Sind, Bhutto told his audience that it had been a mistake for him to accept in 1973 'the system that protected the privileges of the few at the expense of the rights of the many'.[23] Finally, at Gilgit, a small army-cum-trading outpost in the mountainous areas of Northern Pakistan he accused his opponents of

> constraining him in the name of liberty and democracy – concepts that only a few people understand in a nation as poor as Pakistan and from which fewer could expect to benefit – from providing the people with what they needed most, freedom from hunger, freedom from want and freedom from constant deprivation.[24]

The message from these and scores of other speeches was loud and clear. Bhutto was going back to the people to seek a mandate for bringing about a change in the country's political and con-stitutional structure. He was certain that such a change would be resisted by the 'city people' – a term he used repeatedly in his speeches in a derogative sense – but would be supported by the people in small towns and villages. Since three-quarters of Pakis-tan's population in 1977 was still in small towns and villages he was confident that his message would be heard sympathetically by the majority of the people. And, as 1976 came to a close, he did not find any serious economic or political problem that could

divert the attention of the majority to which he was now appealing. He needed a new mandate from the people and March 1977
seemed a good time to seek it.

BHUTTO'S CLASH WITH THE MIDDLE CLASS

Bhutto had sensed correctly that his efforts to change the constitutional structure would be opposed by the middle class. But in
January 1977, when he announced the date for the general
elections, he was confident that he could overcome this opposition
by appealing directly to the classes who had either benefited from
the various reforms and changes in the economic, social and
political system introduced by his regime or who were attracted to
him because of his remarkable charisma. These people, Bhutto
was convinced, greatly outnumbered the middle class. He was
also confident that his opponents would not be able to put
together an organisation that could effectively oppose the government party. When the opposition parties managed to form a
coalition of nine disparate groups, Bhutto dismissed it by calling
the Pakistan National Alliance 'a cat with nine tails'.[25]

But the PNA proved to be more than a marriage of conveni-
ence. Under the PNA umbrella gathered a number of important
social and economic groups that had suffered in one way or
another from the various actions of the PPP government. These
groups that, taken together, constituted the Pakistani middle
class, had been badly hurt by a number of economic, social and
administrative reforms instituted by the PPP during the phase
when the decision-making apparatus had been dominated by the
left. The middle class had been hurt by the economic reforms that
resulted in the transfer of incomes from them to the low income
groups and also by the education policy that resulted in the
government's take-over of the institutions that had specifically
catered to their needs. The restructuring of the administrative
system deprived them of employment opportunities in a sector
that had been their more or less exclusive preserve for a long time
and to which they had access on the basis of merit. The new
administrative structure that began to evolve under Bhutto put a
great deal of premium on political connections and political
loyalty towards the regime. In addition to all this, the middle class
was greatly troubled by what it perceived as a serious deterioration in the law-and-order situation in the country. The departure

of the left from the PPP in 1974 resulted in a restructuring of the party's organisation. One result of this reorganisation was the delegation of some authority to 'district chairmen', who could now influence decision-making by such district-level officials as Deputy Commissioners, in charge of general administration; District Magistrates; Superintendents of Police, responsible for maintaining law and order; Executive Engineers, in charge of the irrigation and road systems in the districts; District Food Officers, responsible for procuring and distributing foodgrains; District Forest Officers; and District Health Officers. Ayub Khan's system of Basic Democracies had introduced an element of political control over these officials by making them responsible to District Councils. The PPP district chairmen exercised control over them without the benefit of any formal arrangement. And since their authority was not formalised, it was at times exercised capriciously without due regard to the rules and procedures that guided the conduct of business by the various parts of the bureaucracy. Accordingly, one critic of the government described the situation that prevailed in the spring of 1977 as follows:

> Justice is no longer a matter of right. It is a matter of accident notwithstanding the elaborate judicial farce. All your rights are suspended and there is no hope that the rulers are ever likely to revive them. All laws are meant only for the convenience of the rulers and to mislead the world. Any law which a citizen can invoke in his defence or for his protection is quickly changed.[26]

This frustration with the law-and-order situation was reflected in the judgement delivered against Bhutto in the murder case under which he was to be tried later by the Punjab High Court:

> According to tradition *amarat* [government] is a trust. The correct rule of law in Islam is much more progressive than the same concept in the modern world. There is, however, similarity to the extent that all governmental authorities are bound by law and are required to act according to law. This principle is the sheet-anchor of our Constitution which specifically provides in its fourth Article that to enjoy the protection of law and to be treated in accordance with law is the inalienable right of every citizen and in particular no action detrimental to the life of a person shall be taken except in accordance with law.[27]

The High Court held that, as the Chief Executive of the administration, it was especially incumbent upon the Prime Minister to
uphold the principle of law:

> Before presuming his ability to guarantee to the citizens the
> enjoyment of the protection of law and their treatment in
> accordance with law he should be a believer and a true adher-
> ent of law. He should consider himself to be as much subject to
> law as he would wish others to be. A person who considers the
> Constitution and the law as the handmaid of his polity is
> neither qualified to be elected to the high office of the Prime
> Minister nor can he be true to his oath.[28]

The Lahore High Court, was, of course, satisfied that Bhutto did
not consider 'himself to be as much subject to law as he would
wish others to be',[29] a belief that played an important part in the
court's decision to impose the death sentence on the Prime
Minister.

Not satisfied with the law-and-order situation that prevailed in
the country even when the 1973 Constitution was operative, the
middle class could not be complacent about the prospect of
further restrictions on their rights and their freedom. Bhutto and
the PPP were aware of the middle class's fears and a section in the
party's 1977 election manifesto addressed itself directly to these
problems and fears:

> The maintenance of law and order today is a world-wide
> problem. It is particularly acute in developing countries which
> are experiencing rapid socio-economic change accompanied by
> a population explosion. In our case, the situation has been
> made more difficult by the fact that previous Governments
> allowed the old colonial structure of the police force to continue
> unchanged.[30]

In other words, the Bhutto government put the blame for the
deterioration of law and order on the forces of change that were
affecting all developing countries. Pakistan, according to this
interpretation, was not in a unique situation. In addition, the PPP
suggested that the institutions that Pakistan had inherited from
colonial rule could not handle the dynamics of the change that
was taking place everywhere in the world. These archaic institu-

tions had been preserved by the governments that had held power in Pakistan prior to Bhutto's PPP because they were representative of the groups that had a vested interest in the maintenance of the *status quo*. In light of all this, the middle class could draw little solace from the manifesto's statement that 'we will take additional steps to ensure the individual the security which is essential to a life of quality'.[31] The Prime Minister's speeches clearly pointed the direction in which the changes were to proceed. They made it clear that Bhutto wanted fairly fundamental changes in the structure of the Constitution. But in order to make these changes, he wanted a clear mandate from the people: a mandate not so much in terms of 'testing his popularity as of restoring his control over the country'. Understanding this, the middle class prepared itself for making it difficult for the Prime Minister to change 'the rules of the game'. The 1977 election gave it the opportunity to challenge Bhutto and the PPP. There was too much at stake for the middle class not to take the election very seriously.

The middle class's disenchantment with Ayub Khan's economics reinforced Bhutto's remarkable charisma in winning him and the PPP victory in the elections of 1970. For the elections of 1977, Bhutto went to the polls without support from large segments of the middle class, in particular from those several groups that had been hurt by his economic reforms, his style of economic management and his party's inability to structure a political system that would have brought the middle class actively into decision-making roles.

In addition the threat of further changes in the system that they already disliked made these groups intensely nervous about a continuation of PPP rule.

In 1970, another class of supporters had been attracted to Bhutto by his socialist leanings and the close ties that he had cultivated during the Ayub years. These were mostly intellectuals from the large urban centres of the Punjab and Sind provinces. In economic terms, they also belonged to the middle class. When Bhutto purged his Cabinet of the socialist elements, he lost the support of this segment of the middle class, too.

These two middle-class segments, who together had formed the vanguard of the PPP movement in the late 1960s and won Bhutto an impressive victory in the elections of 1970, had given the party and its chairman a progressive image. As I argued in Chapter 3 above, it was this image that attracted a wide variety of supporters to Bhutto and the People's Party. They included such social groups as intellectuals in the large cities; urban professionals such as doctors, college and school teachers, university and school students, engineers and government workers. They also included such economic interests as the organised labour in large-scale industries, small merchants and businessmen in large and small cities, and middle-class farmers. Among his supporters, Bhutto could also count those groups who wanted to free themselves from the political hold of such traditional elements as *pirs*, *maulvis*, and *ulemas* (religious leaders of various types); heads of *biradaris* and clans; and large landlords. In 1970, these groups were especially important for Bhutto in the rural areas.

These three sets of groups saw Bhutto and the PPP wielding a modernising influence on the political, social and economic development of Pakistan. The first and third groups saw Bhutto liberating the society from the archaic influence of the traditional elements which had begun to dominate Pakistan when the new country's politics and economics, starting with mid-1950s, came to be gradually indigenised. A number of people within this segment of the PPP's supporters expected Bhutto to bring liberal political and social institution to Pakistan. The left, which was at that time the predominant voice among the big city supporters of Bhutto, read the PPP message differently. It saw the PPP taking Pakistan on a road to political development completely different from the one it had traversed during the British *raj*. There was no clear definition of this course; there were, in fact, remarkable differences among the various socialists represented in the PPP as to the nature of the political structure that was to be created in 'New Pakistan'.[32] But there was agreement on one thing: that Pakistan's new constitutional structure will not be built on the Westminster model. The economic interests that gathered under the wing of the PPP expected to be relieved of the competition of the large industrialists, merchants and farmers who had come to dominate the decision-making apparatus during the latter half of the Ayub era. But these interests, while supporting the PPP's resolve to nationalise large-scale industries and to introduce lower ceilings on land holdings, did not wish or expect a diminished role for the private sector. They did not favour any form of state capitalism; they campaigned only for the elimination of big enterprises who, because of their size, could wield a perverse influence on decision-making. Finally, the PPP supporters in the rural areas expected once again to be put into the positions of influence that they had occupied in the Ayub Khan's system of Basic Democracies but which they lost to the traditional elements after 1965.

There is no way that Bhutto could have reconciled such diverse and, at times, conflicting interests. It was obvious that once he gained power and began to give shape to the deliberately vague promises in the election manifesto the PPP had prepared for the 1970 elections, some of these groups would be disappointed. In fact, some of the earlier defections from the party – such as those of Mahmud Ali Kasuri, Ahmad Raza Kasuri and Miraj Moham-mad Khan – were interpreted in this sense. However, as I attempted to show in this chapter and in Chapter 7, most of the important economic and political decisions taken during the two phases of PPP rule – 1972–4, when the process of decision-making was dominated by the left, and 1974–7, when Bhutto took full command of policy-making – were not aimed at helping any of the more important parts of Bhutto's large middle-class constituency. The Pakistan that emerged in 1977 was not the Pakistan that the various elements that constituted the politically important middle class had wanted to shape. At the time that Bhutto decided to go back to the polls, he had been abandoned by the social, economic and political groups that made up the Pakistani middle class.

SHAPING A NEW CONSTITUENCY

From the manner in which Bhutto prepared himself for the 1977 election, it is clear that he understood that the most important challenge to a continuation of his rule would come from the middle class. He adopted two different tactics to prepare himself for this challenge. First, he sought to broaden the base of his support by cultivating elements from both the upper and lower classes. Second, he attempted to prevent the emergence of a viable coalition among the political parties that represented the various middle-class interests.

Although the available evidence about income distribution changes during the Bhutto period suggests some deterioration, this should not be taken to mean further impoverishment of the poor. In fact, this deterioration may well be a reflection of the decline in the share of middle-level incomes in national wealth.

While hard data on the shares of income of various groups of people is not of the necessary quality to allow one to arrive at a reliable judgement of the exact nature of the change in fortune of these groups under Bhutto, there is little doubt that the middle classes saw a definite worsening in their situation and the urban poor some improvement in their positions. In politics, perceptions can be more important than reality and, for our purpose, it would suffice to note that the poor, particularly in the large cities and in those parts of the rural areas that benefited from the remittances sent home by the migrants to the Middle East, saw a change for the better in their economic situation during the Bhutto period.[33] In several pre-election issues *Nusrat*, the PPP news magazine, carried interviews with people who represented a 'wide segment of the population that had benefited from the reforms instituted by the Prime Minister'. Mazhar Ali Khan, the editor of the left-orientated Lahore weekly *Viewpoint* and no admirer of Bhutto, claimed that 'by and large the working class continue to support him because they benefited in his regime. At the cost of all other economies, Bhutto skilfully manipulated mass loyalty'.[34] Even in those cases in which direct intervention by the state to aid the poor failed to deliver intended benefits to the target population, the poor tended to blame the privileged groups for obstructing the flow of goods and services to them. They credited the government with taking the initiatives but held the middle and upper classes responsible for the failure of the several programmes. In a country in which nearly one-half of the population could be classified as 'absolute poor', and in a political system based, at least in theory, on one-man-one-vote this strategy made a great deal of sense. But, as I will argue later, the system could not be expected to work in an environment in which a wide chasm had developed between the interests of the poor and the middle class.

As indicated above, Bhutto concentrated a great deal of attention on small towns and villages in the year preceding the elections of 1977. The reason for this was once again political arithmetic; the bulk of the poor lived not in the large cities, but in the rural and semi-urban areas. Recognising the influence of the left on the poverty groups in the large cities, Bhutto made little attempt to cultivate their support. This was a major change from the strategy that was pursued during the 1970 election campaign.

As has already been said, following the departure of the PPP left from the Cabinet in October 1974, Bhutto brought the landed interests into the party as well as the administration. He used these groups to help him reach the rural poor, an approach that worked well in the districts that remained socially and economically backward. In districts such as Mianwali, Sargodha, Dera Ghazi Khan, Muzzafargarh, Bahawalpur, Bhawalnagar and Rahim Yar Khan in the Punjab and in the 'Indus West Bank' districts of the province of Sind, the landlords continued to retain considerable social, political and economic influence over the rural population:

> This is not to say that the things have not changed since Ayub Khan's land reforms and as a result of the policies initiated by the Bhutto regime to socially modernize the rural society. These policies had a tremendous impact on the rural areas. They changed the aspirations of the rural people. But it also changed our approach toward the poor. The poor needed a buffer between themselves and the very large bureaucratic structure that emerged under Bhutto. We provided such a buffer. They also needed a channel between themselves and the bureaucracy. We provided such a channel. In return, we kept their votes. There was a change in the relationship of the landlords and the peasants but both were satisfied with the direction of change. The rural middle class did not understand this.[35]

A structure in which the landed interests were the main pillars of support was very different from the one Bhutto and his socialists had erected in the late 1960s. In 1970, the PPP was a party that promised change and modernisation; in 1977, it was a party that sought to preserve the *status quo*. The 1970 manifesto pointing out that 'feudalism as an economic and political force was a formidable obstacle to progress', promised 'to destroy the power of the feudal land owners'.[36] The manifesto for the 1977 election claimed that the party

> had kept this pledge by taking a series of measures in the course of the past five years, including a drastic reduction in the ceilings of land holdings. Together they have brought an end to feudalism in Pakistan and ushered in a new era of progress and prosperity for our rural society.[37]

While Pakistan in 1977 was not a feudal society, the process of eliminating feudalism had begun in 1959, with the land reform of Ayub Khan. The two Bhutto reforms carried the process further, reducing the feudal landlord's hold over the rural areas without seriously destroying his economic and political power. By 1977, the landed aristocracy's power in the countryside did not rest on the traditional feudal links but on the links that had been formed between it and the peasantry on the basis of mutual interests.

Bhutto's dependence on the landed interests was demonstrated by the selection of candidates the PPP was to support in the election of 1977. The Noons and Tiwanas of Sargodha, the Maliks of Mianwali, the Qureshis of Multan, the Hayats of Rawalpindi and Campbellpur, the Legharis and Mazaris of Dera Ghazi Khan were back in the political arena as PPP candidates. Some sections of the opposition interpreted this large-scale induction of old landed families into the PPP as a part of an effort by the chairman, Bhutto, to lend an aura of respectability to the party:[38]

> Mr. Bhutto might have easily calculated that bringing forward the old wealthy families might be a good idea . . . they are not corrupt in the ordinary sense, they are not *goondas* (lawless) and, politically docile, they will be as loyal to the regime as they were to Ayub and their fathers and forefathers were to the government of the day. It is sheer pragmatism that has dictated Mr. Bhutto's choice.[39]

According to this view, by bringing back familiar names and faces into his government, Bhutto could perhaps win over some sections of the middle class that he had lost to the opposition because of their dislike of the way the middle-ranking leadership in the PPP had treated the country's legal and judicial system.

The landlords and their supporters retained power in the districts of the Punjab and Sind, which together did not account for more than 30 per cent of the population. The PPP could not build a victory on the basis of this support. Somehow, it had to attract some urban support. The way Bhutto approached the urban electorate suggests that he was not unaware of the unhappiness of the middle class with some of his policies. He was also aware that without the support of the urban left he could not expect to see unionised labour back in the PPP camp. Accordingly, he focused his attention on the large but unorganised working class. As discussed above, this class had retained confidence in Bhutto. If it was not pleased with the results of the administration's policies, it did not hold Bhutto or his party responsible. The support of these 'urban marginals' was even more important for Bhutto than that of the rural poor. By attending the PPP's rallies in large numbers they gave the impression of a mass following behind Bhutto – an impression that had a deep political significance.

It was with this new constituency of the landed aristocracy, the rural poor and the urban marginals that Bhutto and the PPP approached the election of 1977. That the constituency was new is vividly illustrated by the fact that the PPP slate for the elections did not include 40 out of the 100 PPP members of the old National Assembly. Of the discarded members two had been Ministers in the Cabinet.

By placing himself and his new constituency in the middle of the Pakistani political constituency, Bhutto attempted to divide his opposition into at least two halves: those to the right of the PPP and those to its left. If the 1970 experience was any guide, it could be comfortably predicted that even the left and the right would find it difficult to coalesce into solid blocs. But

> this time [Bhutto] seems to have been had. The opposition shrewdly projected an image of disunity. . . . Assured that the squabbling opposition would never coalesce against his PPP, he announced the election dates. Two days later, the opposition announced the nine-party Pakistani National Alliance.[40]

The nine opposition parties that merged to form the PNA included groups from both the left and the right. Mian Tufail Muhammad's *Jamaat-i-Islami*, Maulana Mufti Mahmud's *Jamiatul-Ulema-e-Islam* and Maulana Shah Ahmed Noorain's *Jamiatul-Ulema-i-Pakistan* were Islamic parties, representing varying points of view regarding the conduct of the affairs of state on Islamic lines. Air-Marshal Asghar Khan's *Tehrik-i-Istiqlal*, Pir Pagaro's Pakistan Muslim League and Nawabzada Nasrullah Khan's Pakistan Democratic Party and Sardar Abdul Qayyum's Azad Kashmir Muslim Conference were essentially parties of the centre, advocating a return to parliamentary democracy and private enterprise. Sardar Sherbaz Mazari's National Democratic Party and Khan Mohammad Ashraf Khan's Khaksar Tehrik were parties of the left believing in some kind of state ownership of capital and decentralised government. The PNA

> grand alliance represented almost the entire spectrum of political thinking and ideologies in the country . . . though giving the impression of a united collective leadership, it was plagued by divided leadership, speaking different languages and subscribing to different, even divergent, ideologies.[41]

Despite these differences, the PNA remained united. It elected Nawabzada Nasrullah Khan as its president and Rafiq Bajwa as its secretary general.[42] And its leadership also managed to agree on a manifesto which on

> constitutional issues . . . stands on firmer ground. While the PPP holds that its five year rule has provided a stimulus to the growth of credible political institutions and stepped up the process of democratic evolution, the PNA is highly critical of the amendments which have disturbed the original balance between the Judiciary and the Executive.[43]

The PNA constituency was essentially a middle-class constituency making, as the government-controlled *Pakistan Times* editorialised, 'a desperate last-ditch attempt to stop the march of history'.[44] The PNA supporters could not allow history to march on the path that was being prepared by Bhutto and the PPP.[45]

9 The 1977 Elections

For forty-five days, the two political coalitions – the PPP representing the landed interests, rural poor and urban marginals and the PNA standing for the powerful middle class – fought what *The Economist* labelled as a campaign 'of whiskey, war and Islam'.[1] These were indeed the symbols of the confrontation that took place between the two different groups, each determined to impose its will on the other. The opposition's charge that Bhutto drank heavily and indulged in 'Bacchanalian orgies'[2] received the response from the Prime Minister that 'he drank wine, not people's blood'.[3] The PNA in charging the Prime Minister, was defending the middle class's values; Bhutto's riposte was meant to remind the opposition and the electorate that he stood for the poor. In the period since 1971 and largely because of the thorough restructuring of society, the Pakistani polity was now polarised. The changes Bhutto and the PPP had introduced had hurt a great many people. They had also benefited a large number. Those who had lost were determined to bring him down; those who had gained were equally resolved to keep him there. But, for the reasons discussed in Part II of the book, the configuration of social groups and economic interests on either side of the political divide was now completely different from the one in 1970.

The environment of polarisation in which the 1977 elections were contested is portrayed vividly by some electoral statistics. In 1970, 12 major parties had fielded a total of 801 candidates for the 138 seats that had been allocated to West Pakistan. This meant 5·8 candidates per seat. The 1977 election to the National Assembly drew only three major groupings into the electoral field, with 741 candidates for 200 seats. This meant only 3·7 candidates per National Assembly seat. The contrast is sharper if independent candidates are excluded. The vast majority of these 'independents' in 1970 and 1977 were essentially non-serious contenders using the elections to articulate little-known or appreciated causes. Excluding the 210 independents who participated in the 1970 elections and 324 who took part in 1977, the candidate–seat ratios declines to 4:3 in 1970 and 2:1 in 1977. The electorate in 1970 could choose between four serious candidates. The 1977 election was an essentially 'either-or' affair: a battle between the sword, the PPP election symbol, and the plough, the symbol of the PNA.

The sword and the plough waged a vicious battle in which a score of people were killed and a few hundred injured.[4] But when the results were announced, the sword had won handsomely in three of the four provinces.

As shown in Table 9.1, the PPP won nearly four-fifths of the National Assembly seats. The PNA managed to win less than one-fifth, while the remainder went to the independents. In fact, the PPP success was even more impressive than the table suggests, since the eight independents from the 'tribal areas' were all quasi-PPP candidates. Following a tradition that went back to the British *raj*, when electoral politics was first introduced into this part of British India, tribal leaders, while not accepting party labels, were always expected to side with the ruling party. Counting the independents with the PPP winners gave the party 81·5 per cent of the National Assembly seats.

TABLE 9.1   Party positions in the 1977 elections

	PPP		PNA		Independent[1]		
Province	Seats won	% of total	Seats won	% of total	Seats won	% of total	Total
Punjab	107	93·0	8	7·0	–	–	115
Sind	32	74·4	11	25·6	–	–	43
NWFP	8	30·8	17	65·4	1	3·8	26
Baluchistan	7	100·0	–	–	–	–	7
Islamabad	1	100·0	–	–	–	–	1
Tribal areas	–	–	–	–	8	100·0	8
Total	155	77·5	36	18·0	9	4·5	200

[1] Independents include one seat won by the Quyum Muslim League in NWFP.
Source: Overseas Weekly Dawn (Karachi), 13 March 1977.

The PPP's popular support, in terms of the total number of votes cast for its candidates, was less overwhelming. It received 58 per cent of the votes against 35 per cent for the PNA. This was not as impressive as its performance in the election of 1970 when, in a field crowded with twelve major political parties, it obtained 39 per cent of the total votes cast. But this wide margin between the number of seats won and popular support is not unusual in parliamentary elections.

The results surprised all parties. The PNA lost in three of the four provinces. It won a majority of seats in only one major city, Karachi, but was roundly beaten in Lahore, Lyallpur, Hyderabad, Multan and Rawalpindi. The PPP's success in the Punjab, where it won 93 per cent of the seats surprised even the party's leadership. The *Pakistan Times*, the paper owned by the government's National Press Trust, admitted that the party had 'done even better than expected in the Punjab'. However, having expressed some surprise, the paper went on to say:

> As in 1970, the people of the Punjab have once again expressed their full confidence in Zulfikar Ali Bhutto, repudiating in no uncertain terms the *halva maulvis* [corrupt religious leaders] in particular, and *Islam pasands* [religious fundamentalists] in general. Many of the self-styled *quaids* [leaders] of Punjab have been rejected, particularly in Lahore where Malik Qasim, Chaudhry Rehmat Elahi and that economic wizard – Rafique Bajwa who was going to lower prices to the 1970 level – have been put in their place.[5]

The opposition and the newspapers supporting it were considerably less exultant: the weekly *Viewpoint* expressed surprise at the gap between the people's enthusiasm for the opposition during the election campaign and their overwhelming endorsement of the PPP candidates at the polls.[6] The Urdu language daily, *Nawa-i-waqt*, predicted that for the Prime Minister the post-election period would be a period not of triumph but of trial.[7] Bhutto was sensitive to the opposition's unease. In a press conference held the day after the elections he warned: 'If the opposition leaders took the law in their own hands and tried to subvert the Constitution and created agitation, in that case, the Government was quite capable of dealing with the situation.'[8]

Stunned by its defeat at the polls, the opposition first decided to boycott the provincial elections. Undaunted, Bhutto went ahead with the provincial polls, where the PPP once again won handsomely. On 11 March, a day after the election to the provincial assemblies, the PNA decided to go to the streets 'to protest against the widespread electoral fraud that had been perpetrated on the nation'.[9] This led to an impasse, with the PPP prepared to grant only minor irregularities and the PNA demanding fresh elections. Pakistan was then clearly headed for a major political upheaval 'One way to deal with this [impasse] would be to show a greater magnanimity towards the opposition than he has done before and to accept its demonstrations of displeasure before coaxing it back into the parliamentary arena,' advised *The Economist*.[10] But it was precisely the suspicion that they were not being coaxed into the parliamentary arena that prevented the opposition leaders from accepting the concessions that Bhutto began to offer in about mid-March. These concessions included an offer to lift the state of emergency under which Pakistan had been governed since the civil war of 1971, to ease restrictions on the press and to release political prisoners. The appointment of a new central Cabinet – 'a better set of men than the previous team'[11] – was also meant as a gesture of good-will towards the middle class, troubled as it was by what it saw as the collapse of the country's institutions during the pre-election period.

The agitation against Bhutto continued to mount; a clash between demonstrators and police in Lahore on 9 April during the visit there of the Prime Minister shifted its focus from the refugee-dominated cities in southern Sind to the large urban centres of the Punjab. The 9 April clash involved a large group of small shopkeepers from the main cloth market in Lahore and a company of the Federal Security Force, a para-military organisation that had been set-up by Bhutto to spare the armed forces from law-and-order maintenance duties.[12] This clash brought on to the streets the confrontation that had first taken place via the ballot box between two groups of people who represented very different interests. As the *Pakistan Times* had put it earlier, the forces that opposed Bhutto were now fighting a desperate last-ditch battle 'to stop the march of history'.[13] After nearly six weeks of agitation, Zulfikar Ali Bhutto imposed limited 'martial law' on 21 April. Karachi, Lahore, Hyderabad, three of the country's four largest cities, were placed under military control. The opposition's movement against him forced Bhutto to invite the military back into the political arena. But the army's appearance on the streets did not daunt the forces of opposition. 'If we surrender to Bhutto now,' the Pir of Pagaro told newspaper reporters in Lahore, 'we must suffer for all time. A little more suffering now at the present time would [however] guarantee a better future.'[14]

Having shown the stick, Bhutto again brought out carrots. These were offered to the opposition leaders – the more prominent of whom were now in jail – in a series of meetings that began in Rawalpindi. It was now the Prime Minister's turn to make a 'last-ditch effort to solve the country's political crisis':

> Bhutto's about turn – he had maintained that he wanted some of his Cabinet colleagues to meet the opposition to iron out some form of agreement before he intervened – was obviously sparked by the continuing stalemate, bloodshed and violence. He had an eye, too, on the country's economy, which has probably been the biggest loser in the anti-Government agitation. Indeed, even if a settlement is achieved, the damage already caused will exacerbate an already problematic economic situation.[15]

When the stalemate did not break, the Prime Minister called for a country-wide referendum to be held in mid-June to ask the electorate if he should continue in office. In making this offer, the Prime Minister 'opted for a course that could either propel him to new heights of power or put an end to his highly controversial political career'.[16] The opposition feared that the first of these two alternatives was the more likely one, for it would 'give Mr. Bhutto the opportunity to ditch the Constitution by which he now feels increasingly constrained'.[17] There was no place for a national referendum in the kind of constitutional system the opposition to Bhutto wanted Pakistan to follow. Victory at the referendum would have increased Bhutto's stature enormously. The opposition was not prepared to grant him this opportunity.

The impasse continued into the first week of July, when rumours began to spread that the PPP was preparing itself for street battles with the opposition. All through the movement against Bhutto, his supporters had stayed in the background. They did not directly challenge the opposition in the streets, possibly because the new Bhutto constituency was much more dispersed than the one he had used to challenge Ayub Khan in the late 1960s. The opposition, with its forces concentrated in the large urban areas, just as Bhutto had deployed his supporters in the large cities in the 1960s, found it much easier to mount, build and sustain the movement against the PPP.

On 5 July, General Zia ul Haq staged a bloodless *coup d'état*, displacing Bhutto and the PPP from the centre of Pakistani politics. Explaining his move in a nationwide broadcast, the general said that he believed that Bhutto's Pakistan People's Party and the nine-party Pakistan National Alliance were incapable of reaching a compromise. This failure to agree, he said, 'Would throw the country into chaos and the country would thus be plunged into a more serious crisis. This risk could not be taken. The army had, therefore, to act.'[18] Thus ended Pakistan's second experiment with civilian rule. The end was brought about by the dynamics of the processes that Bhutto initiated in the six years of his administration. My concluding argument is that the election that Bhutto called in March 1977 could not have averted the crisis that developed in the spring of that year. This conclusion needs a brief elaboration.

By the time the elections were called, Bhutto had lost the support of the bulk of the politically articulate electorate – the middle class. It was the political knowhow of this class, combined with the mass support that Bhutto had been able to build for himself, that had assured him victory in the elections of 1970. Elections as a device for political selection – and if the situation so demands, political succession – are a device that the middle class uses and understands. They are not so used or understood by the large mass of people who are at the fringes of the political arena. Elections can, therefore, lead to political development or political succession only when these two classes – the middle and the lower – work together towards achieving reconcilable goals. In 1946, the Muslim League's remarkable and unexpected victory in all parts of Muslim India was the product of such a coalition between the two classes. Jinnah's demand for the revival of Islam in the Indian sub-continent and the creation of a new Muslim state in the area were popular with the masses. The masses supported not only the Muslim League but helped the middle class that dominated the party to achieve its objectives within the legal and constitutional framework of the day. A similar coalition of the two classes of people made it possible for Bhutto and the PPP in West Pakistan and Mujibur Rahman and the Awami League in East Pakistan to use elections held within Yahya Khan's 'legal framework' order. In fact, in both cases, the coalition was powerful enough to thwart the efforts of other forces and to let the 1970 elections work towards their political and logical ends: the establishment of an independent Bengali state in East Pakistan and the establishment of popular civilian rule in West Pakistan.

But because of the fundamental changes that had occurred in Pakistan's polity and economy since the assumption of political control by Bhutto and the PPP in 1971, elections could not be expected to produce the results that either Bhutto or his opponents hoped for. No matter what results the elections produced, political tension was inevitable. The fact that the tension generated by the elections surprised Bhutto suggests that he had not fully understood the political dynamics of the situation that he had himself created. The type of mandate that he sought from the people could not be given to him by the political process that was now dominated by the social and political groups that opposed him. His continuing popularity with large segments of the population might – and did – get him votes in the elections and win him seats in the central and provincial legislatures, but they would not win him the power that he needed to introduce changes in the political and economic order. These changes the middle class did not approve. Inherent in the holding of the elections of 1977 was, therefore, a great conflict between Bhutto's political objective and the political means and processes available to him under the Constitution of 1973. The groups in the opposition in 1977 approved of the processes but disliked Bhutto's objectives. Accordingly, when Bhutto lost power on 5 July 1977, his Constitution remained in force. It was the only time in the political history of Pakistan, marked by so many coups and counter-coups, that the military retained the legal structure but displaced the politicians who had built it.

Although forced out of power in July 1977, Bhutto continued to dominate Pakistan's politics for another 21 months. For most of this period Bhutto remained in prison. His first incarceration was in the nature of 'protective custody' ordered by General Zia ul Haq to save him from the people's wrath 'in a political climate which is distinctly hostile to the former Prime Minister'.[19] But the political climate began to improve; on 17 July, less than two weeks after the *coup d'état*, Bhutto addressed a large meeting of his followers on the lawn of his improvised prison. The time for launching movements such as the one that had removed him was over, he declared: 'The time had come for a revolution'.[20] Released from custody soon afterwards, he hesitated only for a moment before advising his supporters that he would participate vigorously in the elections promised for October 1977 by the military regime.

His visits to Karachi and Lahore, the two principal cities of

Pakistan, attracted large crowds but 'irrespective of the continuing popularity . . . the local press, including some newspapers that
used to be almost lyrical in his praise, are daily discovering two or
more of his misdeeds'.[21] Freed from the shackles of government
control, the press displayed considerable enthusiasm in inves-
tigating the incidents of abuse of power during the Bhutto years.
These investigations resulted in a clamour for 'accountability', a
process that was begun with a case lodged in Lahore's High Court
that accused Bhutto of participating in a conspiracy to murder a
political opponent. The Court proceedings focused not only on
the criminal charge that was brought against the former Prime
Minister, but also dwelt at length on the way Bhutto had administered Pakistan during his years of stewardship. To help the debate
along, the Government published a number of White Papers
detailing his administration's misdeeds.[22] These investigations
and the people's reaction to them demonstrated vividly how
polarised Pakistan's society had become. The middle class response was articulated by General Zia: 'I said to him "Sir" – I still
called him that – "Sir, why have you done all these things, you
whom I respected so, you who had so much" and he only said that
I should wait and he would be cleared. It was very
disappointing.'[23] Bhutto's followers labelled the campaign
against the deposed Prime Minister as the vendetta of the social
classes that had suffered under him and promised that 'nothing
could avert their skinning'. This was a reference to the PPP's
manifesto for the October elections that resolved to 'skin alive the
capitalists and other property owners'.[24]

Bhutto's judgement that time would clear his name proved
wrong. The Lahore Court announced its verdict on 19 March
1978, finding him an 'arch culprit' in an ambush in November
1974, the object of which had been to kill Ahmad Raza Kasuri, a
one time political protégé turned opponent. The Court ordered
Bhutto's execution.

The execution of the sentence was delayed for over a year while
Bhutto's lawyers explored all possible legal avenues to save their
client's life. The final legal pronouncement came on 31 March
1979 when the country's Supreme Court refused to review their
earlier verdict. On 4 April 1979, Zulfikar Ali Bhutto was hanged
at the Rawalpindi jail.

Notes

NOTES TO PREFACE

1 See Samuel P. Huntington and Joan M. Nelson, *No Easy Choices* (Cambridge, Massachusetts: Harvard University Press, 1976) for a summary statement on the main findings of this group of scholars.
2 Shahid Javed Burki, 'Interest Group Involvement in West Pakistan's Rural Works Program', *Public Policy*, XIX, Winter 1971, pp. 167–206.

1 INTRODUCTION

1 Interview given to Oriana Fallaci and reproduced by her in her book, *Interview with History* (New York: Liveright Publishing Corporation, 1976), pp. 182–209. The quotation is from p. 209.
2 Soon after assuming office, Bhutto gave a number of interviews to foreign correspondents and Pakistani and foreign academics. In addition to the Oriana Fallaci interview (n. 1 above) for Bhutto's assessment of his political rivals, see also the book of an Indian journalist based mostly on his discussions with Bhutto; Dilip Mukerjee, *Zulfikar Ali Bhutto: Quest for Power* (Delhi: Vikas Publishing, 1972).
3 Zulfikar Ali Bhutto, *Political Situation in Pakistan* (Lahore: Pakistan People's Party, 1969), passim.
4 For the belief that Bhutto was serious in bringing back Western-style democracy to Pakistan see Anwar H. Syed, 'The Pakistan People's Party: Phases One and Two', in Lawrence Ziring, Ralph Braibanti and W. Howard Wriggins (eds), *Pakistan: The Long View* (Durham, N.C.: Duke University Press, 1977), pp. 70–116. This article is based in part on Professor Syed's interview with Bhutto. Also see, Zulfikar Ali Bhutto, *Let the People Judge* (Lahore: Pakistan People's Party, 1969) which is an impassioned defence against the charges levelled at him by General Mohammad Musa, Governor-General of West Pakistan (1967–9) and a confidant of Ayub's during the period after Bhutto's departure from the government.
5 Pakistan People's Party, *The Election Manifesto* (Lahore: Pakistan People's Party, 1970).
6 Zulfikar Ali Bhutto, *The Great Tragedy* (Karachi: Vision Publications, 1971).
7 The role of 'idiosyncratic element' in decision-making has received much greater attention in political history than in economic history. Erik Erikson, *Gandhi's Truth: On the Origins of Militant Non-Violence* (New York: W. W. Norton, 1969) is perhaps the best work on an Asian leader.

2 INSIDERS AND OUTSIDERS

1 For an analysis of the geographical distribution of the refugee population see Shahid Javed Burki, *Pakistan: A Demographic Report* (Washington, D.C.: Population Reference Bureau, 1973).

2 For a description of the system of administration introduced by Lord Lawrence in the Punjab, see Sir Charles Aitchison, *Lord Lawrence and the Reconstruction of India Under the Crown* (Oxford: Clarendon Press, 1916). Also see R. Bosworth Smith, *Life of Lord Lawrence* (New York: Charles Scribner, 1883), pp. 155–80.

3 Useful sources for a description of these relationships are J. M. Douie, *Land Settlement Manual* (Lahore: Government of West Pakistan, 5th rev. edn, 1960) and a number of village surveys published by the Punjab Board of Economic Inquiry. As an example of the village surveys see Randhir Singh and W. Roberts, *An Economic Survey of Kala Gaddi Thamman (Chak 73 G.B.): A Village in the Lyallpur District of the Punjab* (Lahore: Board of Economic Inquiry, Punjab, 1932).

4 The term 'little republics' was used originally by F. L. Brayne in *Better Villages* (London: Oxford University Press, 1938).

5 Khushwant Singh, *The Sikhs* (London: Allen & Unwin, 1953).

6 See Philip Mason's account in *A Matter of Honor: An Account of the Indian Army, its Officers and Men* (New York: Holt, Rinehart & Winston, 1974) for the role played by the soldiers recruited in the Punjab in helping to put down the mutiny of the *purbiyas* – the easterners.

7 Quoted in A. B. Rajput, *The Muslim League Yesterday and Today* (Lahore: Mohammad Ashraf, 1948), pp. 19–20.

8 For an account of the attitude of the large landed families towards the Pakistan movement see Azim Husain, *Fazl-i-Husain: A Political Biography* (Bombay: Longmans, 1946).

9 The best analysis to date of the mass migration of people that accompanied the partition of the Indian subcontinent in 1947 is to be found in Joseph B. Schectman, *Population Transfers in Asia* (New York: Hallsby Press, 1949), pp. 5–30. Also see Theodore P. Wright Jr., 'Indian Muslim Refugees in the Politics of Pakistan', *Journal of Commonwealth on Comparative Politics*, XII, March 1974, pp. 189–205.

10 Shahid Javed Burki, 'Migration, Urbanization and Politics in Pakistan' in W. Howard Wriggins and James F. Guyot (eds), *Population, Politics and the Future of Southern Asia* (New York: Columbia University Press, 1973), pp. 147–89.

11 The best modern account of the development of the irrigation system in the Punjab is in Aloys A. Michel, *The Indus Rivers: A Study of the Effects of Partition* (New Haven: Yale University Press, 1967), pp. 22–98.

12 Quoted in Jamiluddin Ahmad (ed.), *Speeches and Writings of Mr. Jinnah* (Lahore: Mohammad Ashraf, 1952), p. 153.

13 J. Russell Andrus and Azizali F. Mohammed, *The Economy of Pakistan* (Stanford: Stanford University Press, 1958), pp. 156–65.

14 See Shahid Javed Burki, 'Economic Decisionmaking in Pakistan' in Lawrence Ziring, Ralph Braibanti and W. Howard Wriggins (eds), *Pakistan: The Long View* (Durham, N.C.: Duke University Press, 1977), pp. 140–72 for an

analysis of economic decision-making during this period.

15 Despite its role in dividing India and founding the independent state of Pakistan, the Muslim League remains to be carefully studied as a political party. Some useful works are available dealing with the founding of the party and its development as a mass organisation. See A. B. Rajput, *Muslim League Yesterday and Today* (Lahore: Mohammed Ashraf, 1948) and Z. H. Zaidi, 'Aspects of the Development of Muslim League Policy', in C. M. Philips and Mary Doreen Wainwright (eds), *The Partition of India: Policies and Perspectives, 1935–1947* (Cambridge, Massachusetts: MIT Press, 1970), pp. 245–75.

16 Khalid B. Sayeed, 'The Personality of Jinnah and his Political Strategy' in Philips and Wainwright (eds), op. cit., pp. 276–93.

17 In counting the families who made up the landed aristocracy in the provinces of the Punjab, Sind and Baluchistan, I have relied on land records as maintained by the Land Administration Department. For an excellent historical survey of the big landed families of the Punjab see Lepel H. Griffin, *Chiefs and Families of Note in the Punjab* (Lahore: Superintendent of Government Printing, rev. edn, 1940). See also Sir Denzil Ibbetson, *Punjab Castes* (Lahore: Superintendent of Government of Printing, 1916), Hugh K. Tresvaskis, *The Land of the Five Rivers* (London: Oxford University Press, 1928) and Craig Baxter, 'The People's Party vs. the Punjab Feudalists' in J. Henry Korson (ed.), *Contemporary Problems of Pakistan* (Leiden: E. J. Brill, 1974), pp. 6–29.

18 For an expression of this view see Reginald Coupland, *The Indian Problem* (Clarendon: Oxford University Press, 1944); see also Khalid Bin Sayeed, *Pakistan: The Formative Phase* (London: Oxford University Press, 1968), p. 224. Sayeed suggests that the landlords with 163 out of 503 members of the Muslim League Council constituted the largest and the most influential interest group within the party.

19 For a good but somewhat biased account of the role played by Nazimuddin in Bengali politics, in particular the way it related to the Pakistan movement, see Kamruddin Ahmad, *The Social History of East Pakistan* (Dacca: Pioneer Press, 1967).

20 Choudhury Khaliquzzaman's autobiography, *Pathway to Pakistan* (Lahore: Longmans, 1961), provides a very good account of the circumstances that led to the involvement of the class of urban professionals in the Pakistan movement. Khaliquzzaman himself was a highly successful lawyer in the United Provinces, the present-day Uttar Pradesh.

21 My estimate based on the somewhat scanty biographical data available in the Muslim League records. These records are bound to yield, once they are carefully analysed, firmer indication of the social and economic background of the more prominent participants in the Muslim League.

22 Hanna Papanek, 'Pakistan's Big Businessmen: Muslim Separatism, Entrepreneurship and Partial Modernization', *Economic Development and Cultural Change*, Vol. 21, October 1972, Table 1, p. 27. Papanek lists the houses of Dawood, Habib, Adamjee, Crescent, Saigol, Valika, Hyesons, Bawany, Amin, Wazirali, Fancy and Colony as the twelve largest in the country in the late 1960s. Of these only two, Wazirali and Colony, both from Lahore, were 'native' to Pakistan.

23 In suggesting that India's industrial development began in the late

nineteenth century, I have followed Alexander Gerschenkron, *Economic Backwardness in Historical Perspective: A Book of Essays* (Cambridge: Belknap Press of Harvard University Press, 1962).

24 S. M. Jamil (ed.), *Muslim Year Book of India, 1948–1949* (Bombay: Bombay Newspaper Co., n.d.).

25 The term is that of Hanna Papanek; see her 'Pakistan's Big Businessmen: Muslim Separatism, Entrepreneurship and Partial Modernization', op. cit., p. 13.

26 The following four companies were set up as a part of Jinnah's efforts to build an independent industrial-commercial sector for the Muslims: Habib Bank Limited, Eastern Federal (Insurance) Union, Muhammadi Steamship Company and Orient Airways.

27 For a description of the economic relations between the states of India and Pakistan in the period immediately following independence in 1947, see C. N. Vakil and G. Raghara Rao, *Economic Relations Between India and Pakistan: Need for International Cooperation* (Bombay: Vora & Co., 1965).

28 Government of the Punjab, *Report of the Court of Inquiry Constituted Under Punjab Act II of 1954: Enquiry into Punjab Disturbances of 1953* (Lahore: Government Printing Press, 1954), p. 387.

29 Government of Pakistan, *Report of Pakistan Pay Commission* (Karachi: Governor-General's Press, 1949), p. 28.

30 Government of the Punjab, *Report of the Court of Inquiry . . .* op. cit., p. 287.

31 Muneer Ahmad, *The Civil Servant in Pakistan* (Oxford: Oxford University Press, 1964), p. 53.

32 These explanations are provided by Gustav F. Papanek in *Pakistan's Development: Social Goals and Private Incentives* (Cambridge, Massachusetts: Harvard University Press, 1967), p. 11, and endorsed by some others who have also analysed Pakistan's development experience during this period. See, for instance, Stephen R. Lewis, *Pakistan: Industrialization and Trade Policies* (London: New York University Press, 1970), pp. 11–35, and Lawrence J. White, *Industrial Concentration and Economic Power in Pakistan* (Princeton, N.J.: Princeton University Press, 1974). See also several articles published on the subject of industrial policy in *The Pakistan Development Review* and *Pakistan Economic Journal*, in particular Mahbub ul Haq, 'Rationale of Government Controls and Policies in Pakistan', *Pakistan Economic Journal*, XIII, March 1963, pp. 70–82.

33 G. F. Papanek, op. cit., p. 95.

34 Henry Frank Goodnow, *The Civil Service of Pakistan: Bureaucracy in a New Nation* (New Haven: Yale University Press, 1964), p. 138.

35 M. Ayub, *Public Industrial Enterprises in Pakistan* (Karachi: PIDC, 1960), p. 13.

36 The author's computations using the Pakistan Industrial Development Corporation, *Annual Reports* for the period 1953/54 to 1960/61, along with the annual reports of the companies listed in the Karachi Stock Exchange.

37 G. F. Papanek, op. cit., passim.

38 This argument is developed more fully in Shahid Javed Burki, 'The Development of Pakistan's Agriculture: An Interdisciplinary Explanation', in Robert D. Stevens, Hamza Alvi and Peter J. Bertocci (eds), *Rural Development in Bangladesh and Pakistan* (Honolulu: University Press of Hawaii, 1976), pp. 290–316.

39 Pieter Lieftinck, Robert A. Sadove and Thomas C. Creyke, *Water and Power Resources of West Pakistan: A Study in Sector Planning* (Baltimore: Johns Hopkins University Press, 1961), p. 23.

40 Herbert Feldman, *Revolution in Pakistan: A Study of the Martial Law Administration* (London: Oxford University Press, 1967), p. 81.

41 These two charges frequently recurred in the cases brought by the state under the EBDO. For instance, see the proceedings against Sirdar Mohammed Khan Leghari as reported in the *Pakistan Times*, Lahore, 14–30 November 1959.

42 This reflects the line of argument adopted by Keith Callard in *Pakistan: A Political Study* (London: Allen & Unwin, 1957).

43 See Khurro's statement in his defence delivered before the meeting of the Muslim League Working Committee on 23 September 1953 and reported the following day in full in the *Civil and Military Gazette*, Lahore.

44 See Safdar Mahmood, *A Political Study of Pakistan* (Lahore: Mohammad Ashraf, 1972), pp. 49–107 and Richard Symonds, *The Making of Pakistan* (London: Faber and Faber, 1950), pp. 130–52.

3 THE SEARCH FOR A NEW CONSTITUENCY

1 Although a number of biographies of Bhutto have appeared in recent years, none of them deals adequately with his childhood and early years. The only exception is the book by Piloo Moody: *Zulfi My Friend* (Delhi: Thomson Press, 1973).

2 Most literature on the Pakistan movement has concentrated on the role of such prominent leaders as Jinnah and Liaqat Ali Khan. Very little is known about the contribution made to the cause of Muslim unity by individuals such as Danyal Lateefi. For some references to Lateefi's influence on Jinnah, see Khalid Bin Sayeed, *Pakistan: The Formative Phase* (London: Oxford University Press, 1968), pp. 108–211.

3 As with a number of other important events that shaped Pakistan's history, no authoritative account is available of the factors that motivated the Rawalpindi conspiracy. Although in his biography, Ayub Khan devoted four pages to the conspiracy, his account is essentially superficial. He blamed it all on General Akbar Khan, the leader of the conspirators, who, according to Ayub, was an ambitious, slightly unstable person with 'political leanings'. See Mohammad Ayub Khan, *Friends Not Masters: A Political Autobiography* (London: Oxford University Press, 1967), pp. 35–9.

4 For a brief account of the treatment of the left during the 1947–62 period see Gerald A. Heeger, 'Socialism in Pakistan', in Helen Desfosses and Jacques Levesque (eds), *Socialism in the Third World* (New York: Praeger, 1975), pp. 291–4.

5 The fall of Ayub Khan in the spring of 1969 has received considerable academic attention. For a summary of a number of different interpretations of the circumstances that led to Ayub's resignation, see Shahid Javed Burki, 'Social and Economic Determinants of Political Violence: A Case Study of the Punjab', *The Middle East Journal*, Vol. 25, 1971, pp. 465–80. Also W. M. Dobell, 'Ayub Khan as President of Pakistan', *Pacific Affairs*, XLII, 1969, p. 307 and Wayne Wilcox, 'Pakistan in 1969: Once Again at the Starting-Point', *Asian Survey*, X, February 1970, p. 73.

6 The term 'revolution' was not initially applied to Ayub Khan's *coup d'état*. This description was adopted later when a number of analysts, impressed with the political, social and economic changes that were being introduced by the regime, started calling it a revolution. The best illustration of this view of Ayub's political intervention is to be found in Herbert Feldman's *Revolution in Pakistan: A Study of the Martial Law Administration*, the first of a trilogy covering the 1958–71 period in Pakistan's history. Feldman was later to change his opinion about the 'revolutionary impact' of Ayub's programmes. See the second book in the trilogy: *From Crisis to Crisis: Pakistan in 1962–69* (London: Oxford University Press, 1970).

7 For a brief description of the social and interest group politics that supported the Pakistan Movement see Shahid Javed Burki, 'Economic Foundations of the State of Pakistan', mimeo paper read at the annual meeting of the Association of Asian Studies, New York, 24 March 1977.

8 Shahid Javed Burki, *Agricultural Growth and Local Government in Punjab, Pakistan* (Ithaca, N.Y.: Cornell University Press, 1974).

9 For a description of the Bonus Voucher Scheme and its impact on industrial development, see Stephen R. Lewis, *Economic Policy and Industrial Growth in Pakistan* (London: Allen & Unwin, 1969), pp. 78–80, and Gustav Papanek, *Pakistan's Development: Social Goals and Private Incentives* (Cambridge, Massachusetts: Harvard University Press, 1967), pp. 130 and 263.

10 Rowland Egger, the first of these experts, was sponsored by the Ford Foundation. His *Improvement of Public Administration in Pakistan* (Karachi: Inter-services Press, 1953) was submitted to Mohammad Ali, the Prime Minister. The report was made public seven years later, in 1960, during the Ayub period. It was highly critical of the Civil Service of Pakistan (CSP). Bernard Gladieux, another Ford Foundation expert, submitted a report in 1955. Titled, *Report of Reorganization of Pakistan Government for National Development* (Karachi: Planning Commission, 1955), it was comprehensive and hard hitting. It too advocated a fundamental reshaping of the country's bureaucratic structure. For a comprehensive review of the reform effort see Ralph Braibanti, *Research on the Bureaucracy of Pakistan* (Durham, N.C.: Duke University Press, 1966), pp. 213–43. For a defence of the CSP's position see Shahid Javed Burki, 'Twenty Years of the Civil Service of Pakistan: A Reevaluation', *Asian Survey*, IX, April 1969, pp. 239–54.

11 W. Howard Wriggins in *The Ruler's Imperative* (New York: Columbia University Press, 1969) treats Ayub Khan's emphasis on economic development as one of the several ways in which the rulers of the Third World sought to legitimise their rule.

12 National income accounts for the period since independence are not available for what is now Pakistan. Since the separation of East and West Pakistan, Pakistan's Planning Commission has prepared national income accounts for the period going back to 1959.

13 David Morawetz, *Twenty-Five Years of Development* (Washington, D.C.: World Bank, 1977) has calculated GNP growth rates for eighty-nine developing countries. This comparison is based on his data.

14 Pakistan's development model won a number of admirers. See for instance, Papanek, op. cit.

15 For a detailed description of the system of Basic Democracies see, Lawrence Ziring, 'The Administration of Basic Democracies', in Guthrie Birkhead

(ed.), *Administrative Problems in Pakistan* (Syracuse, N.Y.: Syracuse University Press, 1966), pp. 31–62. Also see Lawrence Ziring, *The Ayub Khan Era: Politics in Pakistan, 1958–1969* (Syracuse, N.Y.: Syracuse University Press, 1971), passim, and Rahman Sobhan, *Basic Democracies, Works Programme and Rural Development in East Pakistan* (Dacca: University of Dacca, 1968).

16 For a description of the changes in the social composition of Ayub Khan's political support, see Shahid Javed Burki, *Social Groups and Development: A Case Study of Pakistan* (forthcoming). A summary of the main argument in this work can be seen in Shahid Javed Burki, 'Interest Group Involvement in West Pakistan's Rural Works Program', *Public Policy*, XIX, Winter, 1971, pp. 167–206. See also Robert LaPorte, *Power and Privilege: Influence and Decision-Making in Pakistan* (Berkeley, California: California University Press, 1975), pp. 39–74.

17 John McInernery and Graham Donaldson, *The Consequence of Farm Tractors in Pakistan*, World Bank Staff Working Paper No. 210 (Washington, D.C., 1975), p. ii.

18 For a profile of rural-urban migrants see, Shahid Javed Burki, 'Migration, Urbanization and Politics in Pakistan', in Howard Wriggins and James Guyot (eds), *Population, Politics and the Future of Southern Asia* (New York: Columbia University Press, 1973), pp. 147–89.

19 Ibid., p. 155.

20 A. R. Khan, 'Import Substitution, Export Expansion and Consumption Liberalization', *Pakistan Development Review*, XI, Summer 1963, pp. 123–57.

21 Michael Lipton, *Why Poor People Stay Poor: Urban Bias in World Development* (London: Temple-Smith, 1977).

22 John Simmons, 'Can Education Promote Development?', *Finance and Development*, W/15, March 1978, pp. 36–9.

23 Shahid Javed Burki, 'Social and Economic Determinants of Political Violence: A Case Study of the Punjab', op. cit.

24 Ayub Khan, *Friends Not Masters*, pp. 124–37.

25 See Yahya Khan's address to the nation, delivered after assuming political control of the country and reported in the *Pakistan Times* (Lahore), 26 March 1969.

26 Mohammad Ayub Khan, *Pakistan Perspective* (Washington, D.C.: Embassy of Pakistan, n.d.), p. 73.

27 A good account of the leftist literature, its content and the main contributors to it is to be found in Phil Jones, 'Pakistan People's Party', unpublished Ph.D. dissertation, Tufts University, 1977.

28 The terms used here to describe the various groups within the Pakistani left are my own and reflect their ideological orientation and main economic objectives. Also see, Gerald A. Heeger, 'Socialism in Pakistan', op. cit.

29 In order to understand the objectives pursued by various leftist elements, we have to turn to the books and articles available to date in Urdu. See Mubashir Hasan's *Inqalab ki Faraq Rasta* (Lahore: Misawat Press, 1975) and Hanif Ramay's articles in the *Daily Musawat* in the period January 1970–January 1971.

30 *Foundation Documents of the Pakistan People's Party* (Lahore, November 1967).

31 Ibid.

32 Pakistan People's Party, *The Election Manifesto* (Lahore: Pakistan People's Party, 1970).

33 For a good discussion of Jamaat politics, see Charles Adams, 'The Jam'ati Islami: Its Role in the Development of Pakistan', paper delivered at the Wayne Wilcox Memorial Seminar (Duke University, 27–9 September 1974) and his 'The Ideology of Maulana Maudoodi', in Donald E. Smith (ed.), *South Asian Politics and Religion* (Princeton: Princeton University Press, 1966), pp. 352–70.

34 W. Howard Wriggins, *The Ruler's Imperative*, op. cit., pp. 115–16.

35 A quite different interpretation has been presented by G. W. Choudhury in his paper, 'Pakistan's Quest for a Constitution', presented at the Wayne Wilcox Memorial Seminar (Duke University, 27–9 September 1974). Choudhury, a minister in the Cabinet of General Yahya Khan, argues that the regime was well aware of the strength of the Awami League in East Pakistan; General Yahya and his advisers expected the Awami League to return with a majority in the National Assembly. Also see his book on the subject of the management of the Bangladesh crisis by the Yahya regime: G. W. Choudhury, *The Last Days of United Pakistan* (Bloomington, Indiana: Indiana University Press, 1974).

36 See Fazal Muqeem Khan, *Pakistan's Crisis in Leadership* (Islamabad: National Book Foundation, 1973), passim.

37 For a description of the process of modernisation and how it affected the votes in the election, see Shahid Javed Burki and Craig Baxter, 'Socio-Economic Indicators of the People's Party Vote in the Punjab: A Study at the Tehsil Level', *The Journal of Asian Studies*, XXXIV, August 1975, pp. 913–30.

4 RISE TO POWER

1 For an account of Bhutto's role in the development of the political crisis that led to the secession of East Pakistan, see G. W. Choudhury, *The Last Days of United Pakistan* (Bloomington, Indiana: Indiana University Press, 1974) passim. For a defence of his position see Zulfikar Ali Bhutto, *The Great Tragedy* (Karachi: Vision Publications, 1971).

2 A number of accounts have appeared of the political crisis as it developed in the 1969–71 period. In addition to the works cited in n.1 above, see also David Loshak, *The Pakistan Crisis* (New York: McGraw Hill, 1971), Rounaq Jahan, *Pakistan: Failure in National Integration* (New York: Columbia University Press, 1972), Robert Payne, *Massacre* (New York: Macmillan, 1973) and Marta Nicholas and Philip Oldenberg, *Bangladesh: The Birth of a Nation* (Madras: M. Seschachalam, 1972).

3 For a text of the surrender document see, D. K. Palit, *The Lightning Campaign: The Indo-Pakistan War, 1971* (New Delhi: Thomson Press, 1972), pp. 48–9.

4 Ayub Khan, *Friends Not Masters: A Political Autobiography* (London: Oxford University Press, 1967), p. 70.

5 See Mahbub ul Haq, *The Strategy of Economic Planning* (New York: Oxford University Press, 1963) for a description of the strategy adopted by the Pakistani planners and its theoretical justification.

6 For a description of the changes in thinking on the development process see Paul Streeten, 'Development Ideas in Historical Perspective: The New Interest in Development', mimeo (Washington, D.C.: World Bank, 1977).

7 Timothy Nutty and Leslie Nutty, 'Pakistan, The Busy-Bee Route', *Transaction*, 8, February 1971, p. 41.

8 Mahbub ul Haq, *The Poverty Curtain: Choices for the Third World* (New York: Columbia University Press, 1976), pp. 7–8.

9 Ibid., p. 8.

10 This was a common accusation levelled against the regime of Ayub Khan, in particular by the members of the Pakistan People's Party during the election campaign. See Zulfikar Ali Bhutto, *Let the People Judge* (Lahore: Pakistan People's Party, 1969), passim.

11 Government of Pakistan, *The Task of National Reconstruction* (Rawalpindi: Bureau of National Reconstruction, n.d.), p. 3.

12 *Asaf Hussain*, 'Ethnicity, National Identity and Praetorianism: The Case of Pakistan', *Asian Survey*, XVI, October 1976, pp. 918-30.

13 The British administration's approach towards the northern areas is well documented in Philip Woodruff, *The Men Who Ruled India: The Guardians* (London: Jonathan Cape, 1965), passim. Also see, Charles Allen, *Plain Tales from the Raj* (New York: St Martin's Press, 1976), particularly pp. 212–19.

14 Paul Johnson, *Enemies of Society* (New York: Atheneum, 1977), p. 4.

15 For a Marxist discussion of Pakistani 'nationalities' see Yu V. Gankovsky, *The Peoples of Pakistan*, originally published by the USSR Academy of Sciences, Institute of Oriental Studies, and reprinted by People's Publishing House, Lahore, n.d. It should be recalled that the Pakistan Movement, largely on account of its emphasis on the liberation of 'nationalities' received support from the Marxists both inside and outside India. See Gerald Heeger, 'Socialism in Pakistan', in Helen Desfosses and Jacques Levesque (eds), *Socialism in the Third World* (New York: Praeger, 1975), p. 293.

16 For a discussion of constitution making during the Ayub period, see Edgar A. Schuler and Kathryn R. Schuler, *Public Opinion and Constitution Making in Pakistan, 1958-1962* (East Lansing, Michigan: Michigan State University Press, 1967).

17 For a discussion of the role of 'the passions and the interests' in the development of modern capitalism, see Albert O. Hirschman, *The Passions and the Interests: Political Arguments for Capitalism Before Its Triumph* (Princeton, N.J.: Princeton University Press, 1977).

18 For an indictment of Ayub's economic policies, see Mahbub ul Haq, *The Poverty Curtain: Choices for the Third World*, op. cit., pp. 3–26.

19 For an account of this mini-revolt within the army see Herbert Feldman, *The End and The Beginning: Pakistan 1969-1971* (London: Oxford University Press, 1976), pp. 182–9. Feldman was careful to add the following caveat to his account: 'I must make it clear that the contents of this chapter form, in the main, an attempted reconstruction of events. Quite clearly, in terms of great national crisis much happens that is not documented and much which people prefer to forget' (f.n. 4, on p. 185).

20 Fazal Muqeem Khan, *Pakistan's Crisis in Leadership* (Islamabad: National Book Foundation, 1973), pp. 263–4.

21 General Fazal Muqeem had left the army in 1969, just before Yahya took the administration from Ayub Khan. However, primarily because of his writings, he continued to be influential within the army.

22 Pram Chopra, *India's Second Liberation* (Delhi: Vikas Publishing House,

1973), presents estimates of the personnel and material strengths of the two armies at both the western and the eastern fronts.

23 This remark was made by Bhutto in his largely extempore speech delivered on radio after being sworn in as the President of Pakistan.

24 See Henry Bienen and David Morrell, 'Transition from Military Rule: Thailand's Experience' in Catherine Kelleher (ed.), *Political-Military Systems: Comparative Perspectives* (Beverly Hills, California: Sage Publications, 1974), pp. 3–26 for an exposition of this point of view. For an application of this thesis of civil-military hybrid regimes to the case of Pakistan, see Gerald A. Heeger, 'Politics in the Post-Military State: Some Reflections on the Pakistani Experience', *World Politics*, XXIX, January 1977, pp. 242–62.

25 The Legal Framework Order was produced in full by *Dawn* (Karachi) and the *Pakistan Times* (Lahore and Islamabad) in their issues of 31 March 1970. For an analysis of the Order see Feldman, op. cit., pp. 62–75, and Safdar Mahmood, *A Political Study of Pakistan* (Lahore: Mohammad Ashraf, 1972), pp. 360–72.

26 Robert LaPorte, Jr. 'Pakistan in 1972: Picking up the Pieces', *Asian Survey*, XIII, February 1973, p. 196.

27 For an account of Bhutto's conduct of foreign affairs during this period, see S. M. Burke, 'The Management of Pakistan's Foreign Policy', in Lawrence Ziring, Ralph Braibanti and W. Howard Wriggins (eds), *Pakistan: The Long View* (Durham, N.C.: Duke University, 1977), pp. 362–8.

28 See Bhutto's interview with Oriana Fallaci for an assessment of the type of relationship that had developed between him and Mrs Gandhi on the eve of the Simla Agreement. According to Fallaci: 'In judging her [Mrs Gandhi] Bhutto had been heavy-handed and too guided by hatred. I myself was actually embarrassed by it, and in my embarrassment had tried repeatedly to restrain him.' And again: 'It was amusing to watch them on television while they shook hands and exchanged smiles. Indira's smile triumphant and ironical. Bhutto's displayed such discomfort that, even on the black-and-white screen, you seemed to see him blushing to the roots of his hair.' Oriana Fallaci, *Interview with History* (New York: Liveright Publishing Corporation, 1976), pp. 186–7.

5 RESTRUCTURING INSTITUTIONS

1 For a discussion of the role of 'modernisers' in the constituency supporting Bhutto, see Shahid Javed Burki and Craig Baxter, 'Socio-Economic Indicators of the People's Party Vote in the Punjab: A Study at the Tehsil Level', *The Journal of Asian Studies*, XXXIV, August 1975, pp. 913–30. See also Craig Baxter, 'Pakistan Votes – 1970', *Asian Survey*, XI, March 1971, pp. 197–218, and Herbert Feldman, *The End and the Beginning: Pakistan 1969–1971* (London: Oxford University Press, 1976), pp. 76–97.

2 Maulana Kausar Niazi, 'Z. A. Bhutto's Rendezvous with History', in Zahid Malik (ed.), *Pakistan After 1971* (Rawalpindi: Pakistan National Centre, 1974), pp. 1–16. See also Fakhar Zaman and Akhtar Aman, *Z. A. Bhutto: The Political Thinker* (Lahore: The People's Publications, 1973), passim.

3 Dr Mubashir Hasan, *Pakistan Key Jaali Hukmaran Tabqe* (Lahore: Classic

Books, 1976). This is a collection of articles written by Mubashir Hasan during the 1977 election campaign and after he left the office of Finance Minister under Bhutto.

4 *Musawat* (Lahore), 14 May 1970.

5 Zulfikar Ali Bhutto, *Speeches* (Rawalpindi: Ministry of Information, n.d.), pp. 11–32.

6 Zulfikar Ali Bhutto, *Let the People Judge* (Lahore: Pakistan People's Party, 1969), passim.

7 The memorandum has not been published to date.

8 *Nusrat* (Lahore), 14 September 1971.

9 A phrase used repeatedly by Bhutto before as well as after he assumed power. See his *Speeches*, passim.

10 Although the relationship between the development of irrigation systems in the Punjab and Sind and the domination of the political structures in these two provinces by large landlords has not been carefully explored, it seems to me that some of the hypothesis put forward by Wittfogel may well apply. See Karl A. Wittfogel, *Oriental Despotism: A Comparative Study of Total Power* (New Haven, Connecticut: Yale University Press, 1957). Wittfogel's 'hydraulic society' model has been developed somewhat by Marvin Harris in *Cannibals and Kings: The Origin of Cultures* (New York: Random House, 1977). According to Harris:

> My own view of that relationship borrows heavily from Wittfogel's but does not correspond precisely with his formulation. I hold that pre-industrial hydraulic agriculture recurrently led to the evolution of extremely despotic agro-managerial bureaucracies because the expansion and intensification of hydraulic agriculture – itself a consequence of reproductive pressures – was uniquely dependent on massive construction projects which, in the absence of machines, could only be carried out by antlike armies of workers (pp. 237–8).

11 See K. N. Raj, 'Investment in Livestock in Agrarian Economies: An Analysis of Some Issues Concerning "Sacred Cows" and "Surplus Cattle"', *Indian Economic Review*, vol. 4, 1969, pp. 1–33.

12 For an analysis of the conditions under which the *haris* of Sind lived, see M. Masud, *Hari Report: Note of Dissent* (Karachi: The Hari Publications, n.d.). The report was written by Masud in 1948.

13 Pilo Moody, *Zulfi My Friend* (Delhi: Thomson Press, 1973), p. 45.

14 Hans Kelsen, *General Theory of Law and State* (Berkeley: University of California Press, 1968).

15 Hans Kelsen, *Pure Theory of Law* (Berkeley: University of California Press, 1970).

16 J. M. Eekelaar, 'Principles of Revolutionary Legality' in A. W. B. Simpson (ed.), *Oxford Essays in Jurisprudence* (Oxford: Clarendon Press, 1963), p. 25. For an understanding of Kelsen's view, this essay as well as those by A. M. Honoré, 'Groups, Laws and Obedience', and J. M. Finnis, 'Revolutions and Continuity of Law', in the same volume by A. W. B. Simpson are very useful.

17 Hans Kelsen, 'A Reply to Professor Stone', *Stanford Law Review*, 17, vol. 2, 1965, p. 1144.

18 Hans Kelsen, *General Theory of Law and State*, pp. 187–8.
19 Hans Kelsen, *Pure Theory of Law*, p. 285.
20 For a description of the Sindhi stereotype, see books such as H. T. Lambrick, *Sind: Before the Muslim Conquest* (Pakistan: Sindhi Adabi Board, 1973) and Philip Woodruff, *The Men Who Ruled India: The Founders* (London: Jonathan Cape, 1965).
21 Erik H. Erikson, *Gandhi's Truth: On the Origins of Militant Non-Violence* (New York: W. W. Norton, 1969), p. 56.
22 *Dawn* (Karachi), 1 July 1967.
23 Dilip Mukerjee, an Indian journalist, and author of one of the better biographies of Bhutto refers to these stories in what he calls Pakistan's 'yellow press'. Mukerjee also interviewed the brother of Bhutto's mother – a man called Damodar who is still a resident of India. Mukerjee confirms that contrary to speculations in Pakistan, Sir Shahnawaz's marriage to Khurshid, Bhutto's mother was 'regular ... at which Sir Ghulam Hussain Hidayatullah and other notables were present'. See Dilip Mukerjee, *Zulfikar Ali Bhutto: Quest for Power* (Delhi: Vikas Publishing, 1972), p. 27.
24 The quote is from, Phil Jones, 'Pakistan People's Party', unpublished Ph.D. dissertation, Tufts University (1979).
25 As quoted in Anwar Syed, 'The Pakistan People's Party: Phases One and Two', in Lawrence Ziring *et al.* (eds), *Pakistan: The Long View* (Durham, N.C.: Duke University Press, 1977).
26 Malik Ghulam Jilani, 'Time Always Passes' (unpublished essay), quoted in Lawrence Ziring, 'Pakistan: The Campaign Before the Storm', *Asian Survey*, XVII, July 1977, pp. 583–4.
27 Anis Mirza, 'Begum Asghar Recalls Days of Vindictive Politics', *Dawn* (Karachi), 13 November 1977.
28 For an analysis of succession in Pakistan, see Robert LaPorte Jr., 'Succession in Pakistan: Continuity and Change in a Garrison State', *Asian Survey*, IX, November 1969, pp. 842–61.
29 For a brief description of the process of institution-making under Bhutto, see Craig Baxter, 'Constitution Making: The Development of Federalism in Pakistan', *Asian Survey*, XIV, December 1974, pp. 1074–85. For an analysis of the application of the viceregal system to the Pakistan situation, see Khalid B. Sayeed, *Pakistan: The Formative Phase* (London: Oxford University Press, 2nd edn, 1968), pp. 162–92.
30 As reported in *Dawn* (Karachi), 8 October 1972. Similar sentiments were expressed by others.
31 Zulfikar Ali Bhutto, *The Great Tragedy* (Karachi: Vision Publications, 1971), pp. 23–5.
32 Dr Mubashir Hasan, *Pakistan Key Jaali Hukmaran Tabqe*, op. cit., *passim*.
33 *Constitution of the Islamic Republic of Pakistan*, Article 96(5).
34 Herbert Feldman, 'Pakistan – 1973', *Asian Survey*, XIV, February 1974, p. 136.
35 See the editorials in the *Pakistan Times* (Lahore), *Dawn* (Karachi) and *Mashriq* (Lahore) on 17 February 1972 for the impression that Bhutto's administration sought to create in the minds of the public regarding the links between Iraq and the NAP.
36 Quoted in Craig Baxter, 'Constitution Making: The Development of

Federalism in Pakistan', *Asian Survey*, op. cit., p. 1075.

37 Quoted in Lawrence Ziring, 'The Pakistan Bureaucracy: Administration Reforms', *Asian Survey*, XIV, December 1974, p. 1088. The speech from which this quotation comes was delivered by Bhutto on 20 August 1973 when he announced the dissolution of the CSP. The speech is reported in full in the *Pakistan Times* (Islamabad), 21 August 1973.

38 Khalid B. Sayeed, *The Political System of Pakistan* (Boston: Houghton Mifflin, 1967), pp. 62–3.

39 Albert Gorvine, 'The Role of the Civil Service Under the Revolutionary Government', *The Middle East Journal*, XIX, no. 3, 1965, p. 324.

40 For an analysis of the way the CSP survived the initial hostility of the military and later established itself as a full partner in the Ayub coalition of groups, see Shahid Javed Burki, 'Twenty Years of the Civil Service of Pakistan: A Reevaluation', *Asian Survey*, IX, April 1969, pp. 239–54.

41 Hasan Habib, the influential Principal of the Administrative Staff College, wrote a series of articles condemning the CSP. The series appeared in the *Pakistan Times* (Lahore). This quotation is from the collection: 'Nazim' (Hasan Habib), *Babus, Brahmans and Bureaucrats: A Critique of an Administrative System in Pakistan* (Lahore: People's Publishing House, 1973), pp. 4–5.

42 The CSP Association, *Memorandum Submitted to the Service Reorganization Committee* (Rawalpindi: Ferozesons, 1969), p. 2.

43 Ibid., p. 11.

44 The new administrative structure was created with the promulgation and/or passage of the Civil Servants Ordinance, 1973 (XIV of 1973), Service Tribunals Ordinance, 1973 (XV of 1973), the Federal Public Service Commission Ordinance, 1973 (XVI of 1973), the Civil Servants Acts, 1973; the Service Tribunals Act, 1973; the Federal Public Service Commission Act, 1973 and Cabinet Secretariat Memoranda of 14 September 1973 and 20 November 1973.

45 For a Marxist interpretation of the history of Muslim India – a book in which most of their ideas find reflection – see Mubashir Hasan, *Shahrahe Inqilab* (Urdu) (Lahore: Rippon Printing, 1976). The book was written after Mubashir Hasan had left the Cabinet.

46 Pakistan People's Party, *The Election Manifesto* (Lahore: Pakistan People's Party, 1970), p. 24.

47 For a discussion of the curriculum at the Civil Service Academy and its impact on developing the 'CSP character' see Ralph Braibanti, 'The Higher Bureaucracy of Pakistan' in Ralph Braibanti (ed.), *Asian Bureaucratic Systems' Emergence from British Imperial Tradition* (Durham, N.C.: Duke University Press, 1966), pp. 209–353. See also Ralph Braibanti, *Research on the Bureaucracy of Pakistan* (Durham, N.C.: Duke University Press, 1966), pp. 98–101.

48 Ralph Braibanti, 'The Higher Bureaucracy of Pakistan', ibid.

49 For details of the new administrative structure see Robert LaPorte Jr, 'The Pakistan Bureaucracy: Twenty Five Years of Power and Influence', *Asian Survey*, XIV, December 1974, pp. 1094–103.

50 Ibid., p. 1102.

51 *Zindigi* (Lahore), July 1974.

52 *Dawn* (Karachi), 22 August 1973.

53 There is a rich literature on Pakistan's administrative structure as it existed

between 1947 and 1973 and also on its impact on the country's political and economic development. The books by Munir Ahmed, Braibanti and Good- now and articles of Burki, LaPorte Jr and Ziring have been cited already. See also, Anwar H. Syed, *Issues of Bureaucratic Ethics* (Lahore: Progressive Publishers, 1974) for an analysis of the attitude of the civil bureaucracy towards Pakistan's various problems. For a good description of the process that led to the accumulation of power in the hands of a few civil servants see, Robert LaPorte Jr, *Power and Privilege: Influence and Decision-Making in Pakistan* (Berkeley: University of California Press, 1975), especially pp. 55–75.

54   From the statement by Abdul Hafiz Pirzada, Law Minister, in the National Assembly. Reported in the *Pakistan Times* (Rawalpindi), 21 November 1973.

55   Herbert Feldman, 'Pakistan – 1973', *Asian Survey*, XIV, no. 2, February 1974, p. 141.

56   Herbert Feldman, 'Pakistan in 1974', *Asian Survey*, XV, February 1975, p. 115.

6   REDIRECTING ECONOMIC DEVELOPMENT: MANAGEMENT BY THE PPP LEFT

1   For a discussion of the various aspects of the 'economic union' between East and West Pakistan, see Arthur MacEwan, *Development Alternatives in Pakistan: A Multisectoral and Regional Analysis of Planning Problems* (Cambridge, Mas- sachusetts: Harvard University, 1971); Muhammad Anisur Rahman, *East and West Pakistan: A Problem in the Political Economy of Regional Planning* (Cambridge, Massachusetts: Center for International Affairs, 1968); and M. Akhlakur Rahman, *Integration, Economic Growth and Interregional Trade: A Study of Interwing Trade in Pakistan, 1948–1959* (Karachi: Institute of Develop- ment Economics, 1963).

2   'A New Policy Framework for Economic Management', *Pakistan Economist*, 24 February 1972.

3   Government of Pakistan, *Pakistan Economic Survey, 1976–77* (Islamabad: Finance Division, 1977), Statistical Sector, Table 31, p. 85.

4   This point of view is reflected in the contribution of economists from West Pakistan to the Government of Pakistan: *Report of the Panel of Economic Experts* (Islamabad: Planning Commission, 1970), passim.

5   Dr Mubashir Hasan, *Pakistan Key Jaali Hukmaran Tabqe* (Lahore: Classic Books, 1976), pp. 49–58.

6   Ibid.

7   Zulfikar Ali Bhutto, 'Address to the Nation Announcing Nationalization of Ten Categories of Industries', on 12 January 1972, *Speeches and Statements (December 20, 1971–March 31, 1972)* (Karachi, Department of Film and Publications, 1972), p. 33.

8   Dr Mubashir Hasan, *Pakistan Key Jaali Hukmaran Tabqe*, op. cit., p. 51.

9   Ahmed Dawood as quoted in Robert La Porte Jr, 'Pakistan in 1972: Picking up the Pieces', *Asian Survey*, XIII, February 1973, p. 194.

10   See 'Bhutto Follows a Capitalistic Path', *New York Times*, 4 June 1972.

11   See the special issue of *Trade and Industry* (Karachi, March 1972) devoted to the subject of nationalisation.

12 *Outlook*, 'The Road to Socialism', Editorial (Karachi), 5 January 1974, p. 3.
13 World Bank, *Economic Situation and Prospects of Pakistan* (Washington, D.C.: 1 April 1974), p. 1.
14 *Pakistan Times* (Lahore), 17 August 1973.
15 Ibid.
16 MICAS Associates, *A Study of Problems Associated with Procurement, Storage and Distribution of Wheat: Report Submitted to the Prime Minister of Pakistan* (Karachi, May 1976), passim.
17 *Pakistan Times* (Lahore), 6 January 1974. For a review of this reform, see W. Eric Gustafson, 'Economic Reforms Under the Bhutto Regime', *Journal of Asian and African Studies*, vol. 8 (July–October 1973), pp. 241–58.
18 Dr Mubashir Hasan, *Pakistan Key Jaali Hukmaran Tabqe*, op. cit., pp. 49–51.
19 Abdul Ghafoor Ahmad, 'The Economy on the Skids', *Outlook* (Karachi), 8 June 1974, p. 10.
20 Government of Pakistan, *Labour Reforms of 1972* (Islamabad, Labour Division, 1972), p. 34.
21 Ibid., p. 18.
22 *Pakistan Times* (Lahore), 19 December 1972.
23 Dawn E. Jones and Rodney W. Jones, 'Nationalizing Education in Pakistan: Teachers' Association and the People's Party', *Pacific Affairs*, vol. 50, no. 4, Winter 1974–5, p. 581.
24 Ibid., p. 581.
25 The phrase 'dynamic society' was used repeatedly by Zulfikar Ali Bhutto in the speeches dealing with economic reforms. See, for instance, the speech delivered on 1 March 1972 on the occasion of the promulgation of land reform and the speech delivered on 12 March 1972. Both speeches were carried in full by the *Pakistan Times*.
26 For details of the reform see Henry Korson, 'Bhutto's Educational Reforms', in H. Korson (ed.), *Contemporary Problems of Pakistan* (Leiden: E. J. Brill, 1974), pp. 119–46. See also Government of Pakistan, *The Education Policy, 1972–1980* (Islamabad, Ministry of Education, 1973).
27 John Simmons, 'Can Education Promote Development', *Finance and Development*, W/15, March 1978, p. 37.
28 Robert E. Klitgaard *et. al.*, 'Can We Afford a Half-time University?', Applied Economic Research Center, University of Karachi, December 1976.
29 See n. 25 above.
30 This story of the conflict between the *Anjuman-i-Himayat-i-Islam* and West Pakistan College Teachers' Association is taken primarily from Dawn Jones and Rodney Jones, 'Nationalizing Education in Pakistan: Teachers' Association and the People's Party', op. cit.
31 Ibid.
32 Mohammad Hussain Shah, *Urban Problems of Pakistan* (Lahore: People's Press, 1974), p. 15.
33 Ibid, p. 17.
34 Institute of Education and Research, University of the Punjab, *Statistical Profile of Education in West Pakistan* (Islamabad, 1971), Chapters 1 and 2.
35 W. M. Zaki, *End of Misery* (Islamabad: Ministry of Education, 1972), p. 12.
36 In 1960, Sri Lanka reported infant mortality of only 57 per 1000, child mortality of 1 per 1000 and life expectancy of 61 years. See The World Bank,

World Development Indicators, 1978 (Washington, D.C.: June 1978), p. 38. In terms of infant and child mortality and life expectancy, Punjab State in India was also far ahead of Pakistan. See Arun Shourie, 'Meeting Basic Needs in Punjab and Kerala', mimeo, March 1978.

37 Mukhtar Raziq, 'Infant Mortality: Do Pakistanis Still Practice Female Infanticide?', mimeo (Lahore: Punjab University, 1973).

38 See A. Furnia, *Syncrisis: The Dynamics of Health, No. XVIII: Pakistan,* Washington, D.C.: US Department of Health, Education and Welfare, June 1976), for an excellent description of Pakistan's health system. See also Siraj ul Haq and C. Stevens, *Some Account of the Current Situation and Recommendations Regarding the Health Sector* (Islamabad: Government of Pakistan Planning Commission, 1975).

39 For an analysis of the rural health scheme see Akhtar Husain Awan, 'Report of the Preliminary Impact Survey of the Rural Health System of Northern Areas', mimeo (Islamabad: Government of Pakistan Planning Commission, 1976).

40 For a description and analysis of the generic drug scheme in Pakistan, see Khaliq Khan, *Generic Drugs in Pakistan: Their Introduction and Consequences* (Lahore: Model Publishing House, 1976).

41 Ibid.

42 Government of Pakistan, *People's Cloth Scheme* (Islamabad: Ministry of Industries, 1975), pp. 10–18.

43 Ibid., p. 22.

44 Ibid., p. 16.

45 Government of Pakistan, *Pakistan Economic Survey, 1976–77,* op. cit., Statistical Annex.

46 Herbert Feldman, 'Pakistan in 1974', *Asian Survey,* XV, no. 2, February 1975, p. 111.

47 Zulfikar Ali Bhutto, *Speeches and Statements* (Rawalpindi: Ministry of Information, n.d.), p. 51.

48 Zulfikar Ali Bhutto, ibid., p. 62.

49 Ibid., p. 44.

50 For a description of Ayub Khan's Rural Works Programme, see Shahid Javed Burki, 'Interest Group Involvement in West Pakistan's Rural Works Program', *Public Policy,* XIX, Winter 1971, pp. 167–206.

51 For a description of the Comilla experiment, see Arthur Raper, *Rural Development in Action* (Ithaca, N.Y.: Cornell University Press, 1970).

52 Government of Pakistan, *Report of the International Seminar on Integrated Rural Development, Lahore, November 3–10, 1973* (Islamabad: Ministry of Food, 1974), p. 72.

53 Ibid.

7   ECONOMIC DECISION-MAKING WITHOUT CONSTRAINTS: 1974–7

1 For a discussion of the importance of towns and small cities in the agricultural economy of Pakistan, see Hiromitsu Kaneda and Frank C. Child, 'Links to the Green Revolution: A Study of Small-Scale Agriculturally Related Industry in the Pakistan Punjab', *Economic Development and Cultural Change,* vol. 23,

no. 2, January 1975, pp. 249–75, and Shahid Javed Burki, 'Development of Towns: The Pakistan Experience', *Asian Survey*, XIV, August 1974, pp. 751–62.

2 The evolution of the planning system in Pakistan is described in Albert Waterston, *Planning in Pakistan* (Baltimore: Johns Hopkins University Press, 1963).

3 These quotes are from Bhutto's Speech to the nation over radio and television delivered just before the 1970 elections. See Zulfikar Ali Bhutto, *Politics of the People: Marching Towards Democracy* (Rawalpindi: Pakistan Publications, n.d.), p. 157.

4 Quoted from a speech delivered at Sibi in Baluchistan province and reported by the *Pakistan Times* (Lahore), 26 July 1976.

5 Pakistan has adopted a number of different approaches for solving its population problem. For a description of these approaches and the administrative arrangements made for implementing them, see Tine Bussink, 'Major Aspects of Family Planning in Pakistan', in Shahid Javed Burki (ed.), *Prologue to Development Policy and Population Policy – The Pakistan Experience* (Washington, D.C.: Smithsonian Institution, Interdisciplinary Communications Program, 1975), pp. 37–60. See also Lee L. Bean, 'Rapid Population Growth: Implications for Social and Economic Development', *Asian Survey*, XIV, December 1974, pp. 1104–13.

6 Mohammad Nawaz, *Zulfikar Ali Bhutto: A People's Leader* (Lahore: Progressive Publishing House, n.d.), p, 52.

7 Ibid., p. 55.

8 Government of Pakistan, *Pakistan Economic Survey, 1973–74* (Islamabad: Government of Pakistan, Finance Division, 1974), p. 157. See also, *The Fifth Plan, 1977–83, Vol. II (Sectoral Programmes)* (Islamabad: Planning Commission, June 1977), p. 365.

9 Zalmay Khalilzad, 'Pakistan: The Making of Nuclear Power', *Asian Survey*, XVI, June 1976, p. 582.

10 Government of Pakistan, *Pakistan Year Book, 1971* (Rawalpindi: Ministry of Information, 1972), p. 259.

11 Imtiaz Ali Qazilbash, 'Pakistan's Power Potential', *Pakistan Times* (Lahore), 22 June, 1975.

12 Zalmay Khalilzad, 'Pakistan: The Making of Nuclear Power', op. cit., pp. 585–6.

13 Simon Henderson, '. . . And Hopes Founder for Plutonium Plant in Pakistan', *The Middle East*, April 1978, pp. 126–7.

14 Zulfikar Ali Bhutto, *Politics of the People: Awakening the People* (Rawalpindi: Pakistan Publications, n.d.), p. 19.

15 Quoted from a speech at Malakand, *Pakistan Times* (Lahore), 21 May 1975.

16 Anwar H. Syed, 'The Pakistan People's Party: Phases One and Two', in Lawrence Ziring *et al.* (eds), *Pakistan: The Long View* (Durham, N.C.: Duke University Press, 1977), p. 75.

17 Government of Pakistan, *Promotion of Sports and Culture: A Programme of Action* (Islamabad: Ministry of Education, 1976), p. 11.

18 Ibid., p. 14.

19 Ibid., p. 11.

20 For an analysis of 'new directions' in foreign policy, see S. M. Burke, 'The

Management of Pakistan's Foreign Policy' and William J. Barnds, 'Pakistan's Foreign Policy: Shifting Opportunities and Constraints' in Lawrence Ziring *et al.* (eds) *Pakistan: The Long View*, op. cit.

21 Among the better works on this subject are Walter Falcon and Carl Gotsch, 'Lessons in Agricultural Development – Pakistan' in Gustav F. Papanek (ed.), *Development Policy: Theory and Practice* (Cambridge, Massachusetts: Harvard University Press, 1968), pp. 269–315; Carl Gotsch, 'Regional Agricultural Growth: The Case of West Pakistan', *Asian Survey*, VIII, March 1968, pp. 188–206; Carl Gotsch and Shahid Yusuf, 'Technical Indivisibilities and Distribution of Income: Mixed Integer Programming Model of Punjab Agriculture', *Food Research Institute Studies*, XIV, no. 1 (1975).

22 Gilbert Brown and Carl Gotsch, 'Pakistan Agriculture Prices Study', mimeo (Washington, D.C.: World Bank, 1977).

23 Ibid., p. 57.

24 MICAS Associates, *A Study of Problems Associated with Procurement, Storage and Distribution of Wheat: Report Submitted to the Prime Minister of Pakistan* (Karachi), May 1976, p. 52.

25 As reported by the daily *Nawa-i-Waqt* in one of its pre-election issues. See the edition of 27 February 1977.

26 Stephen Guisinger and Norman L. Hicks argue that the common perception that the rapid growth of incomes in Pakistan in the sixties led to a deterioration in their distribution is not supported by facts. See their article, 'Long-term Trends in Income Distribution in Pakistan', *World Development*, vol. 6, November–December 1978, pp. 1271–80.

27 Ibid., p. 7.

28 S. Guisinger and M. Irfan, 'Real Wages of Industrial Workers in Pakistan: 1954 to 1970', *Pakistan Development Review*, XIII, Winter 1974, p. 363.

29 M. L. Qureshi and Faiz Bilquees, 'A Note on Changes in Real Wages of Government Servants', *Pakistan Development Review*, XVI, Autumn 1977, pp. 325–35.

8   PREPARING FOR ELECTIONS IN 1977

1 *Washington Post*, 7 July 1977.

2 In recent years there appears to have been a certain superstition about the dates on which the government leaders announced more important decisions. General Yahya Khan's important decisions were made public, usually in radio and television addresses, on the 28th of the month. Bhutto chose the fifth as his day for important decisions.

3 M. G. Weinbaum, 'The March 1977 Elections in Pakistan: Where Everyone Lost', *Asian Survey*, XVII, July 1977, p. 600.

4 Ibid., p. 614.

5 *The Economist* (London), 15 January 1977.

6 Anwar H. Syed, 'The Pakistan People's Party: Phases One and Two', in Lawrence Ziring, Ralph Braibanti and Howard Wriggins (eds), *Pakistan: The Long View* (Durham, N.C.: Duke University Press, 1977), p. 115.

7 Ibid., p. 115.

8 Zulfikar Ali Bhutto, *Chairman Bhutto's Election Addresses* (Lahore: Forward Publishers, 1978), p. 99.

9 Mubashir Hasan, *Musawat* (Lahore), 17 May 1976.

10 Anwar H. Syed, 'Pakistan in 1976: Business as Usual', *Asian Survey*, VII, February 1977, p. 183.

11 Iftikhar Diwan, 'Students in Pakistani Politics', mimeo (Lahore: Government College, 1977).

12 Ibid.

13 Anwar H. Syed, 'Pakistan in 1976: Business as Usual,' op. cit., p. 182. For a political biography of the Pir, see Peter Mayne, *Saints of Sind* (London: John Murray, 1956).

14 Zulfikar Ali Bhutto, *Chairman Bhutto's Election Addresses*, op. cit., p. 42.

15 Zulfikar Ali Bhutto, 'Let Us Not Be Misguided', *Jang* (Rawalpindi), September 1976. This quotation is my free translation of the *Jang* text.

16 This dissatisfaction was to become an often-repeated theme in Bhutto's speeches in larger cities during the autumn of 1976. For instance, he told an airport reception at Lahore, 'my regime's progress in the economic field has been blocked by a number of interested groups', *Mashriq* (Lahore), 23 May 1976.

17 For an analysis of Bhutto's foreign policy and his negotiating from a position of weakness, see William J. Barnds, 'Pakistan's Foreign Policy: Shifting Opportunities and Constraints' in Lawrence Ziring *et al.* (eds), *Pakistan: The Long View* (Durham, N.C.: Duke University Press, 1977), pp. 309–402.

18 Salamat Ali, 'Sword and Plough Fight it Out', *Far Eastern Economic Review*, 25 February 1977, pp. 33–4.

19 *Mashriq* (Lahore), 7 September 1976.

20 Quoted in G. W. Choudhury, 'New Pakistan Constitution', mimeo, paper presented at the National Pakistan/Bangladesh Seminar, Southern Asian Institute, Colombia University, 2 November 1973.

21 Ibid., p. 45.

22 Ibid., p. 34.

23 Ibid., p. 72.

24 Ibid., p. 33.

25 Ibid., p. 40.

26 From Malik Ghulam Jilani's unpublished essay, 'Time Always Passes', quoted in Lawrence Ziring, 'Pakistan: The Campaign Before the Storm', *Asian Survey*, XVII, July 1977, p. 583.

27 Lahore High Court, *State vs. Zulfikar Ali Bhutto* (Lahore: 1977), p. 132.

28 Ibid., p. 131.

29 Ibid., p. 187.

30 Pakistan People's Party, *Manifesto* (Rawalpindi: Pakistan People's Party Central Secretariat, 1977), p. 58.

31 Ibid., p. 59.

32 For a Marxist interpretation of the political development of Muslim India under the British, see Dr Mubashir Hasan's work in Urdu, *Shahrahe Inqilab* (Lahore: Rippon Printing, 1976).

33 For a coverage of this aspect, see the several pre-election issues of *Nusrat*.

34 This quotation is from Sunil Selti, 'Pakistan: A Nation Adrift', *India Today*, 1–15 March 1978), p. 42.

35 Malik Allahyar Khan in personal communication to the author. Malik Allahyar is the son of Nawab of Kalabagh, who was the Governor of West

Pakistan during the Ayub period. Malik is the brother-in-law of Farouq Leghari, the head of the Leghari Tribe of Dera Ghazi Khan. Leghari was the Minister of Production in the last Bhutto Cabinet.

36 Pakistan People's Party, *The Election Manifesto* (Lahore: Pakistan People's Party, 1970), p. 13.
37 Pakistan People's Party, *Manifesto*, op. cit., p. 20.
38 Abdullah Malik, 'Elections '77: What will be the Bhutto Strategy?', *Viewpoint* (Lahore), 4 February 1977, p. 16.
39 S. R. Ghauri, 'Bhutto Fights for his Political Life', *Far Eastern Economic Review*, 4 March 1977, p. 12.
40 Sharif al Mujahid, 'The Pakistani Elections: An Analysis', mimeo, paper presented at the Quaid-i-Azam International Conference, Columbia University, 9–11 March 1978.
41 A. T. Chaudhri, 'The Battle of Manifestos – I', *Dawn* (Karachi), 14 February 1977.
42 *Pakistan Times* (Lahore), 13 January 1977.
43 A. T. Chaudhri, 'The Battle of Manifestos – I', op. cit.
44 *Pakistan Times* (Lahore), 8 March 1977.
45 *Viewpoint*, the Lahore weekly, published a number of articles on the position taken by the opposition on more important economic and political issues. See in particular, 'opposition protest', in the issue of 28 January 1977, pp. 9–11; 'NDP has own identity' and 'Have your plough, PNA!' both in the issue of 4 February 1977, pp. 9–12.

9   THE 1977 ELECTIONS.

1 *The Economist*, 'Pakistan: Of Whiskey, War and Islam', 5 March 1977, p. 68.
2 Ibid., p. 68.
3 *Pakistan Times* (Islamabad), 22 February 1977.
4 *The Economist*, 'Pakistan: Of Whiskey, War and Islam', op. cit., p. 68.
5 *Pakistan Times* (Islamabad), 8 March 1977.
6 *Viewpoint*, 11 March 1977.
7 *Nawa-i-Waqt* (Lahore), 8 March 1977.
8 Quoted in *Dawn: Overseas Weekly*, 13 March 1977.
9 Statement by the PNA leader, Air Marshal Asghar Khan quoted in *Nawa-i-Waqt* (Lahore), 13 March 1977.
10 *The Economist*, 'Better Bhutto than Not', 12 March 1977, p. 14
11 Salamat Ali, 'Heading for Hard Times', *Far Eastern Economic Review*, 18 March 1977.
12 For a graphic description of this clash, see dispatches by Lewis Simons in the *Washington Post* during the month of April.
13 *Pakistan Times* (Islamabad), 8 March 1977.
14 Quoted in Salamat Ali, 'Bhutto Weathers the Storm', in *Far Eastern Economic Review*, 6 May 1977, p. 9.
15 Salamat Ali, 'Bhutto's Last-Ditch Peace Bid', *Far Eastern Economic Review*, 20 May 1977.
16 Salamat Ali, 'Bhutto Wants Another Mandate', *Far Eastern Economic Review*, 27 May 1977, p. 24.

17 *Nawa-i-Waqt* editorial, 'Don't be Fooled' (Lahore), 24 May 1977.
18 Quoted in Lewis Simons, 'Calm is Welcomed in Pakistan', *Washington Post*, 8 July 1977.
19 *The Times* (London), 7 July 1977.
20 *Musawat* (Lahore), 18 July 1977.
21 Salamat Ali, 'An Orderly Return to the Front', *Far Eastern Economic Review*, 12 August 1977.
22 See for instance, Government of Pakistan, *White Papers on the Conduct of General Elections in March 1977* (Rawalpindi), July 1978, an eleven hundred page long document that gave details of how Bhutto and some members of his administration attempted to influence the results of the polls. See also, Government of Pakistan, *White Paper on Misuse of Media* (Rawalpindi), August 1978. Bhutto's rejoinder to these papers was written in jail and smuggled out to be published abroad. See *Zulfikar Ali Bhutto, If I am Assassinated* (New Delhi: Vikas, 1979).
23 *The Times* (London), 8 September 1977.
24 *Musawat* (Lahore), 9 July 1977.

Selected Bibliography

Adams, Charles, 'The Ideology of Maulana Maudoodi' in Donald E. Smith (ed.), *South Asian Politics and Religion* (Princeton: Princeton University Press, 1966), pp. 352–70.

Ahmad, Jamiluddin (ed.), *Speeches and Writings of Mr. Jinnah* (Lahore: Mohammad Ashraf, 1952).

Ahmad, Kamruddin, *The Social History of East Pakistan* (Dacca: Pioneer Press, 1967).

Ahmad, Muneer, *The Civil Servant in Pakistan* (Oxford: Oxford University Press, 1964).

Aitchison, Sir Charles, *Lord Lawrence and the Reconstruction of India Under the Crown* (Oxford: Clarendon Press, 1916).

Allen, Charles, *Plain Tales from the Raj* (New York: St Martin's Press, 1976).

Andrus, J. Russell and Azizali F. Mohammed, *The Economy of Pakistan* (Stanford: Stanford University Press, 1958).

Anisur Rahman, Muhammad, *East and West Pakistan: A Problem in the Political Economy of Regional Planning* (Cambridge, Massachusetts: Center for International Affairs, 1968).

Ayub, M., *Public Industrial Enterprises in Pakistan* (Karachi: PIDC, 1960).

Baxter, Craig, 'Constitution Making: The Development of Federalism in Pakistan', *Asian Survey*, XIV, December 1974, pp. 1074–85.

Baxter, Craig, 'Pakistan Votes – 1970', *Asian Survey*, XI, March 1971, pp. 197–218.

Baxter, Craig, 'The People's Party vs. the Punjab Feudalists' in J. Henry Korson (ed.), *Contemporary Problems of Pakistan* (Leiden: E. J. Brill, 1974), pp. 6–29.

Bean, Lee L., 'Rapid Population Growth: Implications for Social and Economic Development', *Asian Survey*, XIV, December 1974, pp. 1104–13.

Bhutto, Zulfikar Ali, *The Great Tragedy* (Karachi: Vision Publications, 1971).

Bhutto, Zulfikar Ali, *Let the People Judge* (Lahore: Pakistan People's Party, 1969).

Bhutto, Zulfikar Ali, *Political Situation in Pakistan* (Lahore: Pakistan People's Party, 1969).

Bhutto, Zulfikar Ali, *Politics of the People: Awakening the People* (Rawalpindi: Pakistan Publications, n.d.).

Bhutto, Zulfikar Ali, *Politics of the People: Marching Towards Democracy* (Rawalpindi: Pakistan Publications, n.d.).

Bhutto, Zulfikar Ali, *Speeches* (Rawalpindi: Ministry of Information, n.d.).

Bienen, Henry and David Morrell, 'Transition from Military Rule: Thailand's Experience' in Catherine Kelleher (ed.), *Political-Military Systems: Comparative Perspectives* (Beverly Hills, California: Sage Publications, 1974), pp. 3–26.

Braibanti, Ralph, *Research on the Bureaucracy of Pakistan* (Durham, N.C.: Duke University Press, 1966).

Braibanti, Ralph, 'The Higher Bureaucracy of Pakistan' in Ralph Braibanti (ed.), *Asian Bureaucratic Systems' Emergence from British Imperial Tradition* (Durham, N.C.: Duke University Press, 1966), pp. 209–353.

Brayne, F. L., *Better Villages* (London: Oxford University Press, 1938).

Burki, Shahid Javed, *Agricultural Growth and Local Government in Punjab, Pakistan* (Ithaca, N.Y.: Cornell University, 1974).

Burki, Shahid Javed, 'The Development of Pakistan's Agriculture: An Interdisciplinary Explanation' in Robert D. Stevens, Hamza Alvi and Peter J. Bertocci (eds), *Rural Development in Bangladesh and Pakistan* (Honolulu: University Press of Hawaii, 1976), pp. 290–316.

Burki, Shahid Javed, 'Development of Towns: The Pakistan Experience', *Asian Survey*, XIV, August 1974, pp. 751–62.

Burki, Shahid Javed, 'Economic Decisionmaking in Pakistan' in Lawrence Ziring, Ralph Braibanti and W. Howard Wriggins (eds.), *Pakistan: The Long View* (Durham, N.C.: Duke University Press, 1977), pp. 140–72.

Burki, Shahid Javed, *Economic Foundations of the State of Pakistan*. Mimeo paper read at the annual meeting of the Association of Asian Studies, New York, 24 March 1977.

Burki, Shahid Javed, 'Interest Group Involvement in West Pakistan's Rural Works Program', *Public Policy*, XIX, Winter 1971, pp. 167–206.

Burki, Shahid Javed, 'Migration, Urbanization and Politics in Pakistan', in Howard Wriggins and James Guyot (eds), *Population, Politics and the Future of Southern Asia* (New York: Columbia University Press, 1973), pp. 147–89.

Burki, Shahid Javed, *Pakistan: A Demographic Report* (Washington, D.C.: Population Reference Bureau, 1973).

Burki, Shahid Javed, 'Social and Economic Determinants of Political Violence: A Case Study of the Punjab', *The Middle East Journal*, vol. 25, Autumn 1971, pp. 465–80.

Burki, Shahid Javed, *Social Groups and Development: A Case Study of Pakistan* (forthcoming).

Burki, Shahid Javed and Craig Baxter, 'Socio-Economic Indicators of the People's Party Vote in the Punjab: A Study at the Tehsil Level', *The Journal of Asian Studies*, XXXIV, August 1975, pp. 913–30.

Burki, Shahid Javed, 'Twenty Years of the Civil Service of Pakistan: A Reevaluation', *Asian Survey*, IX, April 1969, pp. 239–54.

Bussink, Tine, 'Major Aspects of Family Planning in Pakistan' in Shahid Javed Burki (ed.), *Prologue to Development Policy and Population Policy – The Pakistan Experience* (Washington, D.C.: Smithsonian Institution, Interdisciplinary Communications Program, 1975), pp. 37–60.

Callard, Keith, *Pakistan: A Political Study* (London: Allen & Unwin, 1957).

Chopra, Pram, *India's Second Liberation* (Delhi: Vikas Publishing House, 1973).

Choudhury, G. W., *The Last Days of United Pakistan* (Bloomington, Indiana: Indiana University Press, 1974).

Coupland, Reginald, *The Indian Problem* (Clarendon: Oxford University Press, 1944).

Dobell, W. M., 'Ayub Khan as President of Pakistan', *Pacific Affairs*, XLII, 1969, pp. 294–310.

Douie, J. M., *Land Settlement Manual* (Lahore: Government of West Pakistan, 5th rev. edn, 1960).

Eekelaar, J. M., 'Principles of Revolutionary Legality' in A. W. B. Simpson (ed.), *Oxford Essays in Jurisprudence* (Oxford: Clarendon Press, 1963).

Egger, Rowland, *The Improvement of Public Administration in Pakistan* (Karachi: Inter-services Press, 1953).

Erikson, Erik H., *Gandhi's Truth: On the Origins of Militant Non-Violence* (New York: W. W. Norton, 1969).

Falcon, Walter and Carl Gotsch, 'Lessons in Agricultural Development – Pakistan' in Gustav F. Papanek (ed.), *Development Policy: Theory and Practice* (Cambridge, Massachusetts: Harvard University Press, 1968), pp. 269–315.

Fallaci, Oriana, *Interview with History* (New York: Liveright Publishing Corporation, 1976).

Feldman, Herbert, *From Crisis to Crisis: Pakistan in 1962–69 (London: Oxford University Press, 1970).*

Feldman, Herbert, *Revolution in Pakistan: A Study of the Martial Law Administration* (London: Oxford University Press, 1967).

Feldman, Herbert, *The End and the Beginning: Pakistan 1969–71* (London: Oxford University Press, 1976).

Feldman, Herbert, 'Pakistan – 1973', *Asian Survey*, XIV, February 1974, pp. 136–42.

Feldman, Herbert, 'Pakistan in 1974', *Asian Survey*, XV, February 1975, pp. 110–16.

Finnis, J. M., 'Revolutions and Continuity of Law' in A. W. B. Simpson (ed.), *Oxford Essays in Jurisprudence* (Oxford: Clarendon Press, 1963).

Furnia, A., 'Syncrisis: The Dynamics of Health, No. XVIII: Pakistan' (Washington, D.C.: U.S. Department of Health, Education and Welfare, June 1976).

Gankovsky, Yu V., *The Peoples of Pakistan*. Originally published by the USSR Academy of Sciences, Institute of Oriental Studies. Reprinted in Lahore, Pakistan: People's Publishing House, n.d.

Gerschenkron, Alexander, *Economic Backwardness in Historical Perspective: A Book of Essays* (Cambridge: Belknap Press of Harvard University Press, 1962).

Gladieux, Bernard, *Report of Reorganization of Pakistan Government for National Development* (Karachi: Planning Commission, 1955).

Goodnow, Henry Frank, *The Civil Service of Pakistan: Bureaucracy in a New Nation* (New Haven: Yale University Press, 1964).

Gorvine, Albert, 'The Role of the Civil Service Under the Revolutionary Government', *The Middle East Journal*, XIX, no. 3, pp. 321–26.

Gotsch, Carl and Shahid Yusuf, 'Technical Indivisibilities and Distribution of Income: Mixed Integer Programming Model of Punjab Agriculture', *Food Research Institute Studies*, XIV, no. 1 (1975).

Gotsch, Carl, 'Regional Agricultural Growth: The Case of West Pakistan', *Asian Survey*, VIII, March 1968, pp. 188–206.

Government of Pakistan, *The Education Policy, 1972–1980* (Islamabad: Ministry of Education, 1973).

Government of Pakistan, *Labour Reforms of 1972* (Islamabad: Labour Division, 1972).

Government of Pakistan, *Pakistan Economic Survey, 1973–74* (Islamabad: Finance Division, 1974).

Government of Pakistan, *Pakistan Economic Survey, 1976–77* (Islamabad: Finance Division, 1977), Statistical Sector, Table 31.

Government of Pakistan, *Pakistan Economic Survey, 1976–77*, Statistical Annex.

Government of Pakistan, *Pakistan Year Book, 1971* (Rawalpindi: Ministry of Information, 1972).

Government of Pakistan, *People's Cloth Scheme* (Islamabad: Ministry of Industries, 1975).

Government of Pakistan, *Promotion of Sports and Culture: A Programme of Action* (Islamabad: Ministry of Education, 1976).

Government of Pakistan, *Report of Pakistan Pay Commission* (Karachi: Governor General's Press, 1949).

Government of Pakistan, *Report of the International Seminar on Integrated Rural Development, Lahore, November 3–10, 1973* (Islamabad: Ministry of Food, 1974).

Government of Pakistan, *Report of the Panel of Economic Experts* (Islamabad: Planning Commission, 1970).

Government of Pakistan, *The Task of National Reconstruction* (Rawalpindi: Bureau of National Reconstruction, n.d.).

Government of the Punjab, *Report of the Court of Inquiry Constituted Under Punjab Act II of 1954: Enquiry into Punjab Disturbances of 1953* (Lahore: Government Printing Press, 1954).

Griffin, Lepel H., *Chiefs and Families of Note in the Punjab* (Lahore: Superintendent of Government of Printing, rev. edn, 1940).

Guisinger, Stephen and M. Irfan, 'Real Wages of Industrial Workers in Pakistan: 1954–1970', *Pakistan Development Review*, XIII, Winter 1974, pp. 325–35.

Guisinger, Stephen and Norman L. Hicks, 'Long-term Trends in Income Distribution in Pakistan', *World Development*, vol. 6, November–December 1978, pp. 1271–80.

Gustafson, W. Eric, 'Economic Reforms under the Bhutto Regime', *Journal of Asian and African Studies*, vol. 8, July–October 1973, pp. 241–58.

Habib, Hasan (Nazim), *Babus, Brahmans and Bureaucrats: A Critique of an Administrative System in Pakistan* (Lahore: People's Publishing House, 1973).

Haq, Mahbub ul, *The Poverty Curtain: Choices for the Third World* (New York: Columbia University Press, 1976).

Haq, Mahbub ul, 'Rationale of Government Controls and Policies in Pakistan', *Pakistan Economic Journal*, XIII, March 1963, pp. 70–82.

Haq, Mahbub ul, *The Strategy of Economic Planning* (New York: Oxford University Press, 1963).

Haq, Siraj ul and C. Stevens, *Some Account of the Current Situation and Recommendations Regarding the Health Sector* (Islamabad: Government of Pakistan, Planning Commission, 1975).

Harris, Marvin, *Cannibals and Kings: The Origin of Cultures* (New York: Random House, 1977).

Hasan, Mubashir, *Shahrahe Inqilab* (Urdu) (Lahore: Rippon Printing, 1976).

Heeger, Gerald A., 'Politics in the Post-Military State: Some Reflections on the Pakistani Experience', *World Politics*, XXIX, January 1977, pp. 242–62.

Heeger, Gerald A., 'Socialism in Pakistan', in Helen Dosfosses and Jacques

Levesque (eds), *Socialism in the Third World* (New York: Praeger, 1975), pp. 291–4.

Hirschman, Albert O., *The Passions and The Interests: Political Arguments for Capitalism Before Its Triumph* (Princeton, N.J.: Princeton University Press, 1977).

Honore, A. M., 'Groups, Laws and Obedience' in A. W. B. Simpson (ed.), *Oxford Essays in Jurisprudence* (Oxford: Clarendon Press, 1963).

Huntington, Samuel P. and Joan Nelson, *No Easy Choices* (Cambridge, Massachusetts: Harvard University Press, 1976).

Husain, Azim, *Fazl-i-Husain: A Political Biography* (Bombay: Longmans, 1946).

Hussain, Asaf, 'Ethnicity, National Identity and Praetorianism: The Case of Pakistan', *Asian Survey*, XVI, October 1976, pp. 918–30.

Ibbetson, Sir Denzil, *Punjab Castes* (Lahore: Superintendent of Government Printing, 1916).

Jahan, Rounaq, *Pakistan: Failure in National Integration* (New York: Columbia University Press, 1972).

Jamil, S. M. (ed.), *Muslim Year Book of India, 1948–1949* (Bombay Newspaper Company, n.d.).

Johnson, Paul, *Enemies of Society* (New York: Altreneum, 1977).

Kaneda, Hiromitsu and Frank C. Child, 'Links to the Green Revolution: A Study of Small-Scale, Agriculturally Related Industry in the Pakistan Punjab', *Economic Development and Cultural Change*, vol. 23, no. 2, January 1975, pp. 249–75.

Kelsen, Hans, *General Theory of Law and State* (Berkeley: University of California Press, 1968).

Kelsen, Hans, *Pure Theory of Law* (Berkeley: University of California Press, 1970).

Kelsen, Hans, 'A Reply to Professor Stone', *Stanford Law Review*, 17, vol. 2, 1965.

Khalilzad, Zalmay, 'Pakistan: The Making of Nuclear Power', *Asian Survey*, XVI, June 1976, pp. 580–92.

Khaliquzzaman, Choudhry, *Pathway to Pakistan* (Lahore: Longmans, 1961).

Khan, A. R., 'Import Substitution, Export Expansion and Consumption Liberalization', *Pakistan Development Review*, XI, Summer 1963, pp. 123–57.

Khan, Fazal Muqeem, *Pakistan's Crisis in Leadership* (Islamabad: National Book Foundation, 1973).

Khan, Khaliq, *Generic Drugs in Pakistan: Their Introduction and Consequences* (Lahore: Model Publishing House, 1976).

Khan, Mohammad Ayub, *Friends Not Masters: A Political Autobiography* (London: Oxford University Press, 1967).

Khan, Mohammad Ayub, *Pakistan Perspective* (Washington, D.C.: Embassy of Pakistan, n.d.).

Korson, Henry, 'Bhutto's Educational Reforms' in H. Korson (ed.), *Contemporary Problems of Pakistan* (Leiden: E. J. Brill, 1974), pp. 119–46.

Klitgaard, Robert *et al.*, 'Can We Afford a Half-Time University?', Applied Economic Research Center, University of Karachi, December 1976.

Lambrick, H. T., *Sind: Before the Muslim Conquest* (Pakistan: Sindhi Adabi Board, 1973).

LaPorte, Robert, *Power and Privilege: Influence and Decision-Making in Pakistan* (Berkeley, California: California University Press, 1975).

LaPorte, Robert Jr, 'Pakistan in 1972: Picking Up the Pieces', *Asian Survey*, XIII, February 1973, pp. 187–98.

LaPorte, Robert, 'Succession in Pakistan: Continuity and Change in a Garrison State', *Asian Survey*, IX, November 1969, pp. 842–61.

LaPorte, Robert Jr, 'The Pakistan Bureaucracy: Twenty Five Years of Power and Influence', *Asian Survey*, XIV, December 1974, pp. 1094–103.

Lewis, Stephen R., *Economic Policy and Industrial Growth in Pakistan* (London: Allen & Unwin, 1969).

Lewis, Stephen R., *Pakistan: Industrialization and Trade Policies* (New York: Oxford University Press, 1970).

Lieftinck, Pieter, Robert A. Sadove and Thomas C. Creyke., *Water and Power Resources of West Pakistan: A Study in Sector Planning* (Baltimore: Johns Hopkins University Press, 1961).

Lipton, Michael, *Why Poor People Stay Poor: Urban Bias in World Development* (London: Temple-Smith, 1977).

Loshak, David, *The Pakistan Crisis* (New York: McGraw-Hill, 1971).

MacEwan, Arthur, *Development Alternatives in Pakistan: A Multisectoral and Regional Analysis of Planning Problems* (Cambridge, Massachusetts: Harvard University Press, 1971).

Mahmood, Safdar, *A Political Study of Pakistan* (Lahore: Mohammad Ashraf, 1972).

Malik, Abdullah, 'Elections '77: What Will be the Bhutto Strategy?', *Viewpoint* (Lahore) 4 February 1977.

Mason, Philip, *A Matter of Honor: An Account of the Indian Army, Its Officers and Men* (New York: Holt, Rinehart & Winston, 1974).

Masud, M., *Hari Report: Note of Dissent* (Karachi: The Hari Publications, n.d.).

Mayne, Peter, *Saints of Sind* (London: John Murray, 1956).

McInernery, John and Graham Donaldson, *The Consequence of Farm Tractors in Pakistan* (World Bank Staff Working Paper No. 210. Washington, D.C., 1975).

MICAS Associates, *A Study of Problems Associated with Procurement, Storage and Distribution of Wheat: Report Submitted to the Prime Minister of Pakistan* (Karachi, May 1976).

Michel, Aloys A., *The Indus River: A Study of the Effects of Partition* (New Haven: Yale University Press, 1967).

Moody, Piloo, *Zulfi My Friend* (Delhi: Thomson Press, 1973).

Morawetz, David, *Twenty Five Years of Development* (Washington, D.C.: World Bank, 1977).

Mukerjee, Dilip, *Zulfikar Ali Bhutto: Quest for Power* (Delhi: Vikas Publishing, 1972).

Nicholas, Marta and Philip Oldenberg, *Bangladesh: The Birth of a Nation* (Madras: M. Seschachalam, 1972).

Nutty, Timothy and Leslie Nutty, 'Pakistan, The Busy Bee Route', *Transaction*, 8 (February 1971).

Pakistan People's Party, *Manifesto* (Rawalpindi: Pakistan People's Party Central Secretariat, 1977).

Pakistan People's Party, *The Election Manifesto* (Lahore: Pakistan People's Party, 1970).

Palit, D. K., *The Lightning Campaign: The Indo-Pakistan War, 1971* (New Delhi: Thomson Press, 1972).

Papanek, Gustav, *Pakistan's Development: Social Goals and Private Incentives* (Cambridge, Massachusetts: Harvard University Press, 1967).

Papanek, Hanna, 'Pakistan's Big Businessmen: Muslim Separation, Entrepreneurship and Partial Modernization', *Economic Development and Cultural Change*, 21, October 1972, pp. 1–32.

Payne, Robert, *Massacre* (New York: Macmillan, 1973).

Rajput, A. B., *The Muslim League Yesterday and Today* (Lahore: Mohammad Ashraf, 1948).

Rahman, M. Akhlakur, *Integration, Economic Growth and Interregional Trade: A Study of Interwing Trade in Pakistan, 1948–1959* (Karachi: Institute of Development Economics, 1963).

Raper, Arthur, *Rural Development in Action* (Ithaca, New York: Cornell University Press, 1970).

Sayeed, Khalid Bin, *Pakistan: The Formative Phase* (London: Oxford University Press, 1968).

Sayeed, Khalid Bin, 'The Personality of Jinnah and his Political Strategy' in C. M. Philips and Mary Doreen Wainwright (eds), *The Partition of India: Policies and Perspectives, 1935–1947* (Cambridge, Massachusetts: MIT Press, 1970), pp. 276–93.

Sayeed, Khalid Bin, *The Political System of Pakistan* (Boston: Houghton Mifflin, 1967).

Schectman, Joseph B., *Population Transfers in Asia* (New York: Hallsby Press, 1949).

Schuler, Edgar A. and Kathryn R. Schuler, *Public Opinion and Constitution Making in Pakistan, 1958–62* (East Lansing, Michigan: Michigan State University Press, 1967).

Shah, Mohammad Hussain, *Urban Problems of Pakistan* (Lahore: People's Press, 1974).

Simmons, John, 'Can Education Promote Development', *Finance and Development*, March 1978, pp. 36–9.

Singh, Khushwant, *The Sikhs* (London: Allen & Unwin, 1953).

Singh, Randhir and W. Roberts, *An Economic Survey of Kala Gaddi Thamman (Chak 73 G.B.): A Village in the Lyallpur District of the Punjab* (Lahore: The Board of Economic Inquiry, Punjab, 1932).

Smith, R. Bosworth, *Life of Lord Lawrence* (New York: Charles Scribner, 1883).

Sobhan, Rahman, *Basic Democracies, Works Programmes and Rural Development in East Pakistan* (Dacca: University of Dacca, 1968).

Syed, Anwar H., *Issues of Bureaucratic Ethics* (Lahore: Progressive Publisher, 1974).

Syed, Anwar H., 'Pakistan in 1976: Business as Usual', *Asian Survey*, XVII, February 1977, pp. 181–90.

Syed, Anwar H., 'The Pakistan People's Party: Phases One and Two' in Lawrence Ziring, Ralph Braibanti and W. Howard Wriggins (eds), *Pakistan: The Long View* (Durham, N.C.: Duke University Press, 1977), pp. 70–116.

Symonds, Richard, *The Making of Pakistan* (London: Faber and Faber, 1950).

Trade and Industry (Karachi) March 1972.

Tresvaskis, Hugh K., *The Land of the Five Rivers* (London: Oxford University Press, 1928).

Vakil, C. N. and G. Raghara Rao, *Economic Relations Between India and Pakistan: Need for International Cooperation* (Bombay: Vora and Co., 1965).

Waterston, Albert, *Planning in Pakistan* (Baltimore: Johns Hopkins University Press, 1963).

Weinbaum, M. G., 'The March 1977 Elections in Pakistan: Where Everyone Lost', *Asian Survey*, XVII, July 1977, pp. 599–618.

White, Lawrence J., *Industrial Concentration and Economic Power in Pakistan* (Princeton, N.J.: Princeton University Press, 1974).

Wilcox, Wayne, 'Pakistan in 1969: Once Again at the Starting Point', *Asian Survey*, X, February 1970, pp. 73–81.

Wittfogel, Karl A., *Oriental Despotism: A Comparative Study of Total Power* (New Haven, Connecticut: Yale University Press, 1957).

Woodruff, Philip, *The Men Who Ruled India: The Founders* (London: Jonathan Cape, 1965).

Woodruff, Philip, *The Men Who Ruled India: The Guardians* (London: Jonathan Cape, 1954).

Wriggins, W. Howard, *The Ruler's Imperative* (New York: Columbia University Press, 1969).

Wright, Theodore P. Jr, 'Indian Muslim Refugees in the Politics of Pakistan'. *Journal of Commonwealth on Comparative Politics*, XII, March 1974, pp. 189–205.

Zaidi, Z. H., 'Aspects of the Development of Muslim League Policy' in C. M. Philips and Mary Doreen Wainwright (eds), *The Partition of India: Policies and Perspectives, 1935–1947* (Cambridge, Massachusetts: MIT Press, 1970), pp. 245–75.

Zaki, W. M., *End of Misery* (Islamabad: Ministry of Education, 1972).

Zaman, Fakhar and Akhutar Aman, *Z. A. Bhutto: The Political Thinker* (Lahore: The People's Publications, 1973).

Ziring, Lawrence, 'The Administration of Basic Democracies' in Guthrie Birkhead (ed.), *Administrative Problems in Pakistan* (Syracuse, N.Y.: Syracuse University Press, 1966), pp. 31–62.

Ziring, Lawrence, *The Ayub Khan Era: Politics in Pakistan, 1958–69* (Syracuse, N.Y.: Syracuse University Press, 1971).

Ziring, Lawrence, 'Pakistan: The Campaign Before the Storm', *Asian Survey*, XVII, July 1977, pp. 581–98.

Ziring, Lawrence, 'The Pakistan Bureaucracy: Administration Reforms', *Asian Survey*, XIV, December 1974, pp. 1086–94.

Name Index

Subject Index